New British Drama in 15 Scenes

Related titles

Good Nights Out: A History of Popular British Theatre Since the Second World War, Aleks Sierz

The Methuen Drama Guide to Contemporary British Playwrights, Edited by Martin Middeke, Peter Paul Schnierer and Aleks Sierz

Modern British Playwriting: The 1990s: Voices, Documents, New Interpretations, Aleks Sierz

Rewriting the Nation: British Theatre Today, Aleks Sierz

The Time Traveller's Guide to British Theatre: The First Four Hundred Years, Aleks Sierz and Lia Ghilardi

The Theatre of Martin Crimp (Second Edition), Aleks Sierz

New British Drama in 15 Scenes

Adventures in Theatre Criticism

Aleks Sierz

methuen | drama
LONDON · NEW YORK · OXFORD · NEW DELHI · SYDNEY

METHUEN DRAMA
Bloomsbury Publishing Plc, 50 Bedford Square, London, WC1B 3DP, UK
Bloomsbury Publishing Inc, 1359 Broadway, New York, NY 10018, USA
Bloomsbury Publishing Ireland, 29 Earlsfort Terrace, Dublin 2, D02 AY28, Ireland

BLOOMSBURY, METHUEN DRAMA and the Methuen Drama logo are trademarks of Bloomsbury Publishing Plc

First published in Great Britain 2026

Copyright © Aleks Sierz, 2026

Aleks Sierz has asserted his right under the Copyright, Designs and Patents Act, 1988, to be identified as author of this work.

For legal purposes the Acknowledgements on p. 181 constitute an extension of this copyright page.

Cover design by Holly Capper
Cover image © Joan Marcus / ArenaPAL

All rights reserved. No part of this publication may be: i) reproduced or transmitted in any form, electronic or mechanical, including photocopying, recording or by means of any information storage or retrieval system without prior permission in writing from the publishers; or ii) used or reproduced in any way for the training, development or operation of artificial intelligence (AI) technologies, including generative AI technologies. The rights holders expressly reserve this publication from the text and data mining exception as per Article 4(3) of the Digital Single Market Directive (EU) 2019/790.

Bloomsbury Publishing Plc does not have any control over, or responsibility for, any third-party websites referred to or in this book. All internet addresses given in this book were correct at the time of going to press. The author and publisher regret any inconvenience caused if addresses have changed or sites have ceased to exist, but can accept no responsibility for any such changes.

A catalogue record for this book is available from the British Library.

A catalog record for this book is available from the Library of Congress.

ISBN: HB: 978-1-3505-6792-4
PB: 978-1-3505-6791-7
ePDF: 978-1-3505-6793-1
eBook: 978-1-3505-6794-8

Typeset by RefineCatch Limited, Bungay, Suffolk
Printed and bound in Great Britain

For product safety related questions contact productsafety@bloomsbury.com.

To find out more about our authors and books visit www.bloomsbury.com and sign up for our newsletters.

'Surely, Criticism is itself an art. And just as artistic creation implies the working of the critical faculty, and, indeed, without it cannot be said to exist at all, so Criticism is really creative in the highest sense of the word. Criticism is, in fact, both creative and independent. [. . .] I would call criticism a creation within a creation.'

Oscar Wilde, 'The Critic as Artist' (1891)

Contents

Introduction: a critic's decade		1
Scene One:	Overview	5
Scene Two:	Social issue plays	17
Scene Three:	Political plays	31
Scene Four:	Brexit plays	45
Scene Five:	Dystopian plays	53
Scene Six:	Experiments	63
Scene Seven:	Monologues	79
Scene Eight:	Plays about family	91
Scene Nine:	Plays about gender	101
Scene Ten:	Plays about race	113
Scene Eleven:	Plays about white privilege	129
Scene Twelve:	History plays	131
Scene Thirteen:	Adaptations	145
Scene Fourteen:	Valediction	153
Scene Fifteen:	Conclusion	163
Book list		165
Play list		167
Notes on sources		175
Acknowledgements		181
Index		183

Introduction

A critic's decade

Hello, reader. Okay. You've got past the title and you've started looking at my book. Great. As you can see, this is an account of new British drama, all those exciting new plays that have recently wowed audiences. But what's the best way of writing about theatre today? Well, my editor is always telling me to start with a story, so here goes:

Let's look back a few years. Remember the pandemic lockdown? Yes, that's when I first started thinking about how to write about contemporary theatre. It was a strange time, with odd sensations: the smell of hand sanitizer, the clouding of my glasses when I wore a face mask, getting used to moving around by keeping a distance between self and strangers, feeling uncomfortable in a crowded room. Not touching anything on the tube with my bare hands. The eerie sense of deserted streets and quiet skies, the empty offices and vacated schools. Beautiful sunlit parks. It's at this weird time in early 2020 that I'm sitting in a room in our house in Brixton, at a crimson-topped desk (slightly chipped) surrounded by crimson-painted walls, all lined with shelves full of faded paperbacks and some even older, more solid volumes. So Instagrammable, maybe – just don't look at that big yellow damp patch in the corner of the ceiling. Obviously, I have spare time, a lot of spare time. Lots and lots. So I decide to write another book.

— *You what? Oh no, not again. Please.*
— *Yes, why not? What else is there to do? Besides, now that I've thought of it I can't get the idea out of my head. It follows me around. When we go for a walk that's what I'm thinking of.*
— *Boh, okay. So what's it about?*
— *British theatre of course. New plays. A sort of follow-up to the other two books I've written.*

This news is greeted with silence. By now, I've been a theatre critic for about thirty years, and have produced several books about contemporary British theatre. Two of them were accounts of the new plays of a particular decade. The first was *In-Yer-Face Theatre*, a polemical and journalistic account of new writing for the theatre in the 1990s, and the second was *Rewriting the Nation*, a follow-up which was an academic monograph about the same subject in the 2000s. So the idea of another book is logical – it would bring the story up to date, and be the third volume of an informal trilogy.

But here's the thing: in the 2010s, I reviewed a whole lot of theatre – from musicals to monologues, from dramas to documentaries, from adaptations to history plays. And I remember a lot of shows. I think of the time as multi-coloured, attention-grabbing, mind-expanding, thought-provoking, vigorous, innovative and vastly entertaining. It really was fun. So what are the memorable plays of the decade?

Well, it's the *Fleabag* decade, the *Bubble Gum Dreams* decade, the *Wanderlust* decade and the decade of *King Charles III* (to name just four plays which were adapted for TV). It's the decade of West End musicals galore, headed by *Hamilton* from New York and homegrown joys such as *Matilda the Musical* and *Everybody's Talking About Jamie*. It's ten years of literary adaptations – the *Wolf Hall* trilogy, *Small Island* and *Harry Potter and the Cursed Child*. A time rich in history plays – *Leopoldstadt* and *Emilia*. A time when heavyweights such as Jez Butterworth and Martin McDonagh (whose 2017 film *Three Billboards Outside Ebbing, Missouri* won Oscars) could transfer to Broadway, of farces like *One Man, Two Guvnors*, of James Graham's political plays and of epics like *The Lehman Trilogy*. Veteran playwrights like Martin Crimp attracted stars of the calibre of Cate Blanchett and James McAvoy to their work, or, like Caryl Churchill, wrote controversial plays such as *Seven Jewish Children*. Black and Asian playwrights, I'm thinking of Roy Williams and Tanika Gupta, were at the height of their powers, and so was Inua Ellams, whose *Barber Shop Chronicles* rocked the night away. It was a time of women playwrights such as Laura Wade (*Posh*), Lucy Kirkwood (*Chimerica*) and Lucy Prebble (*The Effect*, and then the hit TV series *Succession*). It was a time of quirky plays, such as *Constellations* and *Lungs*. Of plays with memorable titles such as *Superhoe*, *Seven Methods of Killing Kylie Jenner* and *My Mum's a Twat*. Of playwrights from all the nations and regions: David Greig and Rona Munro in Scotland, Ed Thomas and Gary Owen in Wales, David Ireland in Northern Ireland. Playwrights such as Simon Stephens and Lee Hall brought northern voices to the metropolis. And, after years in the shadows, trans theatre-makers like Travis Alabanza were finally visible.

— *Are you kidding? Mate, nobody's heard of any of this stuff – who's going to publish a book about all this?*

— *Well, I wouldn't assume that these plays are that obscure. After all, a lot of people go to the West End and the National Theatre. They must remember these shows.*

— *Prove it.*
— *Well, look at some of the Olivier Award winners of those years: plays like* The Curious Incident of the Dog in the Night-Time, Chimerica, King Charles III, Hangmen *and* Harry Potter and the Cursed Child – *they all won the Best New Play award, all were in the West End. So not that obscure. And they're all gonna be in the book.*

Silence again. A shrug. More to the point: I'm bored with writing in a straight journalistic way and a straight academic way, so how could I write in a different style about the 2010s? This is when I discover, in a random google browse, the concept of creative non-fiction. Defined as a genre that employs the creative writing techniques of literature – for example, poetry and fictional narratives – to tell a true story, this experimental way of writing involves using the skills of novelists – or playwrights – to describe factually true situations. So yes, I think, must surely be worth a try.

For this reason I'm not going to write a straight memoir, but a factual account with elements of fiction, of parody and polemic. Since – we are told – form follows function, I'm trying to reflect the variety of 2010s theatre by adopting a different style of writing in each of this book's fifteen chapters, or fifteen scenes. I have created a chorus of different voices, with each section having a different character or narrator: these include a critic being interviewed, some sociologists, a Marxist, a Brexiteer, a diarist, playwrights, Black and Asian speakers, an artist. The diverse writing styles include dialogues, monologues, a listings magazine, an experimental A to Z, informal notes, quotations from genuine interviews, a documentary script and a kind of memory trail. So this book takes a polyphonic approach, in which each section looks at a different theme by using a different linguistic register. At one point, artificial intelligence makes a contribution. And so does a word cloud. In our rather cynical age, all this is an attempt at re-enchantment – at making theatre feel as vivid and urgent to my reader as it does to me.

I can't cover everything – thank goodness! – so I concentrate on new writing. This can be defined as plays which have an identifiable individual voice, something urgent and passionate to say about our world, perhaps also experimental in form or provocative in their taboo-busting subject matter. They tell us, with various degrees of idiosyncrasy, about who we are, how we live and how we relate to other people. Some of these plays were big award winners; others were cutting-edge fringe shows. But all were thrillingly new. And new writing turbocharged 2010s theatre.

And it's worth stressing that new writing for the theatre is a hugely productive cultural area. During those hectic years, I reviewed about two to three new plays every week, mainly in London, which comes to about 1,300 for the 2010s. For the whole of the UK there are some 300 to 500 new plays produced each year, which comes to anything between 3,000 and 5,000 for the decade. And this doesn't include revivals of old plays or modern classics. Obviously, I can't talk about all of these. So what follows is a critical selection of about 250 plays (less than 10 per cent of the total) of what I believe to be the most significant work. Yes, they were mainly staged in the metropolis, but they also include some dramas that came from further afield.

My account covers the crisis-ridden decade, roughly between the election of the Conservative–Liberal Democrat coalition government in May 2010 to the closing of all the country's theatres in March 2020 due to the pandemic. My main argument is that this was a decade of unprecedented theatrical variety. But if I have found a form in which to tell the story of the best of new British theatre of the time, some questions still need to be addressed:

- What was the essential character of the decade's new writing?
- What was the story of those years?
- What were the main themes of these plays?

Okay, now that we know the questions, let's try to find some answers.

SCENE ONE

Overview

What were the 2010s all about? How can you sum up this decade? When Andy Beckett, a journalist and historian who has written comprehensively about British society in the 1970s and 1980s, sat down to record his view of the 2010s for the *Guardian* newspaper, he focused on the crises of the decade. In his article 'The age of perpetual crisis: how the 2010s disrupted everything but resolved nothing', published at the end of 2019, he asks: 'How will we remember the last 10 years?' And his answer is:

> Above all, as a time of crises. During the 2010s, there have been crises of democracy and the economy; of the climate and poverty; of international relations and national identity; of privacy and technology. There were crises at the start of the decade, and there are crises now. Some of them are the same crises, unsolved. Others are like nothing we have experienced before. Some of them are welcome: old hierarchies collapsing. Others are catastrophes.

If the zeitgeist was a time of crisis, how did British theatre respond? Looking at the past decade the first impression is of a huge variety of different plays – there doesn't seem to be any pattern. So how do you even begin to give an account of the times? For a start, it seems like a good idea to embrace this variety, to celebrate it as a time of great creative exuberance. As well as the sheer volume of the thousands of new plays produced, their economic impact can be applauded: a 2023 study conducted on behalf of the Society of London Theatre and UK Theatre argues that this art form is a vital part of the country's lucrative creative industries. The figures are impressive: theatre generates £2.39 billion in gross value added (GVA, a key indicator of economic performance), has a total annual turnover of £4.44 billion and employs nearly 205,000 people. The £1 billion of direct turnover (e.g. from selling tickets, licensing production rights, managing tours) generates a further £1.3 billion in the broader economy. Theatre audiences also contribute additional spending in local economies up and down the land. For every £1 spent on a theatre ticket, an additional spend of £1.40 is generated in local economies, adding up to £1.94 billion per annum of extra value added.

Before examining the most important new plays of the decade, maybe the best way to start is to give an overview of the theatre scene in Britain. Since I've participated in many post-show discussions over the past ten years this seems like a good format with which to start my exploration of the decade. So the following is an imaginary conversation between a Journalist and a Critic, a public Q&A about today's theatre in front of a live audience at a free arts event in central London.

Edited transcript. Location: South Bank, London.[1]

Journalist: Okay, everybody. Okay. Welcome, everybody, to this event in our regular series on the arts. Our guest today is a theatre critic, and for anyone interested in their CV there's a short piece on them in our programme. Or you can just use Google. Anyway, let's start: looking at the past decade as a time of crisis, from austerity through Brexit to the pandemic, can you say something about how British theatre survived?

Critic: Sure. Well, like any art form, theatre both reflects and shapes the wider culture. Obvious really. So – of course – it's been affected by all the various crises, from climate change to political populism, no doubt about that. However, to answer your question directly: the optimistic response is that British theatre did surprisingly well in the 2010s. Despite the climate of austerity, and the various cost of living crises, commercial theatre in London has done really well in terms of profits, and publicly funded or state-subsidised theatre has managed to survive quite well.

Journalist: Okay, thinking about the big picture – can you say something about the West End? After all, that's the kind of theatre most people are familiar with. You know, musicals like *The Phantom of the Opera*, and *Les Mis*, or *Mamma Mia!* and *The Lion King*, the most popular shows...

Critic: Well, yes, the paradox is that, despite an austere decade, commercial theatre in London has thrived. I mean the West End really is a global success story, staging hit shows which delight millions of spectators – and generate billions of pounds in revenue. It's all about millions and billions.

---

[1] During the decade I interviewed many playwrights including Mike Bartlett, Leo Butler, Martin Crimp, Tim Crouch, April De Angelis, Dennis Kelly, Lucy Kirkwood, Tanika Gupta, Gurpreet Kaur Bhatti, Anthony Neilson, Lucy Prebble, Nina Raine, Philip Ridley, Simon Stephens, Laura Wade, Roy Williams and Alexandra Wood, as well as directors such as Katie Mitchell and Rupert Goold, literary managers such as Ben Power and many other theatre-makers.

The annual figures are simply staggering – and the 2010s were no exception – with an average annual attendance near the 15 million mark, with gross revenue of more than £600 million, in turn generating VAT receipts of over £105 million.[2] The real damage to British theatre – I believe – comes after 2020: because of COVID and because of the full effects of Brexit.

Journalist: So it was a good decade for the West End?

Critic: Yes, it's been great for West End theatre producers, people like Cameron Mackintosh, Andrew Lloyd Webber, Nica Burns and Sonia Friedman. When problems arose, they managed to respond. So – following some vocal criticism in the press – several big managements refurbished their theatres. You know, better legroom, more female toilets and improved bar facilities. That kind of thing. Big name theatres like the Theatre Royal Drury Lane, the Dominion Theatre, Victoria Palace and the Adelphi were among those which got a facelift. And there was a celebratory mood – exemplified by the renaming of several venues: the Queen's Theatre was renamed the Sondheim Theatre, after the American composer, and the New London Theatre was renamed the Gillian Lynne Theatre, after the choreographer – in fact, the first named after a woman who wasn't a royal. On the plus side, this was a great way of honouring exceptional theatre-makers. On the minus side, it's part of an unstoppable trend of turning theatres into brands – which risks creating a situation in which the venue's image has a higher profile than the work it puts on stage.

Journalist: But surely theatre wasn't completely free of crises?

Critic: Well, yes, that's true. Bad stuff did happen to commercial theatre. In the West End, the crisis was symbolized by the collapse of the roof of the Apollo Theatre in 2013, in which about seventy people were injured, some very badly. It happened during a performance of *The Curious Incident of the Dog in the Night-Time*.[3] I mean we live in an old country and while many central London theatres are beautiful Victorian – or Edwardian – buildings, they're also ancient, and sometimes dangerous.

---

[2] For example, Society of London Theatre, SOLT Box Office Figures 2015, SOLT website, https://solt.co.uk/about-london-theatre/press-office/solt-box-office-figures-2015/

[3] On 19 December 2013 the ceiling of the Apollo Theatre, Shaftesbury Avenue, collapsed during a performance of Simon Stephens's stage adaptation of Mark Haddon's *The Curious Incident of the Dog in the Night-Time*. Seventy-six people were injured, seven seriously, and fifty-eight people were taken to hospital. The reason for the collapse was caused by the deterioration of century-old cloth and plaster ties holding up timber frames of the decorated plaster ceiling in the Grade II listed building, which was built in 1901 by architect Lewin Sharp.

Journalist: What about the trend towards populism – did that affect theatre?
Critic: In a way, yes it did. Of course, commercial West End is an entertainment industry: it's there to make money as well as making people – its audiences – happy. So it's hardly surprising that theatres put on shows they think'll be popular, from warm-hearted comedies to musicals – in preference to more challenging work. So there've been debates with established playwrights like David Hare, Mark Ravenhill and Simon Stephens, who reckoned that comfortable, safe theatre is in danger of pushing more challenging new work off the stage.[4] In response, Nica Burns – at the time vice-president of the Society of London Theatre – questioned whether this was true. There's still a lot of snobbery about popular musicals being somehow low-quality culture. Designed for tourists. Yet they're the result of highly skilled teams of theatre-makers, and also part of a theatre ecology where there is surely room for everything, from *Phantom* and *Les Mis*, to more obscure work. I think this mix can create cultural collisions that expand our horizons.

Journalist: What about other examples of snobbery – like celebrity casting?
Critic: That's true, but audiences have always loved seeing stars and celebrities on stage. Haven't they? As far as I'm concerned, if a Pussycat Doll wants to appear in a West End musical that's fine – as long as she can play the part. Of course people always complain if the celebrity is not up to the job – so I remember the fuss about TV presenter Amanda Holden playing Princess Fiona in *Shrek the Musical* – she didn't have the stamina to do all eight shows a week – disappointing her fans, and her producers.

Journalist: And then people also complain about rising ticket prices.
Critic: Yes, the main problem with central London theatre is the seemingly inexorable rise in ticket prices. They've continued to rise, with prices by the end of the decade being anything from £125 to £250 for the best seats for popular musicals. Of course, cheaper tickets are also available. But the trouble with cheaper tickets is that you can't see much, and anyway for a typical family a night at the theatre – even excluding transport or an overnight stay in London – could cost about £500. This seems exorbitant to me. But producers argue high prices contribute to the health of the whole sector – I've read articles that say that the performing arts contribute something like £5 billion every year to the economy.[5] And theatre is a big part of that, which is great.

---

[4] For example, Vanessa Thorpe, 'Avant garde theatre: has Britain lost its nerve?', *Observer*, 26 February 2012, https://www.theguardian.com/stage/2012/feb/26/avant-garde-theatre-britain-lost-nerve

[5] For example, Georgia Snow, 'Performing arts contributes £5.4 billion a year to UK economy', *The Stage*, 13 January 2015, https://www.thestage.co.uk/news/performing-arts-contributes-54-billion-a-year-to-uk-economy. The Critic is here conflating the contribution of theatre with other arts such as music and the visual arts.

Journalist: Most people know about musicals, but let's talk about straight plays in the West End.

Critic: Yes, well, the most successful were transfers from the National Theatre such as *War Horse*, *One Man, Two Guvnors* and then *The Curious Incident of the Dog in the Night-Time*.[6] These were mega-hits which ran for years, and then toured globally. I mean, take one of these, *The Curious Incident of the Dog in the Night-Time* – the one that was at the Apollo when the ceiling came down. You know, Simon Stephens's adaptation of Mark Haddon's novel – a terrific show which had a blazing production, telling the story of a teenage boy who has behavioural problems, using a thrilling mixture of physical theatre moves and brilliant lighting and sound. A total theatre experience.

Journalist: What about state-subsidized theatre – how did that do?

Critic: Actually, while the commercial West End flourished – as it always does – even state-subsidized theatre didn't do that badly. In fact, more new theatres opened, more new plays were produced, more people attended shows. But the crisis in state-funded theatre was precisely that – state funding. Under the austerity programmes of the Tory governments, Arts Council money was cut, and many theatres experienced a drop in their regular income, which created pressure to produce more popular drama, and less avant-garde or experimental work. Especially outside London. So although – to generalize hugely – audiences may well have responded positively, and preferred to see comedies with celebrity actors or soap stars in the cast, rather than difficult plays about social problems, the general art of the theatre came under pressure. But art, as well as playwrights, did survive.

Journalist: Can you give us an example of cuts in funding?

Critic: Yes, okay: the National Theatre – the country's flagship theatre, what Wembley is to football – okay, the government's 2010 comprehensive spending review announced a 30 per cent cut to the Arts Council England budget. And private philanthropy can't fill that kind of hole. So in 2011, the National faced a large cut to its income, a £1.4 million reduction in Arts Council funding. But because of its popular programming, it also got £3-million-a-year profit from the West End transfer of *War Horse*. That play also did well in America, bringing in another £2 million. A couple of years later, the global success of *War Horse* and *One Man, Two Guvnors* helped the National to a record year, with its highest ever income of £87 million despite cuts to its subsidy.

---

[6] Nick Stafford, *War Horse* (2007), based on the 1982 novel by Michael Morpurgo; Richard Bean, *One Man, Two Guvnors* (2011), based on Carlo Goldoni's 1743 play *The Servant of Two Masters*; Simon Stephens, *The Curious Incident of the Dog in the Night-Time* (2012), based on the 2003 novel by Mark Haddon.

Journalist: So who was head of the National Theatre?

Critic: Up to the middle of the decade the artistic director was Nick Hytner, who transformed the institution in a really positive way – he pioneered cheaper ticket prices and something called NT Live, the broadcast of shows live to cinemas. I think one of his annual reports includes the inspiring phrase 'Subsidy works'![7] Exclamation mark. He was also a fine showman, creating a series of mega-hits that took the West End by storm. We've already mentioned *War Horse*, and so on. And he had a good record with new plays. But of course his very success provoked criticism: his programming was popular with audiences so he was often accused of being a populist.

Journalist: Yeah, you can't win can you? You mention populism – how did the ongoing culture wars affect the theatre?

Critic: Let me see. The atmosphere in this decade had various cultural flashpoints – but I think culture wars about climate change, gender, race, etc. are less heated in UK than in the USA. But some subjects do stumble into crisis: one example was in the middle of the decade when a play called *Homegrown*, about the radicalization of young Muslims, was cancelled by Paul Roseby, the director of the National Youth Theatre, ten days before it was due to open. The subject matter and its young cast – fifteen- to twenty-five-year-olds – frightened its producers, and its creatives were accused of having an 'extremist agenda'.[8] A lot of right-wing media complain about the so-called wokerati and cancel culture, but this was censorship by those in power.

Journalist: Okay, point taken. But what about the big picture? How did – to take just one example – the controversy about #MeToo play out in theatre?

Critic: Good question. Obviously British theatre is not immune to abusive behaviour by men in power, and there've been accusations of inappropriate behaviour against, for example, Kevin Spacey – star actor who was also head of the Old Vic Theatre – and theatre-makers such as Max Stafford-Clark and Chris Goode. In terms of the bigger picture, most theatres woke up to the fact they needed to protect their more vulnerable workers. One example was Vicky Featherstone, artistic director of the Royal Court – arguably the country's main new writing theatre. She supported the #MeToo campaign, speaking out against sexual harassment in the industry, as well as organizing an event called No Grey Area in October

---

[7] This refers to a National Theatre Annual Report in 2004. See 'National Treasure', *Guardian* editorial, 9 September 2004, https://www.theguardian.com/news/2004/sep/09/leadersandreply.mainsection

[8] For example, Hannah Ellis-Petersen, 'Controversial Isis-related play cancelled two weeks before opening night', *Guardian*, 4 August 2015, https://www.theguardian.com/uk-news/2015/aug/04/controversial-isis-related-play-cancelled-two-weeks-before-opening-night

2017, which resulted in new guidelines to tackle sexual misconduct. She was – at one point – voted the most influential person in British theatre by *The Stage* newspaper, partly because of her #MeToo activism.

Journalist: Yes, women tend to get a bad deal . . .
Critic: That's right. Plays by women rarely go above 30 per cent of the repertoire, but towards the end of the decade things began to improve. And women also contributed to some outstanding theatrical moments. In 2018 Phyllida Lloyd – brilliant director, who did *Mamma Mia!* – staged three women-only versions of Shakespeare plays, with a framing device in which the actors were also prisoners attending a drama group – they performed *Julius Caesar*, *Henry IV* and *The Tempest*. I remember that Lloyd also called on the Arts Council to commit to greater gender equality.[9]

Journalist: Obviously a good thing. Okay, any other flashpoints you can think of?
Critic: Yes, I'd like to mention a couple more. For example, in 2016 Emma Rice – relatively new artistic director of Shakespeare's Globe – quit her job because of pressure from the theatre board who were unhappy about her radical approach to Shakespeare. To me, it's an example of an entrenched conservative mindset pushing out someone who wanted to change things in an imaginative way. Another example is the fuss that happened when Indhu Rubasingham – another new female artistic director – renamed the Tricycle Theatre in Kilburn the Kiln – a lot of local people resisted this change. Needlessly. For soon everyone got used to it.

Journalist: Okay, let's move on – what about class?
Critic: Sure. Yes, in British culture there's always the issue of class: in the middle of the decade some research found that between half and three-quarters of actors come from middle-class professional backgrounds, whereas this group is only about 30 per cent of the general population.[10] And half of British BAFTA winners went to fee-paying schools. And we should also talk about race. I mean Black and Asian creatives have been pretty disadvantaged in British theatre, and theatre-makers such as Madani Younis – who led the Bush Theatre in West London – challenged

---

[9] For example, Georgia Snow, 'Phyllida Lloyd: "Arts Council should stop funding companies that aren't gender-equal"', *The Stage*, 7 March 2018, https://www.thestage.co.uk/news/phyllida-lloyd-arts-council-should-stop-funding-companies-that-arent-gender-equal

[10] For example, Vanessa Thorpe, 'New study exposes "class ceiling" that deters less privileged actors', *Guardian*, 27 February 2016, https://www.theguardian.com/culture/2016/feb/27/class-ceiling-working-class-actors-study

theatre to embrace a more anti-racist agenda. And in mid-decade or thereabouts *The Stage* newspaper led on many debates around diversity.[11] And another theatre-maker, Dawn Walton of Eclipse theatre, made a powerful case for more ethnic diversity onstage and offstage.[12] But although work by women and people of diverse backgrounds became more visible, the people who have the most power in theatre remain mostly male and white. No surprise there – surely?

Journalist: Yes, racism – clearly there's racism in British theatre, as in so many other institutions – can you give some examples?

Critic: Sure. Occasionally there've been some grim incidents: one example is *Harry Potter and the Cursed Child* – you know, the two-play sequel to the Harry Potter novels – it's in the West End. It broke records by selling 175,000 tickets in twenty-four hours, so it was one of the theatrical events of the year. But when it was announced that the role of Hermione was to be played by a Black actress, Noma Dumezweni, there was a storm of protest on social media – most of it disgustingly racist. To be fair, J.K. Rowling defended the casting, saying there's no reason why Hermione has to be white. You know, the books don't mention her race – or skin colour – and she's often portrayed as Black in fan art.[13]

Journalist: Okay, good point. Talking of actors, there's also been controversy about casting, about which actors can play what type of characters.

Critic: Yes, that's true. Obviously you no longer have white actors blacking up to play Black characters, but attention has shifted from race to sexuality. A couple of years ago, Matthew Lopez – who wrote the hit play *The Inheritance* – revealed that his three lead gay characters were played by actors who are straight.[14] Duh. You can see this upsets gay actors – who can bring their own experience to gay roles, but it's not an easy subject. I

---

[11] For example, Georgia Snow, 'Bush Theatre boss complains white voices are dominating diversity debate', *The Stage*, 4 August 2016, https://www.thestage.co.uk/news/bush-theatre-boss-complains-white-voices-are-dominating-diversity-debate

[12] For example, Holly Williams, 'Dawn Walton on what needs to be done to fix British theatre's race problem', *Independent*, 31 January 2016, https://www.independent.co.uk/arts-entertainment/art/features/dawn-walton-on-what-needs-to-be-done-to-fix-british-theatre-s-race-problem-a6841971.html

[13] For example, Rebecca Radcliffe, 'JK Rowling tells of anger at attacks on casting of black Hermione', *Observer*, 5 June 2016, https://www.theguardian.com/stage/2016/jun/05/harry-potter-jk--rowling-black-hermione

[14] For example, Tom Wright, 'Playwright Tom Wright: For now, I applaud straight actors making space for LGBTQ+ talent', *The Stage*, 5 February 2019, https://www.thestage.co.uk/opinion/playwright-tom-wright-for-now-i-applaud-straight-actors-making-space-for-lgbtq-talent

mean, would any producer be comfortable asking an actor about their sexual and gender identity in an audition? So no easy answers.

Journalist: Agreed. Okay, let's shift focus a bit – what about audience behaviour?
Critic: Yes, there've been dozens of incidents of people using their phones, either to film parts of a show – against the rules – or forgetting to turn them off, or even taking calls during the show. Unbelievable. Some stars have had a particularly bad time. In 2015, there was a burst of Cumbermania, when Benedict Cumberbatch played Hamlet – and he complained that during his 'To be or not to be' speech he was being filmed by an audience member. You know, really distracting. Then there was Andrew Scott – also during his brilliant performance as Hamlet – complaining about an audience member taking out their laptop to send emails – also during his 'To be or not to be' speech.

Journalist: Ha, a jinxed speech. Anyway, before we take some audience questions, I'd like to ask you how you think theatre fits into the wider cultural ecology?
Critic: Sure. I suppose the best way of answering that is to say there's an enormous flexibility – in fact mobility – in British culture. The same writers who create plays also write for radio, television, film. A great example is Phoebe Waller-Bridge, whose one-woman fringe show *Fleabag* got two BBC series with the playwright reprising her stage role. A playwright like Mike Bartlett was also a success story on television: he wrote two series of *Doctor Foster*, likewise his television version of *King Charles III*, adapted by him from his play of the same name, with Tim Pigott-Smith, who tragically died before the film was broadcast, playing Charles. But my favourites were more edgy: Nick Payne's *Wanderlust*, brilliantly written series with one entire episode devoted to a single therapy session. Amazing. Equally amazing, and equally well written was Michaela Coel's *I May Destroy You*. And let's not forget film. Couple of examples: Laura Wade's *The Riot Club* and debbie tucker green's film of her brilliant stage show about racism *Ear for Eye*. Theatre directors like Josie Rourke and Rupert Goold have also done film.

Journalist: You haven't mentioned social media.
Critic: Yes, you're right – obviously our biggest social change, which affects so many other things. There have been some theatre plays about the internet like Tim Price's *Teh Internet Is Serious Business* and Jasmine Lee-Jones's *Seven Methods of Killing Kylie Jenner* –

Journalist: Great title. But when we've talked before, you also mentioned a play in which the audience was encouraged to leave their phones on –

Critic: Oh yes, that's right – Javaad Alipoor's *The Believers Are But Brothers*. Instead of being asked to turn off their phones, the audience was encouraged to join a WhatsApp group and to leave their phones on. The play was also contemporary because it talked about lonely young men being drawn to extremism, either Islamism or white supremacism.

Journalist: Talking about social media, can you comment on the state of theatre reviewing in this decade?
Critic: Really? Sure you want to know?

Journalist: Yes, why not – after all, it's your job isn't it?
Critic: Because of the internet everyone can now be a critic – which is great. But it does have consequences – there's much more hype online. On the other hand, social media's greatly expanded the range of the cultural conversation, for sure. Nothing stops you posting a review on TripAdvisor. Website reviewing has increased: platforms such as *What's On Stage* and *The Arts Desk* and *The Theatre Times*, or more leftfield things like *West End Whingers* and *Exeunt* – all proliferated. Individual critics publish reviews on their own websites; bloggers are part of an international exchange of ideas. And, certainly across the decade, the internet became a new frontier where some significant confrontations played out: when the Lyric Hammersmith staged Simon Stephens's new play *Three Kingdoms*, many conventional reviewers were unimpressed, but the buzz on Twitter and in the blogosphere was sensational. The show split reviewers not only down generational lines, but across the media divide. But still – there's always a but still – although in the first part of the decade you could argue that that some of the best writing about theatre was on the internet, by the end of the decade the best bloggers had found jobs in more traditional media or theatre or academia. For them, the internet was merely a step up the career ladder.

Journalist: Can you give an example of good internet reviewing?
Critic: Ha, yes. Sure. I've just read a review of the West End revival of Nick Payne's *Constellations* by Mert Dilek for *Exeunt* online magazine – and it's superb. He uses the same experimental form as the play has – using repetition and restatement to give the reader a sense of the play's radical approach to theatre form. Positively admirable.[15] Other online reviews by committed bloggers, as opposed to casual punters, have also been brilliant. My favourite was Megan Vaughan's review of *Teh Internet Is Serious Business*, which took the form of a WhatsApp exchange – complete with

---

[15] Mert Dilek, 'Review: Constellations at Vaudeville Theatre', *Exeunt*, 6 July 2021, https://exeuntmagazine.com/reviews/review-constellations-vaudeville-2021/

emojis. Wonderful.[16] But – just to say – I also welcome the increased diversity in traditional media: instead of mainly middle-aged, middle-class white guys, there are now new voices like Arifa Akbar and jn benjamin.

Journalist: Now. Okay, we're running out of time – let's take some audience questions.

Audience member one: Could you talk a bit about new writing, you know, new plays about contemporary subjects?

Critic: Yes, sure. Good question. In my mind the 2010s were a bit like the 2000s, but boosted. Turbocharged. The main theme of a lot of new plays was identity: gender, ethnicity and nationality. And a lot of new plays about – as you'd expect – political issues, social issues, international events. There was also a general feeling that the world's in crisis – stories about climate change, pollution, political oppression, poverty, sexual violence. But the keynote is variety – so that variety includes a huge mixture of different forms, from family plays to monologues, adaptations and experimental writing. In the second half of the decade new plays by women and Black and Asian writers became much stronger. And a big rise in stories set in dystopias, as well as a huge number of history plays – which are always popular.

Journalist: Thanks. As a follow-up, could I ask: You've stressed a lot of positive things, but what would you say was wrong with new writing in this decade?

Critic: Yes, good. Historically, most new writing here has been tied to the great British traditions of text-based theatre, where the overall aesthetic is naturalism, realism and in fact social realism. Most mainstream theatre mimics daily life, and what you see is what you get, a kind of snapshot of reality. Although this has a good side, I mean it's very inclusive – no one is excluded because everything is clear – there's a downside. Relentless naturalism can be very boring. Most new plays are rather timid in form and content, not very imaginative. As usual, there are plenty of small plays, with small casts and small imaginations, many of which are soon forgotten.

Audience member two: You've talked a bit about scandals and social issues, and such like. But you didn't say much about international events, such as the invasion of Crimea and Eastern Ukraine, or the Arab Spring and Syria – haven't these also be reflected in new plays?

Critic: Yes, good one, let me think. Such events usually attracted something like one or two plays each, unless there was a direct connection with the

---

[16] Megan Vaughan, Untitled review of *Teh Internet Is Serious Business*, *Synonyms for Churlish*, 23 September 2014, https://synonymsforchurlish.tumblr.com/post/98220912603

UK such as refugees or Muslim kids travelling to Islamic State. So Putin – when he poisoned Alexander Litvinenko – was criticized in Lucy Prebble's *A Very Expensive Poison*, for example. On the fringe, a play like *Dubailand* by Carmen Nasr gave a vivid picture of social and economic inequality in the United Arab Emirates. I think that one trend in new writing in the 2010s was a greater geographical sweep – British playwrights engaged more with the wider world, bit less insular. So the Syrian refugee crisis of 2015 – and migration across Europe – resulted in a variety of responses on stage, such as the Young Vic's *The Jungle*, about the migrant camp in northern France, and included plays such as *Lampedusa* by Anders Lustgarten. Occasionally there was a play about an activist, such as Mike Bartlett's *Wild* which looked at whistle-blower Edward Snowden holed up in Moscow – but our theatre prefers to talk about problems rather than offer solutions. Which is fair enough – who wants to be preached at?

Audience member three: Could you say something more about which areas of the world have been ignored by new writers?

Critic: At the start of the millennium I remember thinking that British theatre had nothing to say about China, South-East Asia, South America or large parts of Africa. In the past decade this has changed, at least a bit. Plays such as Lucy Kirkwood's *Chimerica*, and plays about South Korea and various parts of India and Pakistan, have appeared. There have been seasons of South American drama, but my feeling is that while there've been more and more plays coming from the States, there've been fewer ones from Ireland. Is that okay – does that answer – a bit – your question?

Journalist: Thanks for these questions. Well, actually we really have run out of time now. Which is a shame as I also had another question: what were the characteristics of new writing in the 2010s? Perhaps you should write a book about this subject? Anyway, thank you so much for answering these questions – thanks.

Critic: Yes, thanks for having me – good questions. And that's a great idea about a book . . .

London, July 2021

SCENE TWO

Social issue plays

One of British theatre's specialities is the depiction of contemporary society. And this is also central to the genre known as new writing. During the 2010s, one of the strongest public voices advocating the importance of new writing, and supporting young playwrights and women writers, has been senior playwright David Hare, whose work includes numerous screenplays for film and television, as well as award-winning plays. When asked in December 2017 by the *Guardian* to write about his vision for an 'ideal theatre', he was clear about the centrality of new writing and its importance for society. New plays, he said, should 'represent and reflect the society they are performed in'. For him, playwrights are the Balzacian social secretaries who record the mood of the day; by questioning the zeitgeist they might also help to change it for the better. This is definitely a mainstream tradition in British text-based theatre, and naturally there is a multitude of new work which examines the various crises of our time, from climate change to the state of the NHS. In various ways, they describe Broken Britain.

During the past ten years, as a critic, it was obvious to me that British playwriting has lost none of its heritage of engagement with social issues, with social problems. In fact, I'd say the angriest plays about life under austerity were Alexander Zeldin's *Beyond Caring* and *Love* at the National Theatre. These were hyper-realistic accounts of extreme poverty, in the context of zero-hour contract work in a meat factory and life in a council's temporary accommodation. In a really stark way, both showed the results of cuts to welfare, and were full of grim truths about current social conditions. Across the decade, a huge variety of other issues were staged, from the housing crisis to faults in the legal system, and of course the red thread running through all of them was poverty. One specific example of a pressing social issue is Charlene James's *Cuttin' It*, a really strong play about female genital mutilation. This was timely if not immediate. Often it takes a while for theatre to react to current problems. But not always: one counter-example is journalist Gillian Slovo's verbatim play *The Riots*, about the nihilistic nationwide burnings and lootings of 2011, which followed the police shooting in London of Mark Duggan, a young Black man. Unusually this was staged very soon – about three months – after the events happened. Of course, the danger is that these kind of plays can become like journalism, work that ages badly and is soon forgotten. In fact, they are powerful records of how life was lived in 2010s Britain, and I've chosen to write about these social issue plays in the style of a panel of sociologists.

Theatre and society

§ THE BRIEF A multidisciplinary team of sociologists from various countries was invited to identify key social issues of the 2010s and analyse their representation in British theatre. The task involved examining how themes of crisis, populism and identity were communicated to the public through dramatic works. As is characteristic of sociological inquiry, the team began by establishing a working definition of 'social issues'. This was defined as 'problems that affect significant segments of society, manifesting as undesirable conditions that often result in harm to individuals and groups, typically arising from systemic factors beyond individual control'. These include poverty, anomie, sexism and racism, alongside forces such as climate change, media influence and religious discrimination. Such dynamics frequently materialize in lived experience as inadequate education, poor health outcomes, systemic inequalities and various forms of addiction. The team concurred that such issues provide fertile ground for theatrical exploration, offering a platform to critique the societal conditions shaping such challenges. Theatre's capacity to dramatize the intricate interplay of personal experience and structural inequity makes it a good medium for engaging with the complexities of social relations, fostering public discourse and potentially inspiring social change. Here is their report:

Considering the nature of crises in contemporary society, the team agreed that the logical starting point is climate change. The 2019 declaration by Oxford Dictionaries that 'climate emergency' was the word(s) of the year reflects a critical transformation in public discourse surrounding global warming. This phrase, whose usage surged a hundred-fold, is defined as 'a situation in which urgent action is required to reduce or halt climate change and avoid potentially irreversible environmental damage resulting from it'. Yet, as sociological inquiry reveals, this recognition is deeply enmeshed in power dynamics and conflicting economic interests that resist change. Understanding this phenomenon requires what C. Wright Mills termed the 'sociological imagination', i.e. the capacity to connect individual experiences with broader structural forces, namely the dynamics of power and inequality.

Mike Bartlett's *Earthquakes in London* (National Theatre, 2010) exemplifies this interplay between the personal and the political. Through the lens of an estranged family, Bartlett interrogates how social forces shape individual agency. The patriarch, Robert, is a retired scientist who has studied atmospheric change since the 1970s. He embodies the cynicism of one who perceives humanity as complicit in its downfall. His daughters – Sarah, Freya and Jasmine – navigate their own axis of intersection with the climate crisis: Sarah, an Environment Minister, is defined by political compromises; Freya, a pregnant teacher, agonizes over the morality of bringing new life into a collapsing world; and Jasmine, a hedonistic student, symbolizes the political apathy of the younger generation.

Generational conflict permeates the narrative: Robert, who has compromised his scientific findings by accepting corporate sponsorship, rejects his daughters, and advises Freya to abort her baby: 'I told her to kill it.' Sarah cynically accepts a job with the airline industry – she is tempted to 'clean up the industry, from the inside'. She is also cynical about Tom, Jasmine's lover, an activist whose passionate speech about the socioeconomic effects of climate change ends with: *'Lifestyle?* Fuck your *lifestyle.'* He and Emily, who is Freya's baby, represent hope for the future. Emily appears on a screen as a foetus, then on stage as a newborn baby and finally as a teenage activist, and the play's nonlinear, speculative structure – culminating in a temporal leap to the year 2525 – underscores the interplay of temporality, uncertainty and imagination in constructing societal futures. In its closing moments, the figure of Emily embodies a generational optimism, envisioning 'a new enlightenment' amidst ecological despair.

This thematic exploration resonates with other theatrical engagements with climate change. The multi-authored (by Moira Buffini, Matt Charman, Penelope Skinner and Jack Thorne) *Greenland* (National Theatre, 2011) grapples with the complexities of the Copenhagen Climate Summit, weaving together narratives of protest, scientific inquiry and environmental impact. In contrast, Richard Bean's *The Heretic* (Royal Court, 2011) offers a counterpoint, positioning climate scepticism at the centre of a satirical critique of academia and the hegemonic belief in science. By referencing Climategate – the 2009 hacking of climate researchers' emails – Bean foregrounds the politicization of climate science. It is a provocative play that dares to put a climate change sceptic, the fictional academic Dr Diane Cassell, centre stage in a satire on university life and the role of belief in scientific research. Together, these theatrical works successfully illustrate how climate change is not merely an environmental issue, but a sociopolitical phenomenon. They compel audiences to interrogate their assumptions, consider the interrelation of individual agency and systemic forces, and confront the contradictions inherent in societal responses to ecological crises. In our analysis, through the lens of cultural sociology, they reveal the coalescence of optimism, conflict and critique.

With climate change serving as the broader context, the team's analysis turned to the impact of austerity policies under the UK's Conservative and coalition governments, focusing particularly on the National Health Service (NHS). The NHS, often regarded as central to British national identity, provides a unique lens through which to examine the intersections of public policy, social structures and individual health outcomes. From a sociological perspective, the study of health extends beyond medical conditions to consider the influence of gender, race, sexuality, social class and geography. It also interrogates the institutional dynamics and systemic processes shaping healthcare delivery. During the 2010s, under successive governments, the NHS experienced its most significant reforms and funding constraints. A notable turning point came in 2012, when public satisfaction with the NHS, as reported by the King's Fund, dropped from an all-time high of 70 per cent to 58 per cent. This decline was attributed to a real-terms freeze in funding and polarizing media narratives about hospital conditions.

These challenges and their human impact are dramatized in Nina Raine's *Tiger Country* (Hampstead Theatre, 2011). Set within the environment of a hospital, the play follows Emily, an idealistic new doctor, as she grapples with disillusionment in the face of difficult working conditions. Her relationship with James, a fellow doctor, is strained by the pressures of a system dependent on overstretched staff. The paradoxical central message is that the NHS is so under-staffed that its doctors, in order to survive, need to stop caring. Vashti, an ambitious and experienced doctor, is explicit: 'Try not to care so much.' James also declares, 'There isn't enough NHS' and 'It's what you have to do. Unspoken overtime. That's how the NHS is run. On "goodwill".' One patient says that their doctor looks 'tired to death' and Emily realizes that the hospital 'is making me sick'. It is also a workplace characterized by casual sexism, racism, insubordinate nurses and unhelpful consultants. In terms of class, it is dominated by public-school boys. As Vashti says, 'This job is about being liked by blokes; but men don't like women who act like blokes, and to be taken seriously as a surgeon you have to act like a bloke.' The title, surgical slang for operating near a major blood vessel, serves as a metaphor for the NHS itself, which is working precariously in a landscape of risk and limited resources. The play's characters highlight the emotional toll of the system on healthcare workers.

In view of the NHS crisis, Stella Feehily's *This May Hurt a Bit* (Out of Joint, 2014) takes a more explicitly agitprop approach, juxtaposing the NHS with American private healthcare systems in a family drama where English and American characters debate the merits of the two systems. Whilst the Americans advocate for privatized medicine, the English fiercely defend universal, state-funded healthcare. Instead of using such fictional protagonists,

Michael Wynne's *Who Cares* (Royal Court, 2015) offers a verbatim account of the NHS's recent struggles, drawing on interviews with doctors, nurses and staff to explore the institution's systemic challenges. The play specifically addresses the Mid Staffordshire hospital scandal, in which campaigners – led by Julie Bailey, a local café owner who helped to set up Cure the NHS – exposed widespread failings in care and successfully lobbied for a public inquiry. Together, these theatrical works highlight the sociological dimensions of austerity politics as they relate to healthcare. They reveal how structural constraints, economic ideologies and institutional cultures affect not only the delivery of medical care, but also the lived experience of both healthcare workers and patients. These plays underscore the role of the NHS as both a symbol of collective solidarity and a site of intense social conflict under austerity.

If the NHS is experiencing a crisis, what can be said about the broader landscape of UK institutions? To explore this question, the team turned their attention to the education system, where austerity measures have similarly strained the lives of teachers and pupils. Since much sociological research has focused on the enduring impact of class on life chances, our inquiry centred on how theatre portrays such inequalities. For instance, John Donnelly's *The Knowledge* (Bush Theatre, 2011) offers a vivid depiction of class dynamics within the context of a failing Essex secondary school. The play chronicles a year in the professional life of Zoe, a newly qualified teacher, as she navigates the challenges posed by a frequently unruly classroom. It captures the mutual alienation between this middle-class teacher and her working-class pupils, highlighting the systemic disconnection in many schools. In 2011, this play was staged in tandem with Steve Waters's *Little Platoons*, which shifts the focus to parents, particularly middle-class families in west London, who respond to the education crisis by forming a free school. This initiative, spearheaded by Rachel, a forty-something teacher, reflects an ideological, right-wing reaction to welfare cuts. The play critiques this populist response, offering a commentary on the intersection of class and privatization in education. In contrast, Mark Ravenhill's *The Cane* (Royal Court, 2018) delves into the legacy of authority and punishment within the educational system. It centres on Edward, a retiring teacher whose past includes the administration of corporal punishment at a local comprehensive school. As Edward's daughter Anna uncovers this scandal whilst assisting with the school's OFSTED report, the play becomes a confrontation between generational values and the gendered dimensions of power, with women symbolically challenging the violence of patriarchal authority.

In general, the team noted that the sociology of education examines ways in which social structures, cultural norms and institutional practices influence educational outcomes. Central themes in this field include habitus, hegemony and intersectionality, the frameworks for understanding disparities and power dynamics within the UK educational system. When in 2011 Melissa Benn of the Local Schools Network was researching her book *School Wars: The Battle for Britain's Education*, she visited some of the country's richest and poorest schools, and noted the widening gulf between the wealthiest and most disadvantaged schools, shedding light on systemic issues that perpetuate educational stratification. This concern is dramatized in Vivienne Franzmann's *Mogadishu* (Manchester Royal Exchange, 2011), a play that critiques the state education system and explores the interplay of race, authority and systemic failure. *Mogadishu* – the title refers both to a war zone and to children's ignorance of African geography – centres on a playground altercation where Jason, a Black fifteen-year-old, pushes Amanda, a liberal white teacher, to the ground. When Amanda reluctantly reports him, Jason accuses her of racism, 'a hate crime', and bullies his peers into backing him up. He then gets help from Ben, his father. To the dismay of Amanda, of her teenage daughter Becky and of her Black husband Peter, it is she who is disciplined. When the police and social services are involved, the contentious situation escalates. Yet although Amanda's career is threatened, she is determined to think the best of Jason: 'He just lashed out'; 'No one's unreachable'. Finally, when Jason's lies are revealed he is excluded permanently from school, and his father Ben concludes, 'Permanent exclusion is closure – closing down his future.'

The team understands that the play's themes align with findings from the 2010 Equality and Human Rights Commission report, which underscores deep divisions in the UK education system. Key statistics include:

1. Boys lag behind girls in eleven of thirteen learning categories by age five.
2. Children from the poorest families are half as likely to achieve strong GCSE results.
3. Black pupils of Caribbean descent are three times more likely to face exclusion.
4. Four out of five students with special needs experience bullying.

By integrating sociological insights with dramatic narrative, *Mogadishu* highlights the enduring impact of structural inequalities in education.

Similarly, it was hardly a surprise to discover that the criminal justice system (CJS) – a broad collective term for a wide range of institutions and practices that exist to prevent, detect and prosecute crime as well as to punish and/or rehabilitate offenders/deviants – is also in crisis. In the UK the CJS includes the police, Crown Prosecution Service, criminal courts, and the prison and probation systems. In 2016, Meg Hillier MP, Chair of the Public Accounts Committee, published a report warning that the CJS was close to breaking point. She stated: 'Too little thought has been given to the consequences of cutbacks with the result that the system's ability to deliver justice, together with its credibility in the eyes of the public, is under threat.' This proposition is illustrated in the play *Consent* by Nina Raine (National Theatre, 2017), which explores the issue of sexual violence. The story centres around a group of lawyers and examines two rape cases, neither of which results in a conviction, exposing systemic injustices in the handling of sexual violence. The central characters are two couples: Edward and Kitty, and Jake and Rachel. Edward, a criminal barrister, successfully defends a rapist, leading to devastating consequences when the victim, Gayle, later dies by suicide. Within their personal lives, Edward's marriage to Kitty unravels when she begins an affair with another barrister, Tim. In response, Edward forces himself on Kitty despite her repeated refusals. Kitty says, 'I said "no" several times.' Although Edward acknowledges his guilt, Kitty chooses not to press charges, instead focusing on securing custody of their child.

The play critiques the CJS's systemic treatment of sexual violence victims. Gayle is denied independent legal representation, with Tim, the prosecutor, bluntly stating, 'Strictly speaking I'm not your lawyer ... You don't actually have a lawyer because technically you're a witness.' The court admits evidence of Gayle's mental health history, casting doubt on her credibility, whilst excluding her rapist's violent past. These disparities underscore the structural biases faced by victims. Kitty challenges the ethics of the legal profession, accusing barristers of 'standing up and lying in front of people' as a core function of their work. Even Edward, who takes pride in his career, concedes, 'I'm honestly losing faith in the whole system.' In an argument about his marital rape, when Edward protests, 'That's not the truth', Kitty responds by asserting, 'It's *my* truth!'

Other theatrical representations of similar conflicts, which interrogate the intersections of law, power and personal morality, highlighting the pervasive inequities in the professional sphere, include Rebecca Lenkiewicz's *The Invisible* (Bush Theatre, 2015), about a small law firm which specializes in cases about victims of abuse, those threatened with eviction or loss of their children, and is negatively affected by governmental cuts to the legal aid system. Another angle is explored in Nick Payne's *The Same Deep Water as Me* (Donmar Warehouse, 2013), about a firm of personal injury lawyers who decide to cheat insurance companies by promoting fake car crash claims, using this method until one of these is contested in court. Whilst examples such as these are illustrative of widespread social problems in the UK's institutions, what is the social situation beyond these structures?

The team's analysis next turned to issues of identity and the experiences of ethnic minority communities in the UK. In July 2015, then-Prime Minister

David Cameron commissioned Dame Louise Casey to examine strategies for promoting opportunity and integration in the UK's most isolated and disadvantaged communities. Despite a longstanding commitment to multiculturalism, social exclusion persists among ethnic minority groups, leading to concerns about increasing marginalization. Additionally, the rising incidence of racist and xenophobic hate crimes further complicates questions of integration. John Hollingworth's *Multitudes* (Tricycle Theatre, 2015) offers a powerful exploration of these social tensions, particularly those involving religious belief and tolerance. Set in Bradford, the play centres on a Muslim family grappling with intersecting pressures of identity, faith and politics. Kash, a Pakistani-born secular Muslim widower and local Conservative councillor, prepares to deliver a speech advocating for liberal multiculturalism. His plans are upended when his white partner, Natalie, converts to Islam and becomes involved in an anti-war protest, whilst his teenage daughter, Qadira, adopts a more radical stance, sympathetic to violent activism. Meanwhile, Natalie's mother, Lyn, a staunch Conservative councillor, voices anti-immigrant sentiments: 'It's people like me who keep Britain British.'

The play's central debate interrogates the success of multiculturalism and the social integration of Muslim communities. Kash's declaration that his immigrant father 'loved Britain' contrasts with Lyn's xenophobic view that immigrants undermine British values. Kash counters with a critique of Little Englander attitudes, asserting that it is not immigrants but exclusionary ideologies that harm British society. Qadira's rhetoric, referencing the Qur'an to justify militancy, highlights the appeal of radicalism for some young Muslims, whilst Natalie's decision to wear a hijab reflects broader trends, namely the estimated 100,000 British converts to Islam, predominantly women, in the 2010s. Through its frank representation of ideas, *Multitudes* examines the layered complexities of ethnicity, faith and belonging in the UK, its title echoing Walt Whitman's celebration of multiplicity: 'I am large. I contain multitudes.'

In contrast, Gillian Slovo's *Another World: Losing Our Children to Islamic State* (National Theatre, 2016) employs factual verbatim theatre techniques to explore why young Muslims from Britain and Belgium are drawn to join ISIS in Syria. Through collected testimonies, the play delves into the cultural and ideological forces at play, reflecting broader debates such as Samuel Huntington's controversial clash of civilizations thesis. Slovo's work highlights how some minority ethnic communities prioritize intra-community care and resist external intervention, driven by cultural and religious values. In doing so, the play underscores the tensions between individual agency, collective identity and broader sociopolitical dynamics. Similar questions are raised, in a fictional form, by Hassan Abdulrazzak's *Love, Bombs and Apples* (Arcola

Theatre, 2016). The play comprises four monologues, including one in which Sajid, an earnest Pakistani youth who lives in London, writes what he thinks is the 'definitive post-9/11 novel'. When he sends it to several publishers, he finds himself accused of writing a training manual for terrorists. At one point, Abdulrazzak juxtaposes Osama bin Laden with Kurt Cobain in a highly satirical account of cross-cultural misunderstanding. Other monologues include one about a young Bradford Muslim who compares the devotional aspects of his local mosque with the Apple Store, and finds some surprising similarities between traditional religion and new media, and another about Isaac, a young Jewish man who has an extremely Zionist father and a left-wing peace-activist girlfriend, Sarah, who is pro-Palestine. Together, these plays provide sociologically rich narratives that probe the intersection of faith, ethnicity and identity.

If personal identity is a contested territory in contemporary society, then the issue of substance abuse reflects both individual choices and wider societal trends. The sociology of addiction can be approached as a multidisciplinary field, encompassing diverse yet interconnected perspectives. These include:

1. The sociocultural, which examines the impact of social change, cultural norms and the pressures of modern society;
2. The socio-environmental, which focuses on the role of social learning, environmental settings and experiences of alienation;
3. The ideological, which critiques the cultural, institutional and professional frameworks that shape societal responses to addiction.

Statistics from the UK illustrate the growing social burden of addiction. In 2015, the umbrella organization Collective Voice reported 8,149 hospital admissions primarily due to drug-related mental health and behavioural disorders – a 14 per cent increase compared to previous years. Deaths linked to drug misuse rose by 15 per cent in 2014 to 2,248 cases. Meanwhile, alcohol misuse is estimated to cost the NHS in England £3.5 billion annually. These figures underscore the complex interplay between individual behaviour and structural factors, including cuts to funding for addiction services.

Theatre offers poignant explorations of addiction, shedding light on its subjective as well as social dimensions. Duncan Macmillan's *People, Places and Things* (National Theatre, 2015) examines the struggles of addiction and recovery through the story of Emma, an alcoholic and drug addict who enters rehab and participates in the twelve-step programme of Alcoholics Anonymous (AA). Emma's journey begins with her acknowledgement of her condition, admitting, 'I need help.' Initially resistant to group therapy, she ultimately embraces the process and completes her treatment. The play engages with the controversial aspects of AA, particularly its emphasis on spirituality. Emma rejects the idea of surrendering to a higher power, asserting, 'I can't surrender to a higher person because there isn't one.' This critique mirrors broader debates about whether AA operates as a therapeutic community or a cult. Emma's mother reinforces this scepticism, dismissing AA as 'this new cult of yours'. The title of the play is explained by a therapist: 'People who make us want to relapse, places we associate with using, and things that reactivate old behaviour.' These elements represent the triggers that Emma must navigate as she rebuilds her life. Whilst she acknowledges the attraction of addiction, claiming that 'drugs and alcohol have never let me down' and they 'make the world perfect', the narrative interrogates deeper causes of substance abuse. Her doctor suggests that trauma may underlie her addiction, emphasizing the importance of the psychological dimensions of her condition: 'It's the behaviour, the psychology that is the important thing to address.' Although Emma's subjective experience is central to the story, the play also situates her struggles within a broader social context. By its conclusion, the rehab facility where she finds help is slated for closure due to austerity-driven funding cuts, highlighting the systemic challenges faced by individuals seeking recovery in an era of a crisis in public services.

Contemporary theatrical works offer other valuable sociological perspectives on addiction, with plays such as David Eldridge's *The Knot of the Heart* (Almeida Theatre, 2011) and Nick Grosso's *Ingredient X* (Royal Court, 2010) providing nuanced explorations of this issue. Eldridge's play delves into middle-class addiction through the complex, co-dependent relationship between Barbara and her daughter Lucy, who struggle with alcoholism and heroin use. In *Ingredient X*, Grosso begins with an intimate depiction of drug addiction among a group of women, and then expands the focus to examine obsessive and compulsive behaviours across various aspects of life. These narratives resonate with sociological analysis by linking individual experiences of addiction to broader social dynamics. They highlight how personal struggles with substance use are influenced by structural factors such as class position, personal relationships and social expectations. By embedding the subjective within the structural, these plays challenge audiences to reflect not only on the psychological and behavioural dimensions of addiction, but also on the sociopolitical conditions that perpetuate it.

Finally, the team decided to investigate two other, more expressly cultural areas, namely the media and the music business. The regulation of media ownership is a complex and contentious area, shaped by evolving economic, political and cultural forces. One of the most significant transformations in media ownership over the past four decades has been the globalization of media corporations. Today, major players in the media landscape function as

Scene 2: Social issue plays

transnational corporations (TNCs), operating across national boundaries and consolidating their influence in multiple markets. UK media, particularly its tabloid press, exemplifies this trend, with ownership concentrated in large corporate entities such as Rupert Murdoch's News International. These corporations often resist governmental regulation under the banner of press freedom, a principle that has itself been called into question by occurrences such as the phone-hacking scandal, which reached a critical juncture in 2011. Revelations that the phones of murdered schoolgirl Milly Dowler, victims of the 7/7 London bombings and relatives of deceased soldiers had been hacked by journalists working for News International's *News of the World* shocked the public and highlighted the abuses of unchecked media power. Although the subsequent Leveson Inquiry (2012) scrutinized media ethics and journalistic practices, it failed to produce substantial regulatory changes.

This lack of accountability and oversight underscores the enduring tensions between the principles of a free press and the media's social responsibilities. The dynamics of media ownership and its societal implications have been critically examined in theatrical works which invite a sociological reflection on how power dynamics within the industry influence not only public discourse, but also the ethical fabric of society. For instance, James Graham's *Ink* (Almeida Theatre, 2017) centres on the origins of these dynamics, dramatizing Rupert Murdoch's acquisition of *The Sun* in 1969 and its rapid transformation into a populist tabloid. By examining the strategies used to captivate mass audiences, the play explores the historical roots of sensationalism and the commodification of news. Similarly critical, Richard Bean's satirical drama *Great Britain* (National Theatre, 2014) provides a fictionalized yet incisive portrayal of the phone-hacking scandal. Through the character of Paige Britain, an ambitious news editor at the fictional *Free Press*, the play critiques the ethical compromises and criminal behaviours motivated by profit. Paige's unapologetic declaration, 'We go out there, and we destroy other people's lives. On your behalf', encapsulates the cynical ethos of populist tabloid journalism. The play also highlights the complicity of institutions like the Metropolitan Police, whose chief character quips, 'I can't arrest people just because they've broken the law', illustrating the erosion of accountability in the pursuit of power and profit. The politics of media regulation are further satirized through the *Free Press* owner, who argues, 'The media is over fucking regulated', advocating for an unrestrained press that prioritizes profit over truth. This laissez-faire attitude underscores broader neoliberal ideologies, and their resultant political populism, that often characterize contemporary media governance.

In contrast, on a smaller scale, Lucy Kirkwood's *NSFW* (Royal Court, 2012) shifts focus to gender issues and the exploitation inherent in media content itself. Through its portrayal of two contrasting magazines – one targeting men and the other women – it critiques how the media manipulates gender expectations, objectifies women and deceives its audience for commercial gain. Its title means 'not safe for work', indicating the accessing of inappropriate content by male consumers. Once again, UK culture is represented as problematic.

This conclusion also applies to the music industry. Pierre Bourdieu famously asserted that 'nothing more clearly affirms one's "class", nothing more infallibly classifies, than tastes in music'. Whilst the dynamics of musical taste remain relevant, a more urgent issue today is the persistent underrepresentation and mistreatment of women, a pattern that reflects broader systemic inequalities. In the UK and globally, these inequities are summarized in findings publicized by the 2019 Musicians' Union report. The study highlights the fact that women account for only about 14 per cent of writers signed to publishers and just under 20 per cent of artists signed to labels. Despite the transformative discourse of the #MeToo movement, nearly 80 per cent of women in the study reported experiencing sexism in professional contexts, with many hesitant to report harassment due to fear of retaliation or career repercussions.

This gendered disparity is powerfully dramatized in Joe Penhall's *Mood Music* (Old Vic, 2018), a play that interrogates artistic collaboration, intellectual property and the exploitation of women in the music industry. The narrative centres on Bernard, a selfish populist record producer, and Cat, a vulnerable young singer-songwriter. As they work together on an album, disputes arise over authorship, with Bernard leveraging his influence to claim credit for Cat's creative work. Penhall critiques the industry's commodification of emotional and personal experience, as illustrated by Cat's stark observation: 'The music industry isn't about healing pain and heartbreak and vulnerability. It's about selling it.' The play also delves into the psychological toll of the industry, portraying both characters in therapy sessions that reveal Bernard's narcissism and Cat's insecurity. Whilst Bernard romanticizes music as being 'good for the soul', Cat's therapist counters with a critique of the industry, arguing that it often attracts individuals with sociopathic tendencies due to its normalization of narcissism and lack of empathy. Cat's eventual recognition that Bernard exploited her – creatively and personally – underscores the pervasive socioeconomic dynamics of power and gender in the music business.

The toxic masculinity often associated with the rock and roll archetype is further explored in Simon Stephens's *Birdland* (Royal Court, 2014), which centres on Paul, a fictional rock star whose destructive behaviour epitomizes the egocentric excesses of fame. The narrative examines Paul's inability to process grief and interpersonal responsibility, particularly following the death of Marnie, the girlfriend of a bandmate. Stephens's portrayal critiques the mythos surrounding male rock icons, showing how their unchecked power perpetuates harm. Whilst these theatrical works critique the entrenched sexism and toxicity of the industry, emerging forms like 'gig theatre' have offered more inclusive and innovative spaces for musical expression. By the late 2010s, productions like Debris Stevenson's *Poet in da Corner* (Royal Court, 2018), a grime-inspired semi-autobiographical piece, and Luke Barnes's *All We Ever Wanted Was Everything* (Middle Child, 2017), a vibrant pop opera, exemplified the genre's potential to combine live music with narrative storytelling in ways that challenge traditional norms. Through these examples, the music industry emerges as a microcosm of broader societal structures, where intersecting forces of gender, power and cultural production shape individual opportunities and experiences.

In conclusion, the team notes that UK theatre offers a rich sociological lens through which to examine the structural crises within institutions, e.g. health, education and CJS, often rooted in the political policies of austerity. At the same time, theatre serves as a space for resistance and creative innovation. New works effectively engage with contemporary questions of identity whilst addressing personal responses to complex issues such as addiction. By dramatizing themes like media and creativity, these plays bring to life concepts that might otherwise remain abstract in academic discourse. However, despite the pervasive influence of populism throughout the decade, it is striking that relatively few UK plays explicitly focus on this phenomenon. Apart from the work of Bean and Graham on the UK media, populism remains an underexplored theme. In contrast, some American playwrights, such as Anne Washburn, have addressed figures like Donald Trump, yet equivalent explorations of UK populist leaders, from Nigel Farage to Boris Johnson, are notably scarce. This gap highlights an area of potential growth for UK theatre, suggesting the need for more nuanced artistic interrogations of populism and its politico-cultural impact.

SCENE THREE

Political plays

While plays which discuss society are central to new writing, some of their authors have a strong desire to change the world. However, the context for doing so was rather unpropitious in the 2010s. That decade's atmosphere of political crises was characterized by Niall Ferguson, a historian who specializes in big-picture studies of the British Empire and American imperialism, as a time of triumphant right-wing populism. In an article titled 'The people's decade: how will history come to define the 2010s?', published in the *Spectator* magazine in January 2010, he proposed that 'the past ten years be known as "the people's decade" – a time when nationalist, populist strongmen generally got the better of the "progressive" left'. Certainly, from the middle of the 2010s the most newsworthy politicians were Donald Trump, Boris Johnson and Nigel Farage, as well as Viktor Orbán in Hungary and Jair Bolsonaro in Brazil. Playwrights responded to this trend by reaffirming the oppositional role of political theatre. But this role was also much debated, and the common question was: is political theatre dead? On the one hand, the large-cast political plays – such as work by David Hare or David Edgar – were relatively rare, and critics complained that such state-of-the-nation plays were not radical because they pandered to middle-class audiences, making them feel good while changing none of their opinions. On the other hand, the decade also witnessed the emergence of playwrights such as James Graham (the new David Hare, and go-to political playwright of the 2010s), Mike Bartlett, Lucy Kirkwood, Beth Steel and Jack Thorne, who continued the tradition of critical engagement with contemporary politics.

For me, the decade began with one of the best political plays of those years, which opened at the Royal Court Theatre in April 2010, and was still running when David Cameron's Tories defeated New Labour's Gordon Brown in the general election. This was Laura Wade's *Posh*, about a group of entitled Tory boys behaving very badly. It shows the antics of the Riot Club, a gang of rich Oxford University students who rent a room in a country pub and then trash it for fun, beating up the landlord and sexually assaulting his daughter. Based on the real-life Bullingdon Club, whose past members include David Cameron, George Osborne and Boris Johnson, the play does a good job of portraying posh public-school toffs as bullies fired up by a mixture of testosterone and class antagonism. At one point, the nastiest of the pack blurts out: 'I am sick to fucking death of poor people.' Wade is careful to show the social context of privilege: these young men are connected to the most powerful families in the country, giving them a sense of impunity. Yet the drama also has a magic realist element. At one point, the ghost of an eighteenth-century Riot Club member symbolizes the reactionary's cry that the upper classes should 'take back' England from the 'peasants'. After the show, leaving the theatre you could hear people talking about it – they were not surprised that old Etonians could behave so badly, and they were angry about an elite that doesn't care about decency. Political plays like this are almost always progressive; I mean I can't think of any overtly right-wing plays. They are often openly anti-populist, and sometimes clearly radical and left-wing. So it seems apt to write about them from an ultra-left perspective.

Marxism and contemporary British theatre

The following are five draft chapters for a short book on Marxism and contemporary British theatre, written as part of a critique of the explicit and implicit politics of plays in the 2010s.

1 Theatre and soft socialism

In the era of disaster capitalism what's the role of theatre? Socialists have a rich tradition of thinking about culture and its place in society. Historically, throughout the twentieth century, each new phase of the workers' class struggle, from mass strikes to anti-colonial movements, has thrown up new engagements in radical art. The Russian Revolution – the first time that workers ever took power – released an unprecedented wave of cultural experimentation in the service of society. Whether we like it or not, we live in a society dominated by capitalist hegemony and the entitlement of a greedy bourgeoisie so you'd think that theatre might find it difficult to escape the constraints of this domination. And yet artists – including those working in theatre – always manage to carve out spaces of freedom to create their own ideas. But what kind of ideas are they producing?

During the 2010s, this freedom was evident in plays which advocated social change, but one involving a kind of 'soft socialism', very humane, very warm-hearted, very bourgeois. A good example was Duncan Macmillan's *Lungs* (2011), which stages the discussions that one nameless couple – W and M – have about whether it is ethically right to have a baby in a world where climate change is accelerating into a global emergency (fuelled by the wrong notion of economic growth). In one memorable image the carbon footprint of any new inhabitant of planet Earth is assumed to be, says W, 'Ten thousand tons of CO2 – that's the weight of the Eiffel Tower. I'd be giving birth to the Eiffel Tower.' Thus although this middle-class couple want to change the world, in the end they choose their own selfish interests over those of the community.

Other writers of the 2010s took a more documentary approach. Examples of this include *The Riots* (2011), written by journalist Gillian Slovo, who was responsible for *Guantanamo: Honor Bound to Defend Freedom* (commercially successful on both sides of the Atlantic). *The Riots* is based on interviews with participants and tells the story of the shooting by police of Mark Duggan, a twenty-nine-year-old Black British man, in 2011, and the subsequent riots in Tottenham, north London, which soon spread all over the capital and to other parts of the country. The looting, arson and disorder during that August was so bad that it quite spoilt David Cameron's holiday (he had to fly back from Tuscany). Amid the testimonies, video images of looting and arson were projected on the back wall of the stage, and the carnival atmosphere of shopping without money was joyfully presented. The play also criticizes police stop-and-search practices, and their negative attitudes to working-class youth. It offers a bold panorama of civil disaffection, highlighting issues of race discrimination and class antagonism.

Alecky Blythe's *Little Revolution* (2014) also relies on taped interviews to present an account of the same riots. This time Blythe puts herself into the story, taking her Dictaphone with her during the disturbances – and even plays herself on stage. She shows a community meeting in Hackney, East London, which has been called in order to support Siva, whose convenience store has been looted. Help for Siva comes in the form of a fundraising party (funded by Marks & Spencer). We see a middle-class couple, Tony and Sarah, organizing the fund-raising, ably supported by a local councillor and a rector. A BBC Radio 4 reporter hovers; other people muck in. It's all very polite, very English. One of the problems is that the main protagonists are all irredeemably middle-class. Meanwhile, on the working-class Pembury estate, a group of local mothers is campaigning against the criminalization of young people. This shows the reality of a society fractured by class, but here the emphasis is more on the bourgeoisie than on the proletariat. Shows like these are examples of soft socialism, doubtless well-meaning, but unable to reach those who have nothing to lose – namely the rioters themselves.

By contrast, in *Protest Song* (2013) Tim Price tells the story of Danny, a rough sleeper who has lived for years near St Paul's Cathedral. One day in 2011 he wakes up to find that the Occupy protest movement has set up camp right next to his makeshift home. Thus what follows is a series of encounters with the (mainly) nice middle-class activists that result in Danny at first helping out, but then discovering that his rough-sleeper lifestyle is incompatible with the nine-to-five routines of the middle-class protestors. Although he participates in the big meetings, he gets criticized for making too much noise at night and for bringing drink into the food tent. He eventually becomes disillusioned: as he says, 'Occupy screwed my life up. It could have given me hope.' The play is not just a satirical take on politics, but a concerted way of making the audience uncomfortable – Danny's attack on London Mayor Boris Johnson uses the c-word relentlessly.

More radical in its imagination is the poetically titled *If You Don't Let Us Dream, We Won't Let You Sleep* (2013) by Anders Lustgarten, which joins a small march of work that attempts to make sense of the effects of the global financial meltdown of 2007–8. Unlike other playwrights, Lustgarten offers a solution to the pains and penalties of economic austerity. Set in a dystopic version of current times where, to the tune of David Cameron's plummy praise of the market, the play rapidly paints a picture of triumphant neoliberalism. Prisons are organized on market principles; hospitals function for profit; and the government tries to privatize the air we breathe. In the streets, people riot. Fat-cat bankers and hedge-fund managers are on one side of the barricade, and on the other are Ryan, a young working-class lad in trouble with the police, and McDonald, an African migrant. After a rapid series of tableaux the short play ends in a squatted courthouse in which a group of protestors aim to put capitalism on trial. None of this is likely to convince anyone in power, but that is precisely the point. Lustgarten convincingly argues that austerity is a political coup whose purpose is to open up more areas for the privatization of everyday life. Thus these new markets will enrich the few while the many will only get poorer. Like the activists it puts on stage, the play doesn't care what you think. It simply tells it as it is.

But the point is not just to admire these plays, the point is to change the world.

2 Digital turbo-capitalism

The digital world is everywhere, but can it be used for liberation? Discussions about it are reminiscent of Marx's Introduction to *A Contribution to the Critique of Hegel's Philosophy of Right*, first published in 1844, where he says, 'Religious suffering is, at one and the same time, the expression of real suffering and a protest against real suffering. Religion is the sigh of the oppressed creature, the heart of a heartless world, and the soul of soulless conditions. It is the opium of the people.' In the same way, the new digital religion of Facebook, Instagram and TikTok is our opium. Thus one good argument for going to the theatre is to get away from your screen. Theatre can also offer examples of opposition to today's turbo-charged capitalism, which is the one and only orthodoxy, proclaimed by economists, celebrated by Wall Street and top corporations, and embraced by all the mainstream political parties of Europe.

Two plays illustrate the current malaise: *The Ritual Slaughter of Gorge Mastromas* (2013) by Dennis Kelly, and *Linda* (2015) by Penelope Skinner. Both plays are portraits of individualistic free-market entrepreneurs. In Kelly's play Gorge is a gawky young man who always chooses safety – until he meets a female entrepreneur who asset-strips the company he's working for and teaches him to be ruthless. But as the title signals he eventually implodes in what is an eccentric satire on capitalist values. In Skinner's play, Linda is a fifty-five-year-old senior brand manager for the Swan Beauty Corporation, and she's making a pitch about selling cosmetics and anti-ageing cream to older women. Her high-powered work is compromised by two Nemesis figures, a younger woman at work and a young man who knows her husband. The themes of body image, older women and intergenerational conflict are stated and restated. Both plays are three-hour marathons infused with a kind of sad nihilism. Thus the enjoyable satire on turbo-capitalism is undercut by the absence of any attempt to propose an alternative. Both playwrights are saying: 'Enjoy the fun of taking the piss – there's nothing else you can do about today's super-rich.'

Meanwhile, some work is more explicitly oppositional: Zeldin's *Beyond Caring* (2015) looks at the infamous zero-hours contracts, which have been much debated in recent years. As such, it is a rare representation of the working classes of today, featuring as it does three agency workers, Becky, Susan and Grace, ruled over by Ian, a jobsworth mini-Hitler who evaluates their work and sets their gruelling schedules. The workers are not only poor, but lonely too (loneliness and the lack of nourishing social contacts are a feature of poverty). They have been pushed to a point where they are beyond feelings, apart from desperation. Yes, it's a shit world full of shit jobs! But while much of *Beyond Caring* has the quiet power of suffering humanity, surely it doesn't need theatre to tell us about them. We already know!

If theatre should inspire political change, one example of this is Tim Price's *Teh Internet Is Serious Business* (2014). It is a semi-documentary account of how Anonymous and LulzSec, a collective swarm of hacktivists, took on some of the most powerful capitalists in the world without leaving their bedrooms. The story features online hackers with fictional personas such as Kayla the Japanese tease, Sabu the badmouth, Narcotroll the black-suited punk and Ryan the anarchist. They inhabit the colourful and unpredictable world of internet chatrooms with their Grumpy Cats, Sad Storm Troopers, Socially Awkward Penguins and cruising paedos. Out of this digital Wild West a group, Anonymous, coalesces and vows to right wrongs. Their targets include the FBI, CIA, Rupert Murdoch's Fox News, Tom Cruise and the Church of Scientology. Other case studies include sad stories about the trolling of a suicide's Facebook page, and black humour about the dark net. If the desire of these hackers for social justice is inspiring, some of their rhetoric is naive, with slogans about 'Total freedom' and 'No rules' smacking more of bourgeois individualism than collective protest. But they are welcome on the barricades anyway!

One other play focuses on individual experience. Leo Butler's *Boy* (2016) indicts today's compromised welfare state, which has suffered Tory cuts for years, by showing what happens to Liam, who's just left school, but is not in education, employment or training (NEET in state speak). At a loss about how to survive, he visits doctors and other welfare functionaries, all of whom are unable (or unwilling) to help. Youngsters like him are a symbol of our uncaring society. He's the quintessential loser, except that this play implicitly argues that *we* are the losers to think of him like that and invites us to see him as a casualty of the system. Because that is what he is. Thus while most of these plays give a welcome airing of political issues created by rampant capitalism, they are unable to offer coherent solutions to today's alienation.

3 Going global

Your enemies should have some admirable qualities – otherwise what's the point of opposing them? In the *Communist Manifesto* Marx cannot resist admiring the revolutionary vigour of the bourgeoisie, showing how 'The need of a constantly expanding market for its products chases the bourgeoisie over the whole surface of the globe. It must nestle everywhere, settle everywhere, establish connections everywhere.' As 'all old-established national industries' are 'daily being destroyed', an international global system is created. Thus today's experience of globalization is the inevitable result of this capitalist process, the latest chapter of the evolution of a worldwide market for goods and services. This global new order has also been discussed in the theatre.

For example, the rise of China attracted immediate interest: *Hungry Ghosts*, a play by Tim Luscombe (2010), is about Shanghai lawyer Pin-de trying to save her sister, who has been condemned to death by the Chinese government for political protest. She seeks help from her brother, Zhi-hui, a party member, property developer and journalist. The story shows how reformers try to embarrass the state. By contrast, the hugely successful

Chimerica (2013) by Lucy Kirkwood has a grander global reach. She creates an imaginative epic journey for a fictional American photographer, Joe Schofield, who once snapped a career-defining picture of the 'tank man', the image of the lone activist standing in front of a tank during the Tiananmen Square protests in 1989, and has now heard that the young protestor is alive and living in the United States. Joe's quest takes him through the Chinese community there, while in Beijing his contact, Zhang Lin, engages with his own struggle against the authorities. Angered because his neighbour has died of air pollution, Zhang Lin tells Joe the story. The play's title, a neologism coined by historian Niall Ferguson and economist Moritz Schularick, describes the symbiotic, and toxic, relationship between the two superpowers, China and America, after the end of the Cold War. But Kirkwood's play is not a documentary; it's a rather tragic story of humans caught in two very different cultural binds. In America, the individual is free to pursue any mission they like – just as long as there is a market for it. In China, the individual is free to participate in the market – just as long as they don't go on a reforming mission.

Other globally significant events have also attracted playwrights. For example, the Arab Spring of 2010–11, arguably the most important international event after the credit crunch, is featured in Hassan Abdulrazzak's *The Prophet* (2012). Part of the Gate Theatre's *Resist!* season, it was set in Cairo on 28 January 2011, during the revolution that toppled dictator Hosni Mubarak, and features a young middle-class couple, Hisham and Layla. He is a novelist who wants to be recognized internationally, and she works as a senior engineer with Vodafone and is ordered by her boss to close down the phone network to impede the demonstrators. One of her monologues is a thrilling eyewitness account of a massive demonstration. But Abdulrazzak is not uncritical: he questions how the more privileged classes respond to great historical events, when people are dying in the streets, showing the gap between intellectuals who extol revolution and the workers who create it. Thus the play is great at representing the mass of ordinary humanity which, when it gets moving, is well-nigh unstoppable.

On the other side of the Mediterranean, where Greece is now a symbol of the failure of the euro, and of the iniquity of the IMF, a different historical perspective is given by Alexi Kaye Campbell's *Sunset at the Villa Thalia* (2016), a play which starts in April 1967, on the island of Skiathos. An English thirty-something arty couple, playwright Theo and actress Charlotte, are renting a peasant cottage. After a chance meeting, they invite an older American pair, Harvey and June, over for drinks. It soon emerges that the charismatic Harvey 'works for the Government' (code for CIA), and a right-wing military coup is taking place in Athens. The play's second half is set in

1976, after the fall of the colonels and the start of a new democracy. This is an account of the pressure exerted by America on nations where communists have public support; the power of finance; and the role of art in articulating the anxieties of society.

An even greater historical sweep is offered by Ella Hickson's *Oil* (2016), which focuses on capitalism's exploitation of a fundamental natural resource. Five scenarios span an epic 160 years, showing one character, a strong woman called May, who appears in different incarnations, giving a glimpse of five fictional female lives. At first, in 1889, she is a Cornish farmer's wife, oppressed by patriarchy, and the catalyst for her emancipation is the arrival of an American selling oil. Next, in Tehran in 1908 May is a servant, with an eight-year-old daughter, Amy, at the British colonial residence. In the background the Persian Shah is being courted by the British for his oil. The third episode sees May as a Hampstead businesswoman in 1970. In her forties, she is an oil executive and Amy is her fifteen-year-old daughter. But a revolution in Libya, led by Colonel Gaddafi, means she has to negotiate the nationalization of that country's oil wells. The fourth and fifth scenarios are both set in the future. In 2021 Baghdad, May, now an MP, arrives in the desert to find Amy, now an aid worker, to persuade her to return home. Finally, we're back in Cornwall, in 2051, when the age of oil is over, and May and Amy are much older, sitting in the cold because fuel stocks are low and it looks like only some new technologies from China can save them. Globalization indeed.

Equally astute is *Labyrinth* (2016) by Beth Steel, a good play about the effect that New York bankers have on the fragile economies of Central and South America. Beginning in 1978, she shows how the banks lent millions of dollars to the governments of South American countries in order to fund various infrastructural projects such as power stations. The trouble is most of these projects won't ever get built, and most of the money will disappear into the pockets of the ruling elites. The story moves from Brazil to Argentina to Mexico and Central America. Thus both Hickson and Steel mount strong surgical strikes at the global economy, but in the end they have little to offer in terms of practical politics.

With increasing globalization comes increased migration. *Lampedusa* (2015) by Anders Lustgarten compares two lives: one is Stefano, an Italian fisherman whose job it is to pull drowned bodies out of the sea off the island of Lampedusa, landfall for desperate people being transported to Europe from North Africa in un-seaworthy boats. The other is Denise, who is a debt collector for pay-day loans on the poor council estates of the UK. She is a Chinese-British student and experiences racist insults and anti-migrant hate speech. By showing both of these workers, whose job it is to clear up the mess left by the global system, Lustgarten makes the point that we are all connected.

On a similar theme, Joe Murphy and Joe Robertson's commercially successful *The Jungle* (2017) is a docu-drama about the European migration crisis, and acts as a testament to the individuality and complexity of the refugee experience. Set in an Afghan restaurant in the Jungle camp in Calais, the play's narrator is Safi, a thirty-five-year-old Syrian man and a former Eng Lit student. He takes us back to March 2015, when the camp or shanty town began to fill with people. Soon, after the picture of Alan Kurdi – the child from Syria washed up on a beach – went viral, British volunteers start to arrive. The power of the play tends to obscure just how middle-class this whole venture is: it focuses more on the British volunteers than on refugees. It tells us little we didn't already know, but it's done with integrity and commitment.

Workers of the world unite – you have nothing to lose but the chains of global exploitation.

4 Politics and history

In his essay 'The Eighteenth Brumaire of Louis Bonaparte' Marx memorably writes: 'Hegel remarks somewhere that all great world-historic facts and personages appear, so to speak, twice. He forgot to add: the first time as tragedy, the second time as farce.' This comment can be adapted to any history play: historical fictions always reappear, the second time as entertainment, not necessarily farcical, but certainly drained of politics.

A good example of this tendency is James Graham's 2012 commercially successful *This House*, which looks at the 1970s, a tumultuous decade with runaway inflation, huge strikes and massive social change. It's a docu-drama that takes place in the House of Commons during the 1974–9 Labour government. The protagonists are not the major politicians – Wilson, Callaghan and Thatcher – but the whips, the behind-the-scenes teams responsible for getting MPs to vote. At the time there was a hung parliament and then a minority Labour administration that had to make deals with the Liberals and Scottish Nationalists. Thus the play shows the various tricks used by the whips on both sides to get MPs to vote. It's about the mechanics of power, not ideas; about process, not policy – a political drama without politics.

One of British theatre's favourite past decades is the 1980s, a time of the arch-reactionary Thatcher and overt class struggle. A good example is Moira Buffini's commercially successful *Handbagged* (2013), which stages a fictional account of the weekly meetings when prime ministers see the monarch for 20 minutes to bring her up to speed on current events. The Queen, of course, has devoted herself to a lifelong service of her country while Thatcher, her prime minister, is unashamedly ideological, inflexible and iron-souled. In one amusing scene, Mrs T is appalled by the Queen's Christmas speech, which she sees as criticizing her policies. She asks her husband Denis, 'Is Her Majesty a socialist?', and he replies: 'I don't think she's an actual Trot, old love.' In clashes between the crown and the prime minister, it's a theatrical convention that the Queen comes off best. So this is a play about how a famous handbagger herself gets handbagged – a case of poetic justice, of fair play, but more myth than history.

Simon Woods's *Hansard* (2019) also looks back at the 1980s. Set on 28 May 1988 in the spacious kitchen of a posh Georgian house in Oxfordshire, it is about a marriage in crisis. Robin Hesketh, a Tory junior minister who went to Eton, Oxford and the bar, has just voted in favour of Thatcher's Local Government Bill – with its notorious anti-gay Section 28 – but his wife Diana is more liberal, a *Guardian* reader with less prejudiced attitudes. Thus the clash between homophobia and tolerance echoes around the stage. Like many plays about the problems of upper-middle-class marriages, *Hansard* is also about Englishness, about national identity. A key line is Diana's jibe: 'It's the great mystery of our time: the insatiable desire of the people of this country to be fucked by an Old Etonian.' Despite its title, this story is more about marriage than parliament.

The popularity of plays about the past is further evidenced by Peter Morgan, who went on to create the Netflix global smash *The Crown*. His *The Audience* (2013), like *Handbagged*, creates entertainment from its account of the weekly Buckingham Palace meetings between PM and HM (played by Helen Mirren). We get loving caricatures of once familiar faces: avuncular Winston Churchill, wired Anthony Eden, domineering Thatcher, self-effacing John Major, awkward David Cameron, and Labour leaders such as smug Blair (played by the same actor as Cameron!), agitated Gordon Brown and a bluff Harold Wilson. The Queen is shown not only as a warm human being but also as the mistress of the witty putdown and more progressive than her prime ministers. Republicans, gnash your teeth!

History can also be infused with passion. Beth Steel's *Wonderland* (2014) is an account of the great miners' strike of 1984–5 which looks at both the personal and political lives of a group of workers. In what is clearly a labour of love, the play takes us down the pit, and the sheer physical effort of mining is correctly represented. As well as working, the miners sing working-class ballads and tell jokes. These underground scenes alternate with others which show monetarist economists, Tory government ministers and Coal Board leaders plotting to destroy the National Union of Mineworkers. In a series of documentary snapshots, the Thatcher government is shown planning the destruction of the coal industry. Thus they lay a trap and Arthur Scargill's

NUM walks into it. The painful final 30 minutes show how the strike is broken, and the effects of defeat. It's very moving, but also masculine: why no women on stage?

Similarly passionate is radical playwright David Edgar's one-man show *Trying It On* (2018), which he performs himself as a piece of personal history. Aged twenty in 1968, the year of student revolts, he tells his life story in the form of a conversation between the person he is now at age seventy and his younger self. The show charts the history of the British left and its recurrent theme is the danger posed by right-wing populism. Edgar talks about being the writer for the General Will, a small agitprop company performing Marxist plays to working-class audiences. He memorably conveys the surreal joys of community arts activism and then some of the changes that affected left-wing groups in the 1970s, when identity politics – feminist, gay and Black activism – came into conflict with Marxist ideologies. He explains how straight male lefties saw identity issues as a 'distraction' from the anti-capitalist struggle. He also includes video interviews with comrades from the past, so the voices of feminist activists are present. Although this is a significant contribution to the struggle, Edgar finds himself in the paradoxical situation of middle-class radicals: the object of his desire for change, the working class, is nowhere to be seen; his main instrument of intervention is the pen.

After all, as Marx once wrote, 'Men make their own history, but they do not make it as they please; they do not make it under self-selected circumstances, but under circumstances existing already, given and transmitted from the past.' That's the central lesson of history.

5 Poor Old Labour

Today we have to consider the poverty of social democracy in an era of populist neo-conservatism. In the past, revolutionaries such as Lenin could take a pragmatic view of the British Labour Party, advocating support for it in general elections, while remaining critical of its basic nature. In *What Is to Be Done?*, Lenin argues that workers do spontaneously gravitate towards socialism, but they are influenced even more by bourgeois ideology. Since then, most Marxists have understood that social democratic parties exist to serve capitalism by reforming it, rather than to overthrow the system. Even the election in 2015 of Jeremy Corbyn to the Labour leadership cannot change the fact that this party's hope is to install a more benign form of capitalism than the one currently wrecking the world.

The Labour Party certainly attracts playwrights. One has returned to this subject more than once: Jack Thorne, whose previous work includes not only the commercially successful *Harry Potter and the Cursed Child* (2016), but also *2nd May 1997* (2009), which takes place on the night of Blair's election. In another play, he examines the relationship between the personal and the political: the aptly named *Hope* (2014) is about local politics in a northern town. Faced with another round of Tory austerity cuts, Hilary and Mark, leaders of the Labour council, at first decide to co-operate. But the resistance of Gina, who runs a threatened day centre for adults with learning disabilities and is Mark's ex-wife, shows them that there is another option. Thorne combines contemporary references – to Twitter and YouGov – with more traditional concerns, such as solidarity and the desire to make a difference. Thus he neatly weaves in his characters' family – Mark's girlfriend Julie, his son Jake and Julie's father George, an Old Labourite – into a story which shows how the desire for change can be handed down through the generations. By contrast, Thorne's *The End of History* (2019) is a middle-class family comedy set in the kitchen of David and Sal, two lefties who live in Newbury. Over three different time periods – 1997, 2007 and 2017 – we watch how they relate to their three children, Carl, Polly and Tom (each named after a revolutionary). But despite the play's title, which refers to Francis Fukuyama's 1992 book about the apparent triumph of Western liberal democracy, there is almost nothing about politics here: Blair, Brown and finally Brexit are name-checked, but nothing is discussed. Instead of any political content, what we get is a picture of middle-class generational tensions in a comedy that is both belittling and reactionary.

David Hare, a 1970s radical playwright who moved from the political margins to mainstream theatrical success, is still an important voice. But his *I'm Not Running* (2018) is a disappointment to anyone looking for answers to current political questions. It's about Pauline, a medical student in Newcastle in 1997, but although she's dating Jack Gould, a young law student and Labour activist modelled on the Milibands, she is apolitical. Things change when she starts working as a junior doctor in Corby hospital, especially when one of her patients tells her that the hospital faces closure because of austerity. Galvanized by this, Pauline decides to run for parliament as an independent, but can she resist the lure of joining Labour? Although it examines the role of women in two of our defining national institutions – the NHS and Labour – Hare is more concerned with his fictional female protagonist than with Brexit, the anti-Semitism row or austerity. It's a play about Labour in which it's hard to distinguish the Corbynites from the new Blairites.

Equally deflating is *Labour of Love* (2017) by James Graham, which opens with the familiar chords of the White Stripes' 'Seven Nation Army', the tune of the chant of 'Oh, Jeremy Corbyn!', and tells the story of David, a young Yorkshire-born but Oxford-educated candidate who gets Ashfield, a safe northern Labour seat, in 1990. Because his wife Elizabeth, a lawyer friend of

Cherie Blair, isn't keen on constituency work, David persuades Jean, wife of the retiring MP, to stay on as his election agent. Thus, over the next twenty-seven years, we watch the ups and downs of his life as a Blairite MP, and his arguments with his more left-wing colleagues, especially the feisty Jean. The story of the Kinnock years, the Blair years and the Miliband years is a tale of missed opportunities and betrayal. This image of a party that always fails its radical supporters acts like a compensatory massage for all bruised Blairites, full of centre-left good intentions. In other plays, Labour often gets a mention, usually with a negative twist. In David Eldridge's *Beginning* (2017), for example, Laura is a Labour Party member and supports Corbyn, but she has no time for leafletting or other activity. Definitely a sign of our times.

Labour's attempts to articulate radical policies have often ended in electoral failure. A good example is the party split of 1981, told by Steve Waters in his *Limehouse* (2017), about a group of senior right-wing Labour members – David Owen, Roy Jenkins, Shirley Williams and Bill Rodgers – who meet in secret and set up the Social Democratic Party (SDP). Known as the Gang of Four, their drastic move was a response to the success of left-wing militants within Labour. Several highly intelligent passages have echoes today: at one point, Rodgers asks why Labour members 'always hate our leaders', and 'Why this distaste for office as if power was somehow a betrayal?' But, in the end, the conclusion is that 'The Labour Party's the house hope built for us'. These events resonate with Labour's current woes with Corbyn, who, like Michael Foot in 1981, is seen as unelectable. Thus although senior party figures don't like him, he's still popular among the rank and file. A passionate tale of one of these grassroots radicals is told in James Fritz's *Parliament Square* (2017). Kat is a young wife and mother, both idealistic and energetic. Fed up with political inaction she decides to end her life by setting fire to herself in Parliament Square. It's a form of protest that is chillingly reminiscent of similar cases in Czechoslovakia (1969) and Algeria (2011, Arab Spring). Although the reasons for Kat's self-immolation are a bit vague, Fritz shows her debating the rights and wrongs of staying with her husband Tommy and daughter Jo, against the passionate desire to change the world.

The time has now come to reconsider the options for British social democracy in the era of crises, pandemics and increased global warming. Come on, Labourites, one more effort if you want to become radicals.

SCENE FOUR

Brexit plays

One of the hottest political topics of the 2010s was Brexit, meaning the result of the European Union (EU) membership referendum held on 23 June 2016, when 51.89 per cent of the votes were for Leave and 48.11 per cent were for Remain, a small margin in favour of quitting the EU. By far the most successful fictional account of this divisive campaign appeared not in a theatre, but on television. It was *Brexit: The Uncivil War* (Channel 4, 2019), written by a political playwright – James Graham. The singular thing about it was its very sympathetic account of the Leave campaign, featuring a group of people such as Boris Johnson and Dominic Cummings, personalities despised by most progressives. As Graham says, 'I want to a certain extent to empathize with someone who you politically disagree with.' To make good drama, he argues, 'I want to understand what motivates them.' *Brexit: The Uncivil War* starred Benedict Cumberbatch as Cummings, and was well reviewed. You can see the same empathetic approach in Graham's other plays, such his portrayal of Rupert Murdoch in *Ink* (Almeida Theatre, 2017) or Charles Ingram in *Quiz* (Minerva Theatre, Chichester, 2017): Ingram was the former army major who won a million pounds on ITV's *Who Wants to Be a Millionaire?* before being prosecuted for cheating.

Theatre's failure to engage explicitly with Brexit is perhaps a failure to engage with populism in the wider society. It is, after all, a hugely divisive issue. I can think of only a couple of fringe plays which mention Brexit. One is Stephen Laughton's *Screens* (Theatre503, 2016), about a twenty-five-year-old gay British Cypriot, maybe the first to include a passing mention of this contentious subject. Then there's Sue Healy's *Imaginationship* (Finborough Theatre, 2018), a family drama set in the summer of 2016, in Great Yarmouth, a place which voted 70 per cent to leave the EU and a symbol of left-behind areas impoverished by austerity. So why have theatre-makers been so reluctant to tackle this issue? It may have been because a majority of them were Remainers, but didn't want to appear elitist or anti-democratic by staging anti-Brexit plays; it may be because this was such a hot topic; it may be because the subject is too obvious. Anyway, with a nod to Graham's empathy with the folk I disagree with, here is one Leave voter's view of the subject.

A Brexiteer speaks

RIGHT, let's get one thing straight from the off. I'm a Leave voter, and have no regrets, repeat NO REGRETS. I know, I know, you're already jumping to conclusions: you're thinking – here's another small-minded, knuckle-dragging bigot waving a flag. But hang on a minute. Being a patriot? Loving the Queen? Being proud of this little island of ours? What, pray tell, is so terribly wrong with that?

Look, I'm no thug. When someone like Jeremy Clarkson spouts off about everyone living in a bucket of shame because their great-great-grandad bought a hairbrush that might have been made by slaves, I wince. I do. I properly do.

Anyway, I've been in local government for what feels like centuries now. I'm good at it, and long may it continue. Steady hand on the tiller and all that.

Obviously, I don't agree with the arguments of the Remainers, and have good colleagues at work who practically drool about all things European, although in private, when talking to my wife, I call them papists (being Spanish this gets right up her nostrils!).

That said, listening to Remainers doesn't bother me. I'm not one of those snowflakes; I don't cancel people I disagree with. I wouldn't call myself woke but new ideas don't make me froth at the mouth; they're just fads – like kale smoothies – and I always say to myself: it will pass, it's just a phase.

Unlike some, I still read newspapers, actual ones with ink and paper. None of this 'swipe to refresh' rubbish. I'm quite religious about the *Daily Telegraph* – good journalism and plenty to mull over. I don't watch much TV but have recently discovered Netflix and now I'm hooked on those big series.

But every now and then my wife drags me to the theatre – and sometimes I quite enjoy the experience (okay, I occasionally sneak in a power nap when the pace slackens, all in the name of art of course).

As an unrepentant Brexiteer I was surprised to see that the National Theatre, after all one of our flagship institutions, did actually stage a play that, uniquely as far as I can see, was about Brexit. Yes, you heard me: Brexit, on stage. A rare moment of relevance.

I'm referring to *My Country; A Work in Progress*, which was put on in March 2017 as a quick-fire response to the historic vote. Carol Ann Duffy, our Poet Laureate, teamed up with Rufus Norris, who runs the place, to create a play from a collection of edited testimonials from people living around the UK. Apparently, Norris felt that his theatre should reflect the thoughts of the country. No shit, Sherlock!

It gets better, though. One of my colleagues told me that on 'The Cultural Response', a Radio 4 special some time the previous summer, Norris called the Brexit vote a 'wake-up call' and warned that the arts have become 'out of touch' with some parts of the country. No kidding! So, in a move that's unheard of for a chap so embedded in the metropolitan elite, he sent his staff into the wilds of Britain – yes, outside the M25 – to actually listen to people.

Result? It's a cracking piece. Best bit? No vox pops from people in London. All well and good: who wants to hear the grumblings of Remoaners all over again? And nothing from EU settled migrants – who didn't have a vote anyway. Not their circus, not their monkeys.

Anyway, the play kicks off with Britannia meeting representatives of Caledonia, Cymru, Northern Ireland, South-West England, the North-East and the East Midlands. The play is divided into sections about Europe, patriotism, immigration, the vote and all that jazz.

What hit home for me is the anger of Leavers. In Scotland a state school seethes over the privileges of Fettes public school (most famous ex-pupil arch-Remainer Tony Blair). A Somali refugee gets a cushy flat while the hard-working Midlander gets zilch. The EU dictates the shape of bananas and asylum seekers send money home to criminal mates. A Welsh copper condemns a tenant who claims more in benefits than she earns. Spot on.

Plenty of humour too: Scotland (kilts), Wales (rugby) and Northern Ireland (line dancing) all played for laughs.

A couple of quotes from Boris make everything go with a bang: 'Let's say knickers to the pessimists.' Pure Boris brilliance.

Then there's some glorious eccentricity – a chap called Philip from the North-East equates Britishness with sitting 'in a damp shed, brewing tea, pouring down rain', and don't forget the Geordie chip pizza, terrorists in Wiltshire and a good joke about a brothel. Genius!

I also caught a couple of plays that seemed to understand which way the wind was blowing. One was *Hangmen*, staged at the Royal Court at its smug metropolitan address in Sloane Square. This venue had just had a makeover of a fresh coat of paint, and plastered the place with huge messages: the front doors shout: 'Come In' (as if we couldn't work that one out on our own); the foyer is full of scribblings about the need for fundraising, audiences numbers and how many schoolkids attend. Riveting.

No matter, let's talk about *Hangmen*. It's by Martin McDonagh, the brains behind the Oscar-winning *Three Billboards Outside Ebbing, Missouri*, and it's a scabrous comedy about two executioners: Harry, the main hangman, and his hopeless assistant Syd. The running gag is that, compared to the celebrated real-life executioner Albert Pierrepoint, the fictional Harry is second-best.

Most of the play takes place in 1965 on the day that capital punishment was abolished, and we find ourselves in Harry's pub in Oldham, where he's retired. It's dingy, nicotine-stained and greasy as a chip pan but Harry is a local legend, and the place bursts with his cronies.

Helped by his long-suffering wife Alice and teenage daughter Shirley, he rules the roost. Everyone, especially a nosey newspaper hack, wants to know about his job, and you can understand the interest: Harry certainly has some tales to tell.

But what's this got to do with anything? For one, McDonagh nails the lost world of the northern English working class – warm beer, blokey camaraderie and a steady stream of jokes at the expense of women. He even throws in digs at the Germans, fat people, and, yes, the deaf (which was pushing it a bit). But McDonagh clearly doesn't give a toss about PC-ness. Oh, and there are some excellent cock jokes, of course there are.

The comedy is sharp as a guillotine, and Harry has no moral hand-wringing about his old job. State-sanctioned killing? Just another day at the office. But what struck me most was Harry's seething envy of people who'd done better for themselves – the kind of resentment behind the Brexit vote.

So the play paints a defiant picture of a Britain too long ignored by the pro-European, latte-sipping elites. Unsurprisingly, it was a smash hit, transferring to the West End and then hopping across the pond to Broadway. Proof that a handful of cock jokes can cross any border.

Another play at this address, *The Ferryman*, has also got pedigree. Directed by Sam Mendes – who gave us *Skyfall* and *Spectre* – it was drowning in hype before it even opened. A West End transfer was locked in faster than a speeding Aston Martin. Naturally, there was a lemming-like rush for tickets but I managed to snag one for a Saturday matinee. Worth every penny.

The story, written by Jez Butterworth, is set in rural County Armagh in 1981. Now, I've got an uncle who was a squaddie in Northern Ireland around that time but that's something for another day. The drama takes place in the Carney family home, bursting at the seams. Quinn Carney, the head of this farming family, is ex-IRA. His wife Mary spends most of her time in bed, convinced she's dying of one thing or another. They've got seven children, ranging from nine months to sixteen years. Seven! Imagine the noise.

Add in the old-timers and Caitlin, the wife of Quinn's long-missing brother Seamus, and the house is heaving. Then along comes Father Horrigan with some cheery news: Seamus, who everyone thought had simply vanished, was executed by the IRA a decade ago. The revelation drops right in the middle of the family's harvest fair, which only adds to the chaos as nephews pile in. By the end, the stage is overflowing with people, plus a real baby, a live goose and even a real rabbit. Honestly, it's Noah's Ark crashing a rural Irish kitchen.

Butterworth really nails the community-driven chaos of Northern Irish rural life. The Carneys are steeped in tradition, clinging to old rituals and political beliefs, and enough Catholic guilt to make my wife nod in recognition. It's part *Father Ted*, part Irish folklore, with a dollop of Paddywack on the side. *The Ferryman* is magnificent – a roaring, chaotic, goose-filled reminder of a world far removed from the quinoa of the metropolitan elite.

But looming in the background are the IRA hunger strikes of 1981, a stark reminder of how terrorist thugs tried – and failed – to blackmail Thatcher. Butterworth doesn't sugar-coat the violence of the IRA, showing it for what it was: vile, brutal, morally bankrupt. Although the play isn't explicitly about Brexit, it does confirm one's suspicions about the Catholic community of Northern Ireland. All that political baggage – no wonder they voted Remain.

Ah, Jez Butterworth. The man seems to have his finger on the pulse of rural Britain. His earlier smash hit, *Jerusalem*, has been doing the rounds again, reminding us that he knows exactly how to capture the glorious antagonism of rural pissheads and drug-addled dropouts against all respectable folk and the nanny state. These are the same lads who were told to vote Remain but instead stuck two fingers up at the establishment. With its cheeky nod to my favourite hymn, *Jerusalem* paints a vivid picture of marginalized folk who've had enough of being told what to do.

Now, on to Mike Bartlett. I'd heard of him because he wrote *Doctor Foster*, the BBC show everyone was raving about but I never bothered watching. He also wrote a play called *Albion*, which my wife did see. She got me to read a couple of reviews afterwards, and frankly that's all I needed to get the gist.

Albion is set in an English garden. Of course it is. It's overgrown, crumbling and desperately clinging to past glories – a metaphor for, guess what, the entire country. The story revolves around Audrey, a wealthy, bossy, middle-aged design mogul who's moved into a country house with a historic 1920s garden, called Albion, originally built as a pastoral paradise for First World War heroes, and now a battleground.

Audrey is in conflict with her metropolitan millennial daughter Zara, and Anna, the grieving partner of her son who died in some distant war. Audrey wants to restore the garden, to reclaim some mythical version of Britain that never existed in the first place. Meanwhile, her daughter and daughter-in-law obsess about all the messy stuff – identity, loss, politics. You can imagine.

Even if the symbolism is so thick you could spread it on toast, this seems to be the best post-referendum play out there. Apparently, one character bangs on about the 'European temperament', the 'shocking result of a completely unnecessary plebiscite' and the 'wilfully ignorant people full of hate'. Well, we all know that's Remoaner shorthand for Leavers.

Apart from this sore-loser rhetoric, there's Krystyna, the Polish migrant cleaner who's worked her way up to small-time entrepreneur. She's my kind of migrant: hardworking, practical, no sense of entitlement. According to one review, she delivers a cracker of a line about Britain's respect for money and hard work. She reckons Polish workers are already being accepted because they graft – unlike some of the under-skilled locals grumbling about immigration. Brexit tensions in a nutshell.

All in all, *Albion* sounds like a thoughtful, occasionally preachy and pretty accurate exploration of post-Brexit Britain. If Bartlett's trying to show us the mess we're in, fair enough. At least he's doing it with a bit of style and a touch of dirt under his fingernails.

Oh, yes, our theatre. Apparently, even the fringe brigade has decided to wade into the Brexit debate. My niece – who's very into amateur theatricals (earnest monologues and bad wigs) – told me about a play by someone called Carla Grauls. The play, *Occupied*, features a Romanian character, Alex, whose big speech I found in some blog. Copy and pasted here:

> But you see, it is your problem. Because where Romania go, where do the hundreds, thousands of Romanians come to get jobs, to get a better life? England! It's the pretending I hate. The way the English pretend to care when they don't. Why not be like other Europeans and show your hatred instead of hiding it in your tolerance?

Well, Alex, point taken. Clearly, the Brexit referendum wasn't just about trade or sovereignty. It was also about ripping off the sticking plaster of polite pretence. Which let a lot of people say what they really thought.

Then there's the claim – presumably from someone with an arts degree and too much time on their hands – that Brexit has given classic plays like *Henry V* and *Saint Joan* new meanings. Really? Shakespeare and Shaw, reimagined through the lens of Brexit? Sounds like a desperate attempt by Remoaners to make everything about Europe. Newsflash: Shakespeare didn't write about fishing quotas or freedom of movement.

Look, here's one thing that baffles me: for a group of people who love nothing more than virtue-signalling, why haven't theatre-makers written more plays about Brexit? Is it too difficult for them to engage with the views of 17.4 million people who didn't agree with their vision of Brussels nirvana?

Right, let's do their job for them. Here's a thought: how about a good old-fashioned farce about EU bureaucrats? The joys of laughter! Endless meetings about the curvature of bananas and who can call a Cornish pasty a Cornish pasty. Or how about a gripping drama about the eurozone debt crisis? Greece in flames, Germany playing the stern father and the French shrugging in existential indifference.

And why, oh why, hasn't anyone written *The Nigel Farage Story*? The man is a game-changer. You can't argue with that. Picture it: the pint-drinking, fagin-hand crusader storming the Strasburg barricades. It practically writes itself.

Then there's some juicy historical material. Edward Heath dragging us into the Common Market. Enoch Powell and Tony Benn – strange bedfellows – uniting against it. Or even a play exploring the cultural ties between Britain and Europe. Mozart, Monet and a good Merlot. But no, instead we have endless navel-gazing about how awful it was to Leave.

This lack of courage from cultural bigwigs speaks volumes. They lost because they were too timid, too afraid to confront reality. So let's get this crystal: this lack of guts tells you all you need to know about the Remoaners, and their pusillanimity. Great word! The reason Remainers lost the vote in the first place is that they were weak. Grrr, silence was their safety blanket. Still is. Poor darling ostriches.

SCENE FIVE

Dystopian plays

Although there were few plays about Brexit as a particular political and social moment, the decade did witness an upsurge in shows which had a more generally dystopian theme. This is quite remarkable because British theatre has previously more or less ignored science-fiction scenarios, even while novels, films and television have embraced the genre. The reasons for this include a kind of snobbish distain for ever-popular dystopian imaginings, a sense that serious drama wasn't interested in futuristic visions, or metaphors, and a marked preference for naturalism and realism over fantasy and the imagination. In the 2010s, all this changed. One example of the commercial success of dystopias is Duncan Macmillan and Robert Icke's *1984*, their adaptation of George Orwell's classic novel, which started at the Nottingham Playhouse in 2013, in a co-production with Headlong theatre company, then transferred to the Almeida Theatre, an Off-West End venue in north London. It spent the next five years being repeatedly restaged in the West End, on Broadway and in Australia. When *1984* returned to Nottingham in 2015 as part of the theatre's *Conspiracy Season*, Icke was interviewed for the venue's website. He said:

> There's never been a time when Orwell's book wasn't culturally relevant. But it does feel particularly pertinent to our times with its interrogation of austerity politics, perpetual war, a culture of surveillance, terrorism, torture, the manipulation of the individual by the group, media as an echo-chamber of anger and hatred, and the ways in which our own thoughts can be manipulated. There are many big, complex ideas in the book so it's no surprise that terms like Big Brother and Room 101 have become embedded in our culture and that the word 'Orwellian' is used by people of all political persuasions on a daily basis.

Indeed.

During the 2010s, I remember enjoying examples of dystopian theatre, which seems to me to be a kind of free-form engagement with the sense of crisis pervading the decade. Using the genre of sci-fi, or other imaginatively metaphorical theatrical devices, playwrights could explore extreme states of self and of society. Away from the mainstream, I was impressed by leftfield fringe shows such as Philip Ridley's *Angry* (Southwark Playhouse, 2018), a series of monologues, some of which veered ineluctably towards visions of apocalyptic collapse; Emma Adams's *Animals* (Theatre503, 2015), set in 2046 and about the euthanasia of old people; and Beth Steel's *Ditch* (Old Vic Tunnels, 2010), about the repression of illegal migrants in a flood-sodden near future. Yes, dystopian theatre was booming in the 2010s. In keeping with its popularity, this genre of theatre can be described by using a favourite device of the listings magazine: the top ten list.

Our top ten dystopian dramas

In the 2010s, British theatre got the hots for dystopia. Everywhere we went we could catch plays about fictional bad places, where everything is just about as terrible as it could possibly get. Ever. There are plenty of bad places in reality; dystopias are the awesomely bad places of fiction, of invented reality. As such they come from our desire to fantasize about extreme states of mind. Basically, the opposite of utopia. We've all heard of *The Hunger Games* and its spin-offs, but what about theatrical dystopias? During this decade, we found some forty plays which dived into the black mirror of dark imaginings. Exploring these bleak places gave playwrights the freedom to use all sorts of imaginative devices, such as languages that self-destruct or political systems that are mindbogglingly oppressive. What for? To criticize our social ills. But if zombies are now passé, what are the new threats?

Below is our top ten from a decade of nightmares. But can any human tell the truth about a play? Or is a machine a better guide to dystopian theatre? So we used artificial intelligence to deliver its own verdict (usual disclaimers apply). Who's a better guide: human or AI? You decide!

1 Caryl Churchill, *Escaped Alone* (Royal Court, 2016). No escape: The leader in dystopian imaginings is Caryl Churchill, and this is a superb example of a play about catastrophe.

Plot: Three seventy-something women spend every afternoon having tea in a small back garden. They are Sally, an ex-GP who lives here, and her old friends Vi (ex-hairdresser) and Lena (ex-office worker). Their neighbour, Mrs Jarrett (ex-lollipop lady), pops in to have tea, biscuits and a chat. As you'd expect, they talk about all the normal things people talk about. Every now and then, however, Mrs Jarrett steps out of the garden and addresses us directly: to tell us about various scenarios of catastrophe and chaos. Her monologues are heightened contemporary versions of the ten plagues of ancient Egypt (the play's title is taken, apparently, from the Book of Job) and they offer a wildly inventive illustration of our culture of fear. They include visions of total climate collapse – the planet is fucked and we fucked it. Dystopia is coming!

Darkest moment: Mrs Jarret's description of a global viral pandemic caused by children drinking sugar developed from monkeys. It wipes out most of humanity: watch out!

Human verdict: Wow! What a thrilling imagination.

AI verdict: Unique blend of personal stories and broader societal issues, exploring themes such as aging, loneliness, and the apocalypse. These dystopian glimpses serve as a stark contrast to the everyday interactions of the women, highlighting the fragility of human existence and the looming specter of disaster.

You might also like: Caryl Churchill's *Glass. Kill. Bluebeard. Imp* (Royal Court, 2019).

2 Philip Ridley, *Radiant Vermin* (Soho Theatre, 2015). Gleaming dark: Polymath Philip Ridley is a maestro of the macabre and fantastical; this play is a visionary masterpiece.

Plot: Ollie and Jill, a young couple expecting their first baby, fantasize about buying a lovely new home. Hey presto, a fairy godmother, Miss Dee, arrives to make their dreams come true. She offers them a new house which is a bit rundown, but they accept it anyway. Then gradually they discover that they can use her magic to renovate their new house, but this requires them to commit one murder after another. Yet soon enough they get used to it. After all, their victims are just homeless people, and they don't count, do they? The play ends with an acute sense of how the greed for having more and more possessions can make you insensitive to the horrors you're capable of – especially when you justify any ethically suspect act by rationalising that it's all 'for the sake of the baby'. Bleak magic indeed.

Darkest moment: Ollie's mental meltdown during an ordinary kids party.

Human verdict: Great! Dystopia's answer to the housing crisis, to our nesting instincts.

AI verdict: Thought-provoking and darkly comedic play that explores themes of consumerism, morality, and the lengths people will go to in order to achieve the "perfect" life. The play presents a surreal and satirical look at contemporary society.

You might also like: Philip Ridley's *Karagula* (Styx, 2016).

3 Mike Bartlett, *13* (National Theatre, 2011). Ambitious and amazing: Mike Bartlett is a prolific writer who conjures up, in this epic play, a whole catalogue of bad stuff.

Plot: Every night in a nightmarish metropolis, a bewildering mix of characters – spin doctors, militant protesters, a coke-snorting lawyer, an atheist academic, a part-time sex worker, a forgetful granny, an American advisor, a female Tory prime minister – all have the same disturbing dream. In this parallel universe, 'monsters and explosions' pervade the nights. Then John, a young messiah figure, begins to preach resistance, and a peace movement gathers around him. Time to reject money, materialism and militarism. But the atmosphere is dark with foreboding, as the country sleepwalks into economic disaster. Finally, the PM and John debate the rights and wrongs of supporting an American invasion of Iran, a dystopic escalation of the war on terror, and argue about the pros and cons of Conservative values.

Darkest moment: American religious fanatic Sarah kills her child Ruby because she thinks she's evil incarnate.

Human verdict: Ambitious state-of-the-world drama gives an ominous picture of a nation on the verge of social breakdown.

AI verdict: Set in a fictional future, the play is compelling and provocative, presenting complex characters grappling with their beliefs, loyalties, and the weight of their decisions. The play raises thought-provoking questions about democracy, identity, and the nature of leadership.

You might also like: Mike Bartlett's *Earthquakes in London* (National Theatre, 2010).

4 Alistair McDowall, *Pomona* (Orange Tree Theatre, 2014). Bad harvest: Alistair McDowall's piece is set around a central Manchester wasteland, but the story travels to the limits of the imagination.

Plot: This play is fragmented and ambiguous, so it's uncertain which scenes are real world and which are part of a role-playing game – or just fantasies. (Characters have names derived from cinema history.) The story is mainly about Ollie, a young woman looking for her missing twin sister. In this quest she meets a variety of people, from Zeppo, a local fixer, to Fay, a prostitute, whose boss is Gale. Then there's Keaton, who plays a role-playing game with misfit Charlie, a security guard who works with tough guy Moe. In a fractured non-linear narrative all roads lead to Pomona, a real place in Manchester whose name signifies the Roman goddess of fertility. Under the play's fictional Pomona is a warehouse in which women are forced to give birth to babies, and others have their organs harvested. Real horror show.

Darkest moment: Charlie and Ollie's description of the organ-harvesting ward.

Human verdict: Chilling account of society's exploitation of women's bodies.

AI verdict: Gripping and thought-provoking play that delves into dark and dystopian themes with a skillful blend of suspense and mystery. The play's non-linear structure adds to its sense of disorientation, keeping the audience on the edge of their seats as they piece together the puzzle of Pomona's secrets.

You might also like: Alistair McDowall's *X* (Royal Court, 2016).

5 Rory Mullarkey, *The Wolf from the Door* (Royal Court, 2014). English uprising: Rory Mullarkey is a superbly inventive writer whose best play imaginatively depicts a popular revolt.

Plot: In an alternative reality, Catherine, a steely middle-aged English aristocrat is part of a plan to overthrow the government, and recruits Leo, a young homeless drifter, to be a leader of the revolt. She wants him to be the new ruler of the land, and introduces him to the network of ordinary citizens who have organized the uprising. It's a vision of a Middle England where the Women's Institute makes bombs, Civil War re-enactors assault the capital and a water-polo team shoots rockets at Downing Street. There's a great mix of absurdist humour and provocative ideas, but also a deep sense of dark foreboding: with its ideas about 'the beautiful violence which brings change', the drama is incendiary. It shows nice middle-class people doing horrific things.

Darkest moment: In one dystopic scenario, Catherine asks Leo to behead a supermarket manager.

Human verdict: Playfully absurdist attack on current political apathy.

AI verdict: Bold and inventive play that offers a contemporary twist on classic folklore and political allegory. Sharp, witty, and brimming with dark humor, the narrative unfolds with a surreal and unpredictable energy.

You might also like: Rory Mullarkey's *Pity* (Royal Court, 2018).

6 Stef Smith, *Human Animals* (Royal Court, 2016). Creepy crawlies: Using a mix of bizarre humour and acute discomfort, Stef Smith's macabre tale envisages a world where nature bites back.

Plot: In the near future, nature gets increasingly out of control, and tensions rise in an overcrowded city. As the catastrophe deepens, birds do weird things, insects breed all over the place, and big and small mammals nibble at sleeping humans. Foxes, mice and pigeons infest the streets. In the face of a totalitarian governmental response, each human character reacts differently to the deepening paranoia. They include Si, who works for a chemicals company, middle-aged John and Nancy, Lisa, who lives with Jamie, and Nancy's daughter Alex, who joins local protesters trying to protect a park from being cleansed of all wildlife by fire. Meanwhile. Jamie begins to protect as many animals as he can hide in his garden shed.

Darkest moment: Description of pigeons pecking at the body of woman who has hanged herself, as they gradually turn into humans.

Human verdict: Fast-paced and metaphor-rich account of ecological collapse.

AI verdict: Both poetic and starkly realistic, the play shows a dystopian landscape where the boundaries between the human and natural worlds blur. It raises questions about humanity's place in the natural order and the consequences of our exploitation of the environment.

You might also like: Stef Smith's *Girl in the Machine* (Traverse Theatre, 2017).

7 Thomas Eccleshare, *Instructions for Correct Assembly* (Royal Court, 2018).
Paranoid android: Thomas Eccleshare's engrossing story offers a satirical take on the Frankenstein myth and suburban conformity.

Plot: Harry and his wife Max live in a fantasy Middle England of perfectly nice people who live in perfectly nice families in perfectly nice houses with perfectly nice children. But their teenage son Nick has a problem with behaving like the perfect little boy they think they've brought up. In fact he's wild. When he goes missing, on a drink and drugs bender, they decide to buy a replacement. So Jån is delivered, an android teenager in a flatpack ready to be assembled from an instruction manual. Made up of complicated metal and plastic parts, Jån looks identical to Nick. He is programmed to fit in with suburban family life. At first, things go well. Harry and Max talk about Jån, their perfectly nice new son, to their friends Paul and Laurie, whose eighteen-year-old daughter Amy is on her way to becoming a perfectly nice young woman. But at a dinner party, when Paul, Laurie and Amy visit, Jån starts behaving erratically: he ends up sexually assaulting Amy and trashing the whole house. So the horrified Harry and Max decide to have him terminated.

Darkest moment: Harry and Max's dismemberment of Jån.

Human verdict: Thoughtful exploration of artificial intelligence, robots and the digital world.

AI verdict: This is about me: a thought-provoking play that delves into themes of technology, identity, and the human condition. Innovative storytelling explores the increasingly blurred lines between humanity and artificial intelligence.

You might also like: Thomas Eccleshare's *Pastoral* (HighTide Festival, 2013).

8 Zinnie Harris, *How to Hold Your Breath* (Royal Court, 2015). Topsy-turvy: In this wild epic, Zinnie Harris brilliantly turns the migrant crisis on its head – and then some.

Plot: Twenty-something middle-class professional Dana picks up a man in a bar and takes him home. In this version of reality he turns out to be a demon, a devil, who haunts her. Dana's sister, Jasmine, tries to help. Then the pair set off on a rail journey across Europe to Alexandria in pursuit of getting a better job. Yet just as the devil persecutes them, so they acquire a guardian angel in the shape of a Librarian, who is always on hand to offer advice in the shape of a parody of self-help books. Then suddenly Europe is plunged into a massive financial crisis. The banks fail; card machines are useless; people lose everything; they begin to migrate south. In this collapsing economy, Dana and Jasmine's trip to Alexandria turns into a nightmare; they are desperate for money so they will do anything to survive (including prostitution). By flipping the North–South divide on its head, Harris raises some uncomfortable questions: What if the European economy collapsed? What if all Europeans depended on aid from Africa? Could we survive the perilous boat journey south across the Mediterranean?

Darkest moment: Dana's brutal sex scene after she is forced into prostitution.

Human verdict: Nightmare vision of migration in a crisis-struck consumer economy.

AI verdict: Set in a world where societal structures are crumbling, the play follows the journey of a young woman named Dana as she navigates through a series of surreal and dystopian encounters.

You might also like: Ella Road's *The Phlebotomist* (Hampstead Theatre, 2019).

9 Dawn King, *Foxfinder* (Finborough Theatre, 2011). Creature discomforts: Dawn King explores the use of fear and fake news as an instrument of total state domination.

Plot: In this grim world, the government is using fear of foxes and a mysterious infection as an excuse to keep the population in fear, with farmers required to achieve food production targets – or face investigation. On Samuel and Judith's isolated farm, the family is struggling: their only child has died, they are drifting apart as a couple and can't meet their annual quota of crops while constant rain floods their land. Because of government propaganda, the fox has become a symbol of all the bad stuff in the world. If visited by foxes, the contaminated farm must be repossessed, and cleansed. When William, a foxfinder, arrives to investigate a suspected contamination, the situation becomes increasingly sinister. He is a nineteen-year-old fanatic, having been trained in a seminary to be ideologically pure and puritanical. Although there are no foxes here, he is determined to hunt down any dissidents who dare to question the state's claims about the threat. As William investigates the couple, as well as Judith's friend Sarah, he is increasingly unable to control his own impure thoughts and desires.

Darkest moment: William's sinister evocation of fox infestations.

Human verdict: Double-think and psycho-sexual panic animate this chilling account of total surveillance.

AI verdict: The play is known for its intriguing premise and thought-provoking themes, particularly its exploration of paranoia, control, and the manipulation of fear within a dystopian setting.

You might also like: Sarah Kosar's *Mumburger* (The Archivist's Gallery, 2016).

10 Sam Steiner, *Lemons Lemons Lemons Lemons Lemons* (Warwick Arts Centre, 2015). Word play: Sam Steiner's acidic *Lemons* play shows how censorship can penetrate our deepest thoughts and most intimate moments.

Plot: In this scenario, a populist party has won an election and passed a Quietude Bill through parliament: it radically limits the amount of words any citizen can speak to 140 a day. This stresses out the relationship between Bernadette, an ambitious lawyer, and Oliver, a laidback musician. Having meet at a pet cemetery, they experience all the usual ups and downs of young love – but their daily life is seriously impacted by this new law. Despite all the protest marches, which Oliver helps to organize, the state tightens its grip. This means that Bernadette and Oliver have to relate to each other by finding various other ways to communicate, from Morse code to free-form drumming. The ending is ambiguous because although the constraints of the situation put the couple under intolerable stress, maybe they will somehow manage to muddle through.

Saddest moment: After work, Oliver saves most of his words for Bernadette, but she's not bothered to do the same.

Human verdict: Big issues about populism, censorship, free speech and democracy weave effortlessly though some quick-fire scenes.

AI verdict: The play explores the consequences of a world where individuals are limited to a strict word count each day, prompting audiences to reflect on the importance of communication, freedom of expression, and the impact of language on relationships and society.

You might also like: Lucy Kirkwood's *The Children* (Royal Court, 2016).

SCENE SIX

Experiments

Dystopian theatre was a fresh phenomenon in the 2010s, but it was also a particular instance of a more general development: the expansion of horizons and a renewed openness to different types of new writing, especially in the form of experimental theatre-making. In this decade, the veteran figures of innovative playwriting, such as Caryl Churchill and Martin Crimp, inspired a new wave of creatives: for example, Alice Birch, Tim Crouch, Ella Hickson, Nick Payne and debbie tucker green. This creative richness was acknowledged by Lyn Gardner, a critic who advocates for all kinds of boundary-breaking theatre work and whose highly influential blog and job as theatre reviewer were axed by the *Guardian* in 2017 and 2018 – which was symbolic of the disinvestment from the arts by even progressive media. Undaunted, Gardner moved to *The Stage* newspaper. Among many other pieces, here she wrote an article titled 'New voices challenge our idea of "good" theatre'. This says: 'One of the most interesting developments in the past 15 years has been the way theatre-makers and playwrights have experimented with form', meaning the shape and style of their storytelling. She also added: 'It's all very well to say we want a more diverse theatre, but if we really do, we must be open to a more diverse dramaturgy. If a theatre of different voices also takes different forms, then it follows that we will need to find different ways to think, talk, discuss and write about the work.'

As Gardner's advocacy of innovation shows, the 2010s was a good time for boundary-breaking theatre in the UK. Experimental or leftfield theatre can be defined as work which challenges the pervading naturalism of the great British tradition of text-based social realism. Usually, it opposes the accepted conventions of playwriting or production, and this work often involves new ways of using theatre form. Leftfield theatre also has a political edge: it aims to change audience perceptions, attitudes and beliefs, or to provoke people into action. In the 2010s, you could see shows collectively created by several theatre-makers – which questions the centrality of the playwright – and performed in a variety of locations – which subverts the traditional idea of a theatre building. Companies such as Punchdrunk produced immersive shows, a good example being *The Drowned Man: A Hollywood Fable* (2013), an adaptation of *Woyzeck* performed in a disused postal sorting office in

Paddington, where different scenes took place simultaneously in different locations in the repurposed building. Like an art installation.

I remember the sense of adventure when theatre is delivered to you via headphones, or on the move, and exciting events such as fanSHEN's *Invisible Treasure* (Ovalhouse, 2015), which was billed as 'an interactive digital playspace, an electrifying exploration of human relationships, power structures and individual agency, where your actions can change everything', in short an overturning of normal theatre. By contrast, a new writing venue such as the Royal Court Theatre could be home to a play as wildly experimental as Simon Stephens's *Nuclear War* (2017), whose theme of bereavement used an open text, described by the playwright as 'a series of suggestions for a piece of theatre', and whose key stage direction is: 'All of these words may be spoken by the performers but none of them need to be.' This text, an allusive and metaphorical account of loss, is written as lines of dialogue and descriptive statements without any character names attached, occupying a mere eleven pages. It is a gift for directors and actors to interpret at will. In keeping with this spirit of linguistic experimentalism, here is an A to Z dictionary of 2010s experimental plays and playwrights.

An A–Z of experimental theatre

A is for Anti-Naturalism

Anti-Naturalism (*noun*) is a tendency in theatre that challenges the conventions of naturalism, and is characterized by experimental techniques such as non-realistic settings or fantastical themes. Unlike the realistic tradition, which aims for clear, accessible storytelling, Anti-Naturalism embraces abstraction, ambiguity and genres such as science-fiction, encouraging audiences to engage with the work on multiple levels.

Key features include:

- Non-Realistic Elements: incorporates fantastical or surreal aspects.
- Collaborative Creation: multi-authored works are common, challenging traditional notions of individual authorship.

E.g. *A Thousand Stars Explode in the Sky*, co-written by David Eldridge, Robert Holman and Simon Stephens, premiered at the Lyric Hammersmith in May 2010. The play explores an extraordinary premise: what would humanity do if scientists confirmed the imminent end of the universe? Rather than focusing on a financial or political crisis, the narrative grapples with the ultimate destruction of the cosmos. At its heart is the Benton family, who respond to this apocalyptic news by coming together at their home, Mill

Farm, near Stockport. Being Anti-Naturalistic, the play reframes the end of the universe as a gradual, transformative process rather than a single catastrophic event. Phenomena from outer space affect everyday life – telepathy becomes possible, ghosts materialize, injuries miraculously heal and dead birds return to life. What begins as a seemingly conventional family reunion evolves into a science-fiction narrative, weaving domestic intimacy with cosmic wonder. As a multi-authored work, the play is inherently experimental. The collaborative writing process fosters an unpredictable creativity, inviting audiences to reflect on which writer wrote which part of the play. But the drama's interest lies not merely in identifying its authors' individual contributions, but rather in the merging of its domestic and otherworldly dimensions.

B is for Birch, Alice

Alice Birch (b. 1986) is a playwright and screenwriter renowned for her bold, experimental style and incisive critique of patriarchal structures. Her screenwriting credits include the critically acclaimed *Lady Macbeth* (2016) and the BBC adaptation of Sally Rooney's *Normal People* (2020). Birch's theatrical works are distinguished by their formal innovation and sharp social commentary. Her plays often deconstruct traditional narrative structures, employing wit and structural fragmentation to explore themes of gender, power and violence. E.g. *Revolt. She Said. Revolt Again.* (RSC, 2014) abandons conventional notions of setting, character and plot to present a vision of radical feminism. Reflecting on her creative process, Birch notes: 'I write plays for myself. I don't write for an audience. Anyone who is making anything should have that process as well, but there has to be recognition of a play's further impact on an audience. There's responsibility there as well.' Her play *[Blank]* (Donmar Warehouse, 2019) also epitomizes her avant-garde approach. Composed of 100 scenes within a 516-page script, the play allows each production to select its own combination of scenes. In director Maria Aberg's interpretation, twenty-two scenes were chosen to create an exploration of how the criminal justice system affects women. The result is a work that combines creative freedom with a profound engagement with societal issues. Birch's oeuvre continues to challenge and redefine the boundaries of contemporary theatre and storytelling.

C is for Crouch, Tim

Tim Crouch (b. 1964) is an innovative theatre-maker, actor, writer and director known for pushing the boundaries of theatrical conventions, particularly naturalism. His works invite audiences to play an active role in shaping the performance. Notable among his plays from the 2010s is *Adler & Gibb* (Royal Court Theatre, 2014). Crouch's earlier plays exemplify his commitment to experimental forms. E.g. *My Arm* (Traverse Theatre, 2003) tells the story of a man who holds one arm aloft for thirty years. This narrative unfolds through a blend of live performance, digital film and the animation of everyday objects provided by the audience. Similarly, *An Oak Tree* (Traverse Theatre, 2005) involves a guest actor each night who has not seen the script prior to coming on stage. The play explores the interaction between a hypnotist and a grieving man, creating an unpredictable and collaborative dynamic. In a 2007 interview, Crouch said: 'Theatre in its purest form is a conceptual art form. It doesn't need sets, costumes and props, but exists inside an audience's head.' This philosophy is evident in *Total Immediate Collective Imminent Terrestrial Salvation* (National Theatre of Scotland, 2019), which examines the influence of a messianic cult leader. Audience members are given copies of the sect's bible and invited to participate by reading lines of dialogue, simultaneously engaging with the text, its illustrations and the production's live actors. By transforming the audience into co-creators of the event, this layered interaction challenges the traditional illusion of text-based theatre, where the same words are spoken by the same characters every night.

D is for Digital Theatre

Digital Theatre (*noun*) emerged as a significant innovation in the 2010s, distinct from simply broadcasting or streaming live artistic events. It usually blends live performance with digital media, creating a hybrid art form. Digital technology is integral to the experience, often incorporating interactivity and a strong narrative. With roots in the multimedia experiments of early twentieth-century theatre, it aims to rejuvenate the live theatre experience.

E.g. Eve Leigh's *Midnight Movie* (Royal Court Theatre, 2019), which examines the concept of being 'Extremely Online'. The protagonist is unable to sleep because of a painful medical condition, and instead spends the night surfing the internet. Leigh integrates found digital material – unusual images, ideas and stories – into the production. Using visual projections and two performers representing avatars of the playwright (a large bearded man and a deaf Asian woman), the play invites the audience into Leigh's mind. This distancing device, where alternative versions of herself speak her words, showcases the creative freedom afforded by digital theatre.

Another example is Philip Ridley's *The Beast of Blue Yonder*, a play which was unable to be staged because London theatres closed on 16 March 2020 due to COVID-19. Instead Ridley wrote fourteen monologues titled *The Beast Will Rise*, as weekly monologues performed by the cast and streamed for free via the We Are Tramp website. The pieces vary: the shortest, *River*, is about two minutes long, featuring a single line of dialogue and filmed outdoors, while the longest, *Eclipse*, is a complete narrative. In this piece, which has echoes of *The Handmaid's Tale*, a posh former teacher of creative writing and art history reflects on pandemic anxieties. Together, these monologues offered a rich experience, full of inventive storytelling, emotional depth and bold ideas, showcasing the creative potential of digital theatre.

E is for *Either*

Either by Ruby Thomas premiered at the Hampstead Theatre in October 2019. The story concerns a relationship that begins with a chance encounter at a Pride march. A and B meet, reconnect, fall in love, move in together, explore polyamory and eventually break up – repeating cycles of passion, connection and separation. A and B are deliberately undefined in terms of gender, sexuality and ethnicity; the playwright emphasizes that they can be performed by any combination. This choice allows the characters to shift between heterosexual, gay and lesbian relationship dynamics. In the original production, six actors alternated as A and B, exploring themes of shifting personal identity. With A and B played by actors of diverse genders and ethnicities, the audience is invited to consider how relationships might differ – or remain consistent – depending on these changes. The dialogue remains unchanged, but the diverse casting allows the same lines to take on different meanings. A line like 'I just came out of a long relationship so – I think I'm having an identity crisis' resonates differently when spoken by different performers. The play includes comedic episodes such an encounter in a gender-neutral bathroom and an argument over email etiquette during an intimate moment. Thomas cleverly uses innovative structure and casting to explore gender as a social construct.

F is for Form

Theatre Form (*noun*), or the structure of how a story is told on stage, is one of the most common areas of experimentation. Traditional plays typically follow a linear structure with a clear beginning, middle and end. By contrast, experimental theatre often employs a non-linear approach, characterized by a fragmented or fractured representation of time, where events occur out of chronological order. This non-linear structure can be used for:

- Creating dramatic irony or revealing unexpected plot twists;

- Reflecting the fractured mindset of the characters or representing unstable situations.

    E.g. *Shivered* by Philip Ridley, premiered at Southwark Playhouse in March 2012. The story concerns the lives of two twelve-year-old boys and their parents over a period of more than a decade using fragmented storytelling. The play's structure deviates from linearity so the first scene is chronologically the fifth, the second is the twelfth, and so on. The effect of this structure is to amplify the intense emotions of the characters, which disrupt the traditional linear narrative, creating an experience in which reality has been 'shivered'.

G is for Gig Theatre

Gig Theatre (*noun*) is a dynamic performance art that merges music and theatre, characterized by the immersive use of music, storytelling and audience interaction, to create a shared experience.

Key features include:

- Multitasking Artists: performers are typically both musicians and actors, and transition between these roles. They often engage directly with the audience, breaking the fourth wall.
- Participant Audiences: the atmosphere encourages a live, social experience where audiences are made to feel part of the show.

    E.g. *The Strange Undoing of Prudencia Hart* by David Greig, premiered during a National Theatre of Scotland tour in 2011. Drawing inspiration from the border ballads, the show blends site-specific and immersive elements with a playful script written in rhyming couplets. It includes surreal, mythical storytelling, lively music, audience participation and karaoke, all evoking the spirit of a Highland ceilidh. The folk-tale atmosphere is filled with devilish characters and underworld journeys, an example of the exuberance of the Scottish theatrical tradition.

    Similarly engaging is *Hole* by Ellie Kendrick, premiered at the Royal Court Theatre's experimental Theatre Upstairs in December 2018. Directed by Helen Goalen and Abbi Greenland of RashDash, the show features an all-female cast and employs music, song, movement and striking visual set pieces to explore themes of power and gender. The performance includes the cosmological metaphor of the black hole and critiques the violence of ancient Greek myths through a feminist lens, using examples like Medusa and Pandora's Box. The production combines slogans, music and impassioned performances to celebrate female empowerment, critique the male gaze, creating an electrifying experience infused with rage.

H is for Hickson, Ella

Ella Hickson (b. 1985) is a playwright and academic whose recent work challenges the conventions of naturalism. Notable 2010s plays include *Oil* (Almeida Theatre, 2016) and *ANNA* (National Theatre, 2019). In an interview, Hickson described how an eight-week retreat in the USA allowed her to write freely, unbound by commissions, and to explore new forms. She says:

> I gave myself full freedom. I did a lot of automatic writing and wrote down lots of my dreams, and all kind of woo-woo stuff. It came from quite an instinctive place. I was angry, let's be clear, really angry, I'd been in the industry for ten years so I had an anger, but it was less about men in the industry and more about restriction, and feeling that artistry was hitting up quite hard against creative control in a lot of venues. And commercial values as well.

This anger fuelled her play *The Writer* (Almeida Theatre, 2018), which has a non-linear narrative, plus a play within a play, and includes a scene titled 'The Provocation', which represents female experience as a vivid tribal fantasy. The play's theme is gender fluidity – two sex scenes represent similar dynamics, one heterosexual and the other lesbian – and it critiques male dominance in the cultural industries. *The Writer* examines both sexual politics and the politics of playwriting, and the fractured storytelling mirrors Hickson's refusal to offer easy answers.

I is for *In the Republic of Happiness*

In the Republic of Happiness by Martin Crimp premiered at the Royal Court Theatre in December 2012. The play is divided into three overtly political parts: 'The Destruction of the Family', 'The Five Essential Freedoms of the Individual' and 'In the Republic of Happiness'. The first part begins as a family drama, with three generations gathered for a tense Christmas meal. They are interrupted by the unexpected arrival of Uncle Bob, whose cryptic message triggers an implosion of fragile family dynamics. In the second part, the play shifts into an experimental mode: all eight cast members deliver an open text reminiscent of Crimp's 1997 masterpiece *Attempts on Her Life*. This section satirizes individualism and its narcissistic tendencies, critiquing contemporary obsessions with self-centred narratives, apathy towards politics, personal trauma, therapy culture, physical appearance and the quest for immortality. The final section evokes an ambiguous, otherworldly setting – perhaps a kind of heaven. The framing suggests that part one represents hell, while the satirical critique of part two is purgatory. Uncle Bob and his wife Madeleine reappear in the concluding part, but Bob is transformed into a dethroned ruler grappling with dementia, and the couple face a 'high-tech deletion'.

J is for Jenner, Kylie

As in *Seven Methods of Killing Kylie Jenner* by Jasmine Lee-Jones, premiered at the Royal Court Theatre in July 2019. This provocative two-hander explores the relationship between two young Black women, Cleo and Kara, as their friendship is tested. The tension begins when Cleo, enraged by a Forbes tweet declaring Kylie Jenner the youngest self-made billionaire, starts posting death threats under the handle @INCOGNEGRO, including tweets like 'METHOD #1 #DEATHBYPOISON'. Kara disapproves, leading to an argument that unearths painful childhood memories and forces the pair to confront their identities – Cleo as dark-skinned and straight, Kara as light-skinned and queer. The play's experimental structure alternates between real-life interactions and 'Twitterludes' (scenes set in cyberspace). Written with a rich use of slang, abbreviations, emojis, memes and other digital elements, the text looks as much like a piece of visual art as a script.

K is for *King Charles III*

King Charles III by Mike Bartlett is a 'future history' play written in blank verse, and premiered at the Almeida Theatre in April 2014. It is experimental in its mixture of Shakespearean-style language and contemporary themes. Opening with the funeral of Queen Elizabeth II – still alive at the time – it follows the ascension of King Charles III as he becomes embroiled in a constitutional crisis. He refuses to sign a parliamentary bill restricting press freedom, so Parliament bypasses his formal assent and Charles dissolves it in a dramatic echo of Charles I's actions in the seventeenth century. This decision divides the nation, and threatens civil war. The younger royals, Prince William and Kate, play pivotal roles in the unfolding drama. Meanwhile, a subplot concerns Prince Harry's relationship with Jess, a politically active republican and art student squatter. The play combines commentary on the responsibilities of monarchy and the challenges of republicanism with entertaining moments, such as Princess Diana's ghost haunting Buckingham Palace.

L is for *Love and Information*

Love and Information by Caryl Churchill premiered at the Royal Court Theatre in September 2012, and, like much of her work, is an experimental play. The central themes – our need to know and our need to love – are explored through dozens of characters in approximately fifty scenes, some very brief. These scenes are grouped into seven sections and unfold in a dazzling variety of settings. The characters are equally varied: lovers, couples, married partners, families, mothers and their children, office colleagues, friends, and so on. They represent a spectrum of beliefs and experiences, from faith in God to mental distress. The play has a distinctly English tapestry of everyday life, including Radio 4 jingles, Big Ben chimes and eccentric fads. The central question asks: is it better to seek knowledge (information) or to remain in the dark? Through confessions, disclosures, betrayals and musings, the play shows how some secrets can be beneficial, others profoundly destructive. The overarching impression is of a fragmented world dominated by information overload. The disjointed structure mirrors the content, creating a fast-moving panorama that reflects the chaos of contemporary life.

M is for Middle East

How can one address the complex economic, political and social conflicts of the Middle East without resorting to journalism? British-Egyptian writer Sabrina Mahfouz tackles this challenge in *A History of Water in the Middle East* (Royal Court Theatre, 2019), using the Form of gig theatre to offer a fresh perspective on these geopolitical issues. Partly autobiographical, the play is both a documentary – examining Britain's colonial role and the importance of water in the Middle East – and a personal narrative of Mahfouz's own interview for a job in the UK's secret services. The play has a historical framework, including Elizabeth Taylor's portrayal of Cleopatra in 1963 and the Sumerian myth of Ninhursag and Enki. Its narrative traverses time and space, from Iraq in the 1920s to an imagined Jordan in 2050. Mahfouz introduces fictional females who include Zakiya, an Iraqi freedom fighter; Miriam, a Jordanian plumber; and Amalah, a Dubai resident who develops an app called 'Shagging in the Shower'. The script is infused with entertaining theatrical elements, such as a British spy performing a karaoke mashup of Egyptian history and Neil Diamond's 'Sweet Caroline'.

N is for Neilson, Anthony

Anthony Neilson (b. 1967) is a playwright known for his innovative approach to theatre, often experimenting with Form. He frequently incorporates improvisation into rehearsals, sometimes placing under-rehearsed casts onstage to heighten their adrenaline and spontaneity. In the 1990s, Neilson's work often featured explicit depictions of sex and violence, as in *Penetrator* (Traverse Theatre, 1993). However, his later plays have showcased a broader creative vision, such as the fantastical *The Wonderful World of Dissocia* (Tron

Theatre, 2004), a landmark work. Notable plays from the 2010s include *Narrative* (Royal Court Theatre, 2013) and *The Prudes* (Royal Court Theatre, 2018). Neilson himself has stated: 'It's not that I'm against realism *per se*, it's just that I'm looking for the theatrical form that will best express whatever I'm interested in expressing at the time.' E.g. *Unreachable* (Royal Court Theatre, 2016) tells the story of Maxim, a self-destructive director grappling with his latest post-apocalyptic film. Written in the style of a farce, the play merges serious themes about the ineffability of art with sharp satire and humour. Developed through improvisation, this devised work critiques the creative process itself, delivering its sombre message through comedy.

O is for *On Bear Ridge*

On Bear Ridge by Ed Thomas is a rare piece of experiment: the use of metaphysical theatre, blending elements of absurdism and realism. Premiered at the Sherman Theatre in Cardiff in September 2019, it is set on a remote mountain at Bear Ridge Stores, a family-run butcher shop managed by John and Noni, with help from their young slaughterman. Following an unspecified catastrophe that has left the area depopulated and the store's shelves empty, the trio faces starvation. Their fragile existence is disrupted by the arrival of an army captain, part of a military operation carrying out ethnic cleansing. The play explores themes of loss and the fragility of language. John, who claims to speak the 'old language', describes it as a repository of memory and identity. But the erosion of language mirrors the disintegration of his sense of self. Thomas's writing is marked by a stark, flinty prose that combines Beckettian incantations of bleakness – 'Nothing moving. Nothing growing. Snowing heavy' – with absurdist humour and metaphysical reflection. This tragicomic sensibility results in emotionally strong speculative theatre.

P is for Payne, Nick

Nick Payne (b. 1984) is a theatre and television writer whose work is characterized by innovation in Form and content. Reflecting on his shift away from naturalistic plays, Payne remarked:

> I had written a few plays that were naturalistic in their form, and I found something unsatisfying about it. I hadn't quite cracked those plays. And then just by sheer chance, I read a few books on physics – just because I was interested and didn't know anything about it. I came across the multiverse thing and thought I could tell a story in a nonlinear way. I found that really freeing. It's funny; it's less about the science and more

that the science freed me from having to worry about doorknobs and bedroom suitcases.

This applies to his masterpiece, *Constellations* (Royal Court Theatre, 2012), whose story concerns Marianne, a theoretical physicist, and Roland, her love interest. Drawing on Marianne's background in quantum mechanics and the concept of parallel worlds, Payne structures the play as a series of repeating scenes. Each event is presented multiple times, with variations in mood, tone or outcome, interspersed with moments set in the present. This experimental Form, inspired by the multiverse theory, adds layers of depth and complexity, creating a moving exploration of love, loss and choice.

Q is for Queer Theatre

Queer Theatre (*noun*) has developed considerably in the 2010s. Just as queer theory challenges gender binaries and embraces the fluidity of identity and sexuality, queer theatre questions the boundaries of genre, often blending diverse theatrical styles into a single work. E.g. Ben Buratta and Outbox Theatre's devised play *And the Rest of Me Floats* (Bush Theatre, 2019), which features performers from the trans, non-binary and queer communities. The production defies traditional theatrical conventions by combining autobiographical storytelling with creative experimentation, weaving together elements of documentary and entertainment. It includes monologues, stand-up comedy, dressing-up, karaoke, dance and movement, creating a multifaceted experience. Both angry and joyous, it is a celebration of identity and a challenge to the confines of conventional theatre.

R is for *Rules for Living*

Rules for Living by Sam Holcroft is an inventive take on the traditional Christmas family reunion play. Premiered at the National Theatre in March 2015, it combines absurdist comedy with observations about family dynamics and personal habits. Edith, in her sixties, is married to Francis, a hospitalized retired judge. She is hosting a festive Christmas Day celebration to welcome him home. The family includes their two sons, Matthew and Adam. Matthew brings his new girlfriend, Carrie, who serves as the outsider figure. Adam arrives with his wife, Sheena, and their teenage daughter, Emma, who suffers from chronic fatigue syndrome and requires cognitive behavioural therapy. As the title suggests, and inspired by Emma's therapy, *Rules for Living* explores the characters' adherence to rigid behavioural patterns that dictate their daily lives and reveal their inner motives. For instance, Matthew must sit to tell a lie, Sheena must drink to contradict and Edith must clean to keep calm. These behavioural quirks create both tension and insight as the characters' psychological make-up becomes increasingly exposed. Innocent actions turn into moments of embarrassment, emphasizing the conflicts of family life. A games board displayed above the stage tracks the characters' 'scores', adding a playful meta-theatrical dimension.

S is for Stephens, Simon

Simon Stephens (b. 1971) is a versatile playwright whose body of work includes both popular successes and more challenging pieces. His most acclaimed work, the 2012 adaptation of Mark Haddon's *The Curious Incident of the Dog in the Night-Time*, was in his view an experiment: 'I wanted to do it as an experiment in form, because I'd never done an adaptation before.' He also says:

> For me the play structure is fundamental and increasingly creative and exciting. As playwrights rather than writers our work concerns itself with shaping and making. Dramatic structure is like song structure in music. It contains the force of the melody and idea more than any other element. I try to be as creative with the structure of my pieces as I would be with language or image or action.

Among his 2010s experimental works are *Carmen Disruption* (Almeida Theatre, 2015) and *Nuclear War* (Royal Court Theatre, 2017). One of the decade's most controversial experiments was his *Three Kingdoms* (Lyric Hammersmith, 2012), a collaboration with German director Sebastian Nübling and featuring actors from the UK, the Munich Kammerspiele and Estonia's Teater NO99. This dark thriller, which explores themes of sex trafficking across Europe, was a multilingual, dreamlike experience, a phantasmagoria. It was celebrated for its striking visuals and surreal storytelling, including scenes such as a petty criminal delivering a speech with a photograph stuck to his face, a coroner's assistant peeling an apple while giving an autopsy report and a corpse gripping a detective's hand. Other visual elements included a surreal rendition of The Beatles' 'Rocky Raccoon', sex workers dressed in furs and deer heads, and eerie figures in wolf masks. The production's experimental character provoked mixed responses from critics.

T is for tucker green, debbie

debbie tucker green (b. 1975?) is an innovative playwright and filmmaker whose work is defined by its experimental Form. Since her debut *Dirty*

Butterfly in 2003, every piece has adopted a different structure, blending elements of play, poem and song lyrics. Her writing process is exploratory, as she explains:

> I never set out to write plays. I was just messing about, writing stuff down and throwing it away or keeping it if it interested me. Then the writing started to get longer. I didn't know whether it was a poem, the lyrics to a song or a play. It is all much of a muchness to me. It's all words, ain't it?

Her 2010s work includes *hang* (Royal Court Theatre, 2015) and *a profoundly affectionate, passionate devotion to someone (-noun)* (Royal Court Theatre, 2017). One of her most striking works is *nut* (National Theatre, 2013), which explores themes of mental illness, depression and emotional connection. The play concerns a young Black woman struggling with mental distress, and includes themes of post-natal depression, suicide and the complicated patterns of emotional dependency. Her writing maintains its signature intensity, but beneath its restrained dialogue lies a powerful subtext, suggesting a world steeped in anguish. The play's ambiguity further deepens its impact: is the narrative confined to a single woman's mind or shared among multiple perspectives? Which moments are real, and which imagined? What, or whom, can the audience trust? This experimental approach reflects the playwright's commitment to exploring complex psychological and emotional landscapes.

U is for Uncertainty

The concept of Uncertainty (*noun*) in experimental theatre involves the deliberate acceptance of ambiguity, unpredictability and the unknown in both the creative process and final performance. This challenges traditional working methods, creating space for spontaneity and diverse interpretation. It reflects the theatre-maker's willingness to venture into uncharted territory, take creative risks and defy conventional expectations, resulting in work that is often open-ended and subjective. Unlike risk, which refers to situations where outcomes can be quantified, Uncertainty deals with outcomes that cannot be measured or anticipated. Experimental theatre operates within this realm, where the potential for failure is an inherent and accepted part of the process. This dynamic invites dialogue about the boundaries of theatrical Form.

V is for *Very Expensive Poison, A*

A Very Expensive Poison by Lucy Prebble, premiered at the Old Vic in September 2019, is an anti-documentary exploration of the search for justice following the

2006 assassination of Alexander Litvinenko in London, orchestrated by Vladimir Putin. Litvinenko's wife, Marina, successfully campaigned for a public inquiry into his death, which was eventually held in 2016. The story is based on *A Very Expensive Poison* by the *Guardian* journalist Luke Harding. However, Prebble doesn't approach the story as a straightforward docu-drama. Instead, she adopts a more experimental, multi-genre method to examine the interplay between storytelling and truth. The play combines intimate moments with epic ones, naturalistic dialogue with direct audience address, dance sequences with songs and comedy with horror. It includes shadow play, large puppets and surreal elements to create a fractured, dream-like narrative that challenges traditional theatre conventions. Prebble deliberately eschews clear-cut genres, leaving the audience uncertain whether they are witnessing a spy story, a tragedy, a farce, a surreal nightmare or a political thriller.

W is for Wade, Laura

Laura Wade (b. 1977) is a playwright whose work is characterized by innovation in form and content. One of her earliest works, *Breathing Corpses* (Royal Court Theatre, 2005), features a mind-twisting, MC-Escher-style time sequence. In the 2010s, Wade adapted Sarah Waters's novel *Tipping the Velvet* for the stage (Lyric Hammersmith, 2015) and reimagined Jane Austen's *The Watsons* in a postmodern format (Chichester Festival, 2018). She reflects on her creative process:

> Getting started is very often the hardest thing. I often find I just make myself write the rubbish version of the thing that I'm trying to write because the inner critic is, before you even get your pen on the page, is saying 'that's rubbish', and actually thing number one that you have to do is get words onto paper.

An example of Wade's experimental storytelling is *Home, I'm Darling* (Theatre Clwyd, 2018). The play tells the story of Judy and Johnny, a contemporary couple who have chosen to live as if they are in the 1950s, from their clothing to their furnishings. For Judy, this is more than just a hobby; it's a lifestyle choice. However, as the story progresses, Judy's sense of security begins to unravel as her fantasy of the past disintegrates. The play is both a satire on traditional female domestic roles and a commentary on society's nostalgic escapism.

X is for X

X by Alistair McDowall, premiered at the Royal Court Theatre in April 2016, and is a science-fiction play set in a research station on the planet Pluto.

Science fiction offers exceptional freedom to playwrights, liberating them from Earth-bound conventions and allowing for inventive storytelling. *X* embraces this freedom with its non-linear structure and haunting narrative. As the station loses contact with Earth and its characters grow increasingly isolated and anxious, time begins to warp. Clocks fail, day and night lose their natural patterns, and the passage of time starts to erode the characters' memories. One of the most innovative moments in the play is a daring five-page sequence entirely covered with the repeated letter X. This bold visual and textual choice represents a complete breakdown of language, reflecting the psychological unravelling of the characters. McDowall's *X* explores themes of isolation, time and the disintegration of communication – reminding audiences that, in the emptiness of space, no one can hear you.

Y is for Youth

Youth (*noun*) is often seen as a time of life marked by heightened experimentation in theatre and greater artistic creativity. However, neither of these assumptions is entirely accurate.

Z is for Zoom Theatre

Zoom Theatre (*noun*) was developed after the COVID-19 pandemic brought live performance to a halt in March 2020. Several theatre companies began experimenting with Zoom – a video conferencing platform – as a new medium for creating theatre. This raised fundamental questions about the nature of theatre: must it involve all participants in the same physical space at the same time, or can it exist in a virtual format? Zoom Theatre relies on the immediacy of live performance, but delivered by means of digital tools. The technical mishaps – wobbly audio, frozen screens, blackouts – add an unpredictable, spontaneous quality to such performances, contributing to the liveness of the remote experience. During the lockdowns, Zoom Theatre became an important way to reach audiences. E.g. *My White Best Friend (And Other Letters Left Unsaid)* (Royal Court Theatre, 2020) was an online festival curated by playwright Rachel De-Lahay and director Milli Bhatia in response to the resurgence of the Black Lives Matter movement. Over the course of a week, ten Black writers shared personal, often deeply emotional, reflections on their relationships with white individuals. Each night, letters written by two of them were performed live online by actors reading them in real time, without rehearsal, making the experience raw, spontaneous and immediate. This innovative Zoom Theatre event was powerful also in its active privileging of a non-white audience. One critic saw it as 'generous in feeling, brave in its honesty and urgent in its politics'.

SCENE SEVEN

Monologues

In the 2010s, there was an explosion of monologue or one-person shows. If the increasing passion of identity politics can be partially explained as a reaction to the various crises of this decade, the monologue is the perfect theatre form for the exploration of a personal sense of self. It is also one answer to the challenge of representing subjectivity on stage. When playwright and academic Sarah Grochala was asked to contribute a programme note to Duncan Macmillan's *People, Places and Things* (2015), she asked, 'If drama is an inherently objective medium, then how can it be possible to tell a story from a subjective perspective in a play?', and added:

> Whilst the majority of plays continue to offer us an objective viewpoint of the world, there has been an increase in the number of subjective plays on the British stage in recent years. This is interesting in terms of the way in which it reflects a change in how we view both ourselves and the world that we live in.

Of course, there are other reasons for the popularity of monologues: they offer a mixture of individual vision (a playwright's personal voice) and theatre economics (a one-person show is cheaper to stage than a large-cast play). The monologue form also other advantages: it has an immediacy of voice that is exciting and satisfying; as a narrative form it is extremely flexible, conveying character easily and telling stories with immense economy and speed. It's also the most intimate of forms (it puts you right inside the head of the character). In defiance of populism, this offers the freedom to be as provocative or painful, direct or violent, as you like. Paradoxically, the monologue is a kind of objective voiceover which at the same time has a subjective point of view. It can be both an expression of our increasingly self-centred society and a criticism of it. And the agonized version, whether male or female, suggests the embrace of the notion of an angry national identity.

My memory of monologues in this decade is that of a carnival of variety. From intriguing titles, such as *The Hijabi Monologues*, to brilliant performances, such as that of the eighty-four-year-old Maggie Smith as Brunhilde Pomsel, secretary to Nazi propaganda minister Joseph Goebbels, in Christopher

Hampton's beautifully succinct monologue *A German Life* (Bridge Theatre, 2019). Whether the one-person shows were edgy – like Travis Alabanza's *Burgerz* (Hackney Showroom, 2018), an effective trans polemic, or Natasha Marshall's *Half Breed* (Talawa, 2016), a semi-autobiographical story about growing up non-white in the English countryside – or using onstage music – like Kae Tempest's *Brand New Ancients* (BAC, 2012) – they always had a compelling quality. I remember some lovely shows – like Ian Kershaw's beguilingly warm *The Greatest Play in the History of the World* (Traverse Theatre, 2018), which was performed by the playwright's wife Julie Hesmondhalgh – and some instant classics – like Chris Goode's *Men in the Cities* (Royal Court, 2014), which illustrates by means of two violent deaths (the murder of Fusilier Lee Rigby and the suicide of a young gay man) how several lonely men are connected in an alienating metropolis. Anyway, it's not that difficult to decide on how to write about monologues. So here are fifteen different characters who share their thoughts on fifteen monologues they have seen on stage.

Fifteen monologues

Chewing Gum Dreams by Michaela Coel (Yard Theatre, 2012)

Oh gawdddd! Yes. This is a little firecracker of a one-woman show, written and performed by the playwright herself – it's about Tracey, a fourteen-year-old Black schoolgirl, who's trapped in a cycle of poverty, but has no illusions, says things like 'I'm not smart enough to be someone; I'm just smart enough to know I'm no one.' Worse, she sees herself as stuck in 'the cracks in the floor'.

She's from Hackney and she kind of knows her place: back of the bus and back of the class, bottom of the pile. But this means she's free, free to say anything she likes. Her favourite comment for her buff best friend Candice, whose hair is PERFECT, is 'Fuck you, bitch', and she has a real talent for putdowns, whether it's Candice's abusive boyfriend or Fat Lesha ('DIY vagina licker'), who's a teen entrepreneur selling condoms and bagels at school. Yeah, teen girls are queens of taunts.

Like so many monologues, this one is semi-autobiographical (allegedly) and Coel's performance – with a garage soundtrack – as her feisty girl is ace. I can still picture it: she sits up, then slouches, then walks around the stage, then runs, then dances a bit. The stage is hers. Yeah. She also brilliantly impersonates the monologue's other characters: vicious Aaron, vulnerable Candice, Tracey's maths teacher and an unhelpful pharmacist.

Tracey tells us about being scared of sex, how Fat Lesha suggests using a maxi tampon to break your hymen, how to time your kiss and how her white friend Connor's dick is like a pink balloon with raw chicken skin. The writing is fast, funny, and quite strong: cos the piece is about sexual violence too. Bad things happening to good people. Who'd be a young teenager again? Not me!

Fleabag by Phoebe Waller-Bridge (Edinburgh Fringe, 2013)

So, this is an hour-long play about a young, sex-obsessed, angry, dry-witted woman, written and performed by Phoebe Waller-Bridge, who's famous now but back then was no one. The character is called Fleabag and she runs a guinea-pig-themed café, which she opened with her best friend Boo, who is now dead. She died by walking into a busy cycle lane after she found out her boyfriend slept with someone else – she wanted to punish him by ending up in hospital, but accidentally killed herself. The café is out of cash and is going to close because Fleabag can't afford the lease and her sister won't help her. Why? Because Fleabag lied to her about her husband trying to touch her up at Christmas.

Fleabag says she's a bad feminist, and she's a sex addict, and pisses everyone off by some, um, saying some nasty stuff (about everything). The play is a kind of catalogue of boyfriend trouble, wanks, one-night stands and porn. Sorry. But it's not all about using shock tactics: Waller-Bridge has also honed her technique. For example, she often sets up a situation, say a threesome during her period, then suggests how anyone might react to this: the event was 'sticky and awkward' and they all 'went home a little bit sad and empty', before pausing, and then delivering the punchline, in this case: 'It was lovely', followed again with a twist, in this case an insincere apology: 'Sorry.'

Waller-Bridge has this direct relationship with the audience, moment by moment – she tries to seduce, amuse and shock us, manipulate even, until eventually revealing her truth. She has this really posh voice, and a way of looking aghast at herself whenever she says something outrageous – which is, like, every minute. It's a kind of stand-up routine, except she's sitting on a high stool all the time. She has one liners like: 'I'm not obsessed with sex. I just can't stop thinking about it.' She also mimics the people in Fleabag's life: Joe, her loud cockney friend, her sister and Boo. Her face when she does the impression of the rodent guy she met on the tube is priceless. Priceless. But she's also good at pain, anguish. After all, she's lost her mum as well as her best friend Boo.

Fleabag in all her fucking glory became iconic (shit word I know). Sorry. She's a 'naughty' character, with her big mouth and restless mishaps – representing this group of young angry women, mostly middle-class, all reacting against pressure, the pressure of being good women, high-achieving, perfect types. I guess they hate the idea of being good girls, glossy girls.

Sometimes they just want to be a bit grubby and a bit out of control. Show up at work in make-up from the night before, after two cigarettes for breakfast – or want to fuck their sister's boyfriend. Prone to oversharing. But with, um, dry humour and twinges of guilt. Yeah, it's a recognizable female, and Fleabag is the prototype.

Dark Vanilla Jungle by **Philip Ridley (Edinburgh Festival, 2013)**

Philip Ridley? Yeah I'm a total fangirl – he's the master of the monologue, and he's so brilliant because he started his career not at drama school, but at art college, where he himself performed solo stuff, kind of live art, you know? Hours and hours of monologuing. Anyway, on my way to see *Dark Vanilla Jungle* I was almost stung by a wasp, which is very weird because that's how this one-woman show begins. It's performed by Gemma Whelan – Yara Greyjoy in *Game of Thrones* – who is Andrea, a fifteen-year-old from the East End of London whose upbringing has been damaged by parental indifference.
Slight pause.
Okay, let me see. I suppose I've got to tell you the plot. What happens is that Andrea and her friend whose name I've forgotten meet a pair of men, who take them out, treat them to cocktails and clubbing, to fun nights out in glamorous venues. But what happens is that the naïve Andrea is groomed for sex by an older guy, pushed into this pimp's world of abuse. So, um, there's violent sex, extreme violence, unwanted pregnancy and mental collapse. Hell, perhaps.
Slight pause.
Pain. Some bits really turned my stomach, so uncomfortable. But at least I felt something – most theatre is so bland! And the text is so sensuous, razor-sharp contrasts, blasts of rage. Hallucinatory intensity. Desperation nightmare, paranoia central – that kind of thing. Whelan monologues at high speed, barely pausing for breath, talking directly to us, exhausting but also exciting. And I remember a song about 'My lover's hands'. At the end, her scream tore through my spinal cord like high-voltage wasp sting. On my way home I swear I saw puddles of blood reflecting the lurid street lights. OMG!

True Brits by **Vinay Patel (Edinburgh Fringe, 2014)**

This one has a good start. It's about Rahul, a young British-Asian Londoner, who – during the 2012 London Olympics – is asked by a BBC reporter: 'Do you feel British?' He's upset by the question, which reminds him of the time around the 7/7 bombings in 2005, when anti-Muslim feelings range from suspicious glances at any Asian guy wearing a backpack to violent assaults on innocent kids.

This is a well-observed coming-of-age story about the eighteen-year-old who falls for a girl, Jess, while on a protest march on the second anniversary of the Iraq War, takes his A-levels and goes on a wild Spanish holiday. Like so many guys, he loves pop music (in his case Blur). Other characters, such as the intellectual and politically engaged Jess, family friend Mihir and school mate Rhys, are sketched in by performer Sid Sagar, who narrates and plays all the parts with a light touch.

London is quite a grumpy city, but for the two weeks of the Olympics everyone seemed to be happy. It was really strange. I think as part of a minority, Rahul usually forgets about skin colour. But 7/7 was the first time in his life when he is made to be aware of it for an extended period of time. I mean, it really put him on the outside. In the street, people would say racist things, and just get tense whenever they saw him.

The play's main theme is Britishness, what this means at a time of heightened racist feelings and how it might change when times are good. Patel suggests that love has a healing force and that sometimes you can dare to hope that things will turn out well after all. And what can it mean to for him to be proud to be British today. By the end, he's as true a Brit as any.

Iphigenia in Splott by Gary Owen (Sherman Theatre, 2015)

Well, boys and girls, ladies and gents, I'd like to introduce Effie.

Often seen pissed first thing in the morning, wandering around. People in this monologue think: 'Stupid slag. Nasty skank.'

Young, unemployed. A bucket for alcohol and drugs. Promiscuous and aggressively confrontational.

Then one evening she meets Lee, a wounded soldier, and falls in love with him. What happens next is a crazy story that takes off and roars, screeches and powers through a dozen twists and turns until it crashes right through the barriers of our emotions.

Because the show is based on a Greek tragedy, *Iphigenia*, Effie has to make a sacrifice. Too bad.

Sophie Melville's performance kills it. Her voice is her instrument and she snarls, she whispers, she yells, she mutters, she curls her lip in contempt. Then she starts to move, she strides, she jumps, she pirouettes, she dances, she climbs on top of a chair. She's angry, she's funny, she's coy, she's enraptured.

But Effie's monologue ends on a note of breath-taking defiance, with one of the most highly charged declarations of recent times – a special moment I cannot hope to paraphrase so here it is (she's talking about how the most deprived areas have to take the most government cuts):

It seems, it's always places like this
And people like us who have to take it,
When the time for cutting comes.
And I wonder: just how long
Are we gonna have to take it for?
And I wonder –
What is gonna happen
When we can't take it any more?

An Evening with an Immigrant by Inua Ellams (Soho Theatre, 2016)

I always love it when the playwright performs their own monologue.

Poet, playwright and performer Inua Ellams begins *An Evening with an Immigrant* by saying that he comes from a long line of troublemakers.

His story is about being born in Nigeria to a Muslim father and a Christian mother, and how, after they came under pressure from religious extremists, the family left for England in 1996, moved to Ireland for three years, then came to London and then how, despite experiences of racism, Ellams began his creative life as a performance poet, and achieved great success.

He performs the show with a compelling blend of reminiscence, poetry, alliterative and allusive, and music, inspired by hip-hop.

He also gives an acutely critical account of applying for asylum and of the failures of the UK immigration system.

His story reminds us about how this nerdy guy, who calls himself the 'Black Matilda' because he also has a passion for reading, found his calling by becoming a poet. He has this effortless charm, both confident and seductive, eloquent and graceful. Still makes me smile, and go 'Hey!' Long live the poets and troublemakers!

Living with the Lights On by Mark Lockyer (Young Vic, 2016)

Mental health issues are one of the most difficult subjects to talk about in a theatre production, and one of the shows that affected me most strongly was *Living with the Lights On* by Mark Lockyer, who is a Shakespearean actor. It is an autobiographical piece about his experiences of bipolar disorder.

I remember how he welcomed us all into the studio theatre at the Young Vic, with a warm friendly smile, and offered us tea and biscuits, and asked us our names. This encouraged all of us to sympathize. The space was designed to look like a rehearsal room, but, oh, then it also had a picture of the Devil on the wall. Ominous I thought!

Anyway, how does the story go? After he gets offered the part of Mercutio in an RSC production of *Romeo and Juliet*, he starts hearing the Devil's voice in his head, and is tempted to do some weird shit. Like get off with some woman in the company, even though he already has a girlfriend in London, then he is tempted to break up with his girlfriend; then he is tempted to do other much worse stuff, like forgetting his lines on stage, committing arson and even attempting suicide.

Lockyer manages to communicate how it feels to experience an acute manic-depressive episode. Starting with the emotional confusion of sexual infidelity, his monologue spirals into ever more extreme incidents that become increasingly toe-curling to listen to. You can feel his distress. Because, despite all the energy in its most manic phases, having bipolar is sad.

Ultimately, the manic-depressive is utterly alone.

The Shape of the Pain by Chris Thorpe (Edinburgh Fringe, 2017)

Hello. I am going to talk about this unique show, which is all about pain. Physical pain. A rare condition called complex regional pain syndrome. It's a neuropathic condition which causes constant chronic pain, which has no apparent source.

This one-woman show is an experiment. About how we talk about pain. It is based on the experiences of Rachel Bagshaw, a theatre-maker, who developed this condition as a teenager, after an accident, and has lived with it ever since. Not only does she experience various degrees of chronic pain, but she also has a synaesthetic response to its intensity, seeing and hearing it as colours and sounds. At its worst, it feels like an out-of-body experience, an extreme sense of dissociation.

Although based on personal experience, the narrative of this monologue is fictional. It is presented as a love story, a story about how two people try and live together when one of them has a frightening medical condition. A condition that is hard to explain. It's a really touching account of mutual understanding, with all of its ups and downs.

The show is a mix of the scientific and the personal and is performed by Hannah McPake, who is funny, serious, sad, touching, empathetic, then even more funny, intense and also moving. No coyness; no excess. And, as she herself says, she has really expressive eyes. She manages to make the sense of feeling depersonalized into a very personal journey.

Bagshaw's production uses projections of Thorpe's words, bright changes of colour, with music by Melanie Wilson, to create another dimension to rational understanding. Even the most dramatic moments, when the whole set pulses with the overwhelming agony of confusion, or the passages of rage and hatred, are perfectly controlled. But the confusion is real. After all, sometimes it's just impossible to be understood.

My Mum's a Twat by Anoushka Warden (Royal Court, 2018)

This is an 'unreliable' version of a true story filtered through a hazy memory and vivid imagination. It's a comic semi-autobiography with an amazing title in which Anoushka Warden gives a brightly written humorous account of being a teenager, one whose mother twatishly shacks up with an unsympathetic man, a Canadian stepfather the girl calls 'the Moron'.

But she thinks her mum was not always a twat.

She says that when she was young her mum used to buy her presents on her birthday, and kiss her goodnight. She remembers her as a normal mum.

Then her mum meets 'the Moron', and everything changes. They move to Canada because her mum has been sucked into a cult and wants to open The Heal Thyself Centre for Self-Realization and Transcendence.

The story of this girl is played brilliantly by Patsy Ferran. You know who I mean? She has this really mischievous puckish presence, she moves with a pixie-like alertness and has some great grimaces. Always seems on her toes – ready to dance.

Anyway, the monologue is full of memorable incidents, like when the speaker and her best friend hide in a cupboard in the meditation room, pissing themselves with silent laughter, while the adults squat silently for chilled deep breathing. This is one of those vivid moments which stays with you. And there's lots of music, with Tupac Shakur being, for the speaker, the go-to guy for empowerment.

Girls & Boys by Dennis Kelly (Royal Court, 2018)

I met my husband in the queue for returns to see this show, and I have to say that at first, unlike in the monologue, I took an instant like to him. I'd just got back to London after travelling because I didn't know what else to do with my life, and I'd heard that this play was by the guy who'd written *Matilda the Musical*, and was starring Carey Mulligan. So I went to see it.

She plays a gutsy, feisty young woman who is ambitious, and has both incisive intelligence and 360-degree emotional awareness. Speaking in a Cockney accent she tells the story of her marriage and career. In between her direct chats to the audience, she mimes scenes with her two kids.

Then, as she says, 'Things with us started to go properly wrong' and the story turns into a horrific account of toxic masculinity.

Put simply, men are the problem. Their obsession with control, being boss and capacity for extreme violence is all bad news for women. On the other hand, women have courage and generosity – in fact, this monologue is all a bit like #MeToo on speed.

Anyway, Mulligan's performance of a text that glories in vulgarity as well as being deeply emotional was absolutely magnetic. Her freshness and vitality informed this confessional monologue with a bright honesty and detail of feeling that came alive at every turn. The audience ate from her elegant hands. Kelly's plotting is faultless, and the piece is full of theatrical tricks that shock as well as entertain. And the play concludes: 'We didn't create society for men – we created it to stop men.'

Baby Reindeer by Richard Gadd (Edinburgh Fringe, 2019)

This powerful and engaging monologue portrays a man brought to the edge by the fallout from his frivolous attitude to Martha, a forty-something woman he meets while working in a bar. The man is stand-up comedian Richard Gadd. After he makes a fleeting mistake, an inappropriate sexual joke to Martha, she becomes obsessed by him. Apparently based on a true experience with a female stalker, this is a story about obsession. She starts phoning and emailing him constantly, incontinently, and then starts turning up at his gigs. In total, he says she sends him 40,071 emails, 350 hours of voicemail, 744 tweets, 46 Facebook messages, sets up three fake Facebook accounts, 106 pages of letters and even sends a cuddly toy with soft antlers. Her name for Gadd is Baby Reindeer. But because she never threatens him directly with violence, the police say that they are powerless to stop her. Also in the mix is Gadd's love interest, Teri, a politically active trans woman who tries to help him. As the Gadd says, 'Sometimes the truth is messy: I had a convicted stalker stalking me', and so it is that Gadd the victim becomes as obsessed as Martha the stalker. It's a cautionary tale.

Superhoe by Nicôle Lecky (Royal Court, 2019)

Thanks for coming. I wanna tell you about Sasha Clayton, a mixed-race twenty-four-year-old living with her mum, stepdad and irritating little sister, in Plaistow, East London. She spends most of her time on her own in her bedroom scrolling through social media. Working on her songs, recording tracks. She says she's a singer-slash-rapper and not the sort of girl to work in 'fucking' Wetherspoons for eight pounds an hour. FUCK SAKE – DON'T INTERRUPT.

After Sasha has a bust-up with her folks and leaves home, she is broke, with nowhere to go, so she stays with various friends but runs outta options and eventually finds herself in a world of sexual exploitation and misery. The superficial glamour of posh clubs and hotels can barely hide the squalid nature of these transactions. If female friendship is the main defence against exploitation by rich and powerful men, then occasionally even this proves fragile.

Lecky peppers her text with memorable sayings – such as 'the hoe wife never becomes the housewife' – and her writing has all the vividness of fully imagined situations. During the occasional rap songs, to the music of The Last Skeptik, her humour and singing makes the studio space come alive, and the writing offers wry observations, lightning-quick perceptiveness and emotional intelligence: selling her 'premium pussy' mixes filthy chat with heartbreak. She manages to effortlessly suggest the innocent child within the sassy woman. Reminds us of what we already knew: the internet is a place of fake imagery – and celebrity culture is shit.

Death of England by **Roy Williams and Clint Dyer** (**National Theatre, 2020**)

Look, I got things to say about this one. Alright? It's about Michael, who feels powerless and angry. So it's like Michael's an angry white working-class guy whose dad dies suddenly during the England football team's defeat in the World Cup. As Williams and Dyer say: 'Three lions? More like three kittens.' Dad was a traditional working-class man, Tory voter, *Sun* reader and bleeding Leave voter. His views on race, always Black this, Chinky that, shit. But Michael's different. His best friend is Delroy, who's Black and is going out with Carly, Michael's sister. But then Michael, when it comes to his dad's funeral, is out of control. He really is. Fuelled by Charlie and drink, he decides to say a few words about his dad – with predictably awful results. So this is how it was on that night. On a stage that looks like a red cross, like the flag of Saint George, Michael, played by Rafe Spall – you can see his battered face looking out the cover of the playtext – interacts with the audience, building up a rapport, and then launches into stuff that is so out of order it almost beggars belief. As Delroy's mum says: 'Typical white bwoi foolishness.' But the authors also have tricks up their sleeves. The monologue ends up overturning our first impressions. Wake up will yer! Never judge a book by its cover, eh?

Shoe Lady by **E.V. Crowe** (**Royal Court, 2020**)

I love Katherine Parkinson.
 So I was keen to see *Shoe Lady* because she was in it.
 She's on all the posters for the show.
 Virtually a one-woman show.
 Quite short.
 Quite surreal.
 All about Viv, a middle-class mum who works as an estate agent in London.
 The kind who wants to make a whale of a sale.

She loses her shoe, doesn't know what to do and starts to feel more than a little overwhelmed.

The shoe's a metaphor, and what starts as a comedy slowly becomes a nightmare.

And what a nightmare!

It feels like she's right on the edge.

She says sorry a lot.

And no problem.

No problem at all.

Viv is angry about life.

She says she's a good person, but she feels insecure.

She's worse off than her parents.

But still goes to Waitrose twice a day.

Um, the playwriting has a kind of musical quality which works well with Parkinson's nasal voice. I think a good word for her voice is querulous. She does self-esteem issues very well, doesn't she?

The play ends with a speaking tree which listens to the little squeaky voices of the humans who walk past.

As it turns out, this is the last play I get to see before the pandemic closes theatres for months.

No matter.

SCENE EIGHT

Plays about family

Monologues are the most personal of theatre forms, but other traditional genres, such as the family play, also focus on intimate relationships. At a time when social attitudes to marriage and the family were, in the view of traditionalists, in crisis, most British people seemed to be taking change in their stride. A typical example is Damien Gayle's article 'Survey finds UK is abandoning traditional views of gender roles', published in the *Guardian* in 2018, which reported that the latest survey of social attitudes by the National Centre for Social Research (NatCen) found that 'Traditional views of gender roles have continued to decline, with 72% disputing the conservative view that women should dedicate themselves to housework, compared with 58% 10 years ago.' Nancy Kelley, NatCen's deputy chief executive, was quoted as saying: 'The people of Britain are moving away from the idea that men should be breadwinners and women homemakers.' While attitudes to gender roles were changing, there was also a widespread perception that broken families were at the heart of Broken Britain, and that family breakdown has negative effects on mental health, earning power and social status. Reports found children from 'broken homes' have fewer friends, earn much less and are more likely to stay single. By the end of the decade a cost-of-living crisis was severely impacting on the family life of millions.

While the family play is the oldest genre of drama – going back to ancient Greek tragedies which charted the fall of the house of Atreus and the story of Oedipus – it has not always had a dominant presence in contemporary theatre. In the 1990s, for example, most young playwrights wrote stories about 'me and my mates', or about boy gangs and girl gangs, rather than about families, which involve interactions between the generations. In the 2000s, however, the family play returned to prominence, perhaps because the young writers of the previous decade had become more ambitious, embracing more complex relationships, and maybe because they now had their own families so could write from personal experience.

I remember many impactful family plays, to take examples just from one year: 2014. From the ferocious – Polly Stenham's *Hotel* (National Theatre) with its shocking scenes of brutality – to the charming – Gurpreet Kaur Bhatti's *Khandan* (Birmingham Rep) whose title means family in Urdu and

Punjabi and whose plot criticized the illusions of traditional family life. One of the best was *3 Winters* (National Theatre) by Tena Štivičić, a Croatian-born London resident who created a complex and moving epic spanning four generations and seventy years of Croatian history – and she did it with such playwriting skill that it struck me as one of the best new plays of that year. Looking back, I sometimes wish that I'd kept a more coherent diary of my theatregoing in the 2010s, but instead, to make up for this oversight, I am adopting a fictional diary form as a way of recording the various shapes taken by family plays during the decade.

A theatregoer's diary

So, excuse me, where were we? Oh yes. Well, since you ask, the pandemic did rather put a stop to my theatre outings, and, truth be told, even now I'm still a bit on edge about it all. I *do* still go, mind you, but whenever someone behind me gives a particularly hearty cough, I can feel every nerve in my body tensing up. Yes, I'm one of those 'vulnerables', a fact I've had to make peace with, though it does come with its own little set of anxieties. As I've got older, I've noticed that I'm gradually becoming less visible, if you know what I mean. People seem to look right through me these days, as if I'm some sort of old biddy rather than a proper, living human being. It's a strange feeling, I must say. Anyway, I'm still managing, though my asthma isn't showing any signs of improvement. This morning, for instance, I was up in the loft, clearing out some old bits and bobs to make a bit of space. And wouldn't you know it, between all the dust and forgotten junk, I found my old theatre notebooks.

These notebooks are a bit of a time capsule, really. For over a decade, I recorded every single theatre trip. The handwriting is exactly the same as my schoolgirl script, which hasn't changed a jot in all these years: neat, controlled and unmistakably me. Looking at them now, I must admit, I felt a touch of shame. I mean, who do I think I am, passing judgement on the work of actors and playwrights who've put so much time and effort into their craft? And yet, I can't help but feel a bit entitled to share my opinions.

Now that I look back on it all, from the perspective of a civil servant with plenty of time to reflect, the 2010s feel like such an intriguing time. I can see from my notes that I was clearly drawn to plays about family struggles: parents passing, siblings misbehaving, all the emotional baggage that comes with those sorts of stories. I think it might've been the thrill of watching other people's families fall apart on stage while I could go home at the end of it all, safe in the knowledge that *my* baggage wasn't anything of the sort. A guilty pleasure, if you like. Since leaving my family to settle in London, I haven't really looked back. I find I rather like my own company. Yes, I've got my hobbies, and theatre is one of them. It keeps me busy, keeps me thinking (safely ensconced in the stalls). So here we are, then. A little selection of my thoughts over the years. Make of them what you will:

Friday, 24 September 2010

Saw Wanderlust, a new play about sex and intimacy by Nick Payne, and what a lovely solo trip it was to the Royal Court. There's something very satisfying about an evening out by oneself, especially when you can immerse yourself in this season's theme of middle-class family anxieties. Set in suburban England, it's about Alan and Joy, who have been married for about 25 years: she's a GP, he's head of English at a secondary school, and they live with Tim, their 15-year-old son. Tim's a classic case of a teenage boy discovering the effects of hormones for the first time: a virgin, he wants to have sex, so he turns to his friend Michelle, same age, but more experienced. Can she teach him how to 'do it'? Meanwhile, his parents are wrestling with their own dilemmas about infidelity. Payne has a knack for scenes of excruciating embarrassment and tender little glimpses at human foibles; good at sharp observation. And goodness, am I glad I stayed single: sexual desire really does have a talent for unravelling families, doesn't it? Terrific cast especially Pippa Heywood as Joy, who (unlike me) always seems to be on the verge of exploding with feeling. I've always preferred to keep a lid on things. Now we know this play has been made into a terrific TV series. Payne is undoubtedly funnier and more 'out there' than Stephen Frears and Moira Buffini's Tamara Drewe film, which I saw around the same time. Poor Tamara, shouldn't have gone back home, bit off more than she could chew.

Friday, 29 October 2010

At the Royal Court again, this time for Nina Raine's Tribes. It's set in the bustling, middle-class chaos of a noisy family home and is about Billy, a 20-something who's been deaf from birth, and his father, Christopher, a sharp-witted ex-academic with attitude, and his mother, Beth, aspiring novelist. Other siblings are Daniel (struggles with schizophrenia) and Ruth (perpetually adrift and lonely). Raine has a knack for capturing that unmistakable rhythm of parental squabbles and sibling rivalries, and this play is brimming with clever jokes, sharp observations and thoughtful musings on the three Ls: language, listening and loneliness. Billy's deafness is tempered by his skill at lip-reading (another L), and his life takes a turn when he meets Sylvia, a young woman who's losing her hearing. This encounter sends Billy on a journey to try and build an independent life away from his family. The problem is that Christopher has a distinct disdain for other social 'tribes', particularly those defined by their disabilities. He takes a particularly dim view of Sylvia, who is connecting with the deaf community, and is horrified when Billy expresses interest in learning sign language, a language his father sees as unnecessary, given that he's always insisted Billy is perfectly 'normal' and doesn't need other forms of communication. Directed by Roger Michell with a fantastic cast: Jacob Casselden as Billy, Stanley Townsend as Christopher, Kika Markham as Beth, Michelle Terry as Sylvia, Harry Treadaway as Daniel and Phoebe Waller-Bridge as Ruth. Made me reflect on the loneliness that can come with having a disability, much like my work colleague Martha. She once tried to teach me sign language over our M&S sandwiches; I managed just one sentence about the weather.

Friday, 18 March 2011

Just seen Ryan Craig's excellent The Holy Rosenbergs at the National Theatre. Set in a Jewish family home in Edgware, the story opens with the arrival of the local rabbi on the eve of a funeral. One son, Danny, has been killed fighting on the Israeli side against Hamas, while his sister Ruth (human rights lawyer based in Geneva) is branded a traitor by the Jewish community for her work on war crimes in Gaza. Then there's Jonny, another son, who's more interested in having a good time. The father, David, once a successful kosher caterer, now finds himself the head of a struggling business. The play explores that familiar family dynamic: the way the truth can remain unspoken because it's too painful to face. Secrets become the glue that holds families together, even when they threaten to pull everyone apart. Play captures the strong sense of a social group that is unforgiving of any member who doesn't conform. There's this chilling idea that if Ruth isn't kept 'under control', the whole family will suffer. Brought back memories of my own father, though Henry Goodman as David is much more attractive, blend of softness and strength. This evening also included an interesting Platform event with Ryan Craig and director Laurie Sansom discussing the show, hosted by a critic whose name, must admit, escapes me.

Monday, 14 November 2011

Drizzle all day long. My joints are aching, and I can't help but wonder if this constant damp is a sign I might be developing arthritis. Oh, the joys of middle age. Still, it was a much-needed distraction to see Jumpy by April De Angelis at the Royal Court: exceptionally funny and sharp, this one. The play is about Hilary (Tamsin Greig), a 50-year-old living with her husband Mark and their

15-year-old daughter Tilly. At first glance, they are your typical middle-class, suburban sort of family. But of course, things take a turn when Tilly introduces her boyfriend Josh, who is, like her, underage. And naturally, it becomes clear what they're getting up to. So what do Hilary and Mark decide to do? Well, mainly Hilary, actually. She tries to sort things out by talking to Josh's parents, Roland and wife Bea. And then there's Frances, Hilary's best friend and a proper sort of feminist warrior who's managed to dodge the parenting life entirely: her choice, of course. She's one of those friends you always need in your corner; honest, loyal, and also, by some miracle, child-free. Makes me think of someone else I know . . . The play really spoke to the complexities of that friendship: two women who can be completely themselves with each other, warts and all. The most laugh-out-loud moment? Frances's impromptu striptease routine. Oh, it had the audience in absolute stitches. I laughed so hard. But, as much as this is a comedy, it tackles some rather thorny issues too, particularly the reactions of parents to underage sex. De Angelis has a clever way of showing the misjudgements that can come from liberal middle-class parents, as well as the way children can so easily misread their parents. You could feel it as the audience watched: parents chuckling nervously at their own foibles while the younger ones fidgeted, unsure whether to giggle or wince. Smartly directed by Nina Raine (her again!). A proper night out, even with the damp weather following me on the way home.

Friday, 2 March 2012

Chilly day, so quite glad to retreat once more to the Royal Court, this time for David Eldridge's In Basildon. It's a story about Len, who's dying of prostate cancer, surrounded by his fractured family. His two sisters, Doreen and Maureen, haven't spoken in nearly 20 years, and yet here they are, brought together by his impending death. Also present are Doreen's son, Barry, and Len's best mate, Ken. The atmosphere? Thick with old grudges and unspoken grievances. Now, while Doreen and Maureen can't stand each other (sisters, eh?) their children, Barry and Shelley, are as close as can be. Barry is a plumber drowning in debt, and Shelley, the first in the family to make it to university, brings along her middle-class boyfriend, Tom (lefty playwright, no less). In the course of the play, Len finally dies, and instead of bringing the family together, this tears them even further apart. The bone of contention? Property, of course. Len owned his house outright, and the sisters go at each other hammer and tongs over who gets what. Barry, with a knowing grin, sums it up: family feuds are a working-class tradition. Eldridge captures the nuances of class differences so well: the cultural tastes, the political divides. I found it refreshingly unsentimental, which suits me just fine. Life's messy, isn't it? And this play doesn't try to tie it all up with a neat little bow. Directed by Dominic Cooke, with Linda Bassett as sharp-tongued Doreen, it was funny in places, but heartbreakingly honest. I left the theatre pondering family loyalties and grudges, and once home, I couldn't resist revisiting The Queen on TV. That old Peter Morgan and Stephen Frears film with Helen Mirren. The royals, now there's another dysfunctional family for you! Mind you, I do have a bit of a soft spot for Her Maj. Bless her . . .

Wednesday, 23 May 2012

Goodness me, I've just seen Love, Love, Love by Mike Bartlett, again at the Royal Court. Honestly, I must be besotted with that place! A three-hour marathon on a midweek evening: quite a commitment, especially with work in the morning. But here we are. The play's about a pair of brothers: Kenneth, the cool and groovy one, and Henry, a bit more buttoned-up. It spans three time periods: 1967 during the Summer of Love, when Sandra (Henry's girlfriend, no less) finds herself drawn to Kenneth; then 1990, with Kenneth and Sandra now married and raising two kids, Rose and Jamie; and finally 2012, when their grown-up daughter Rose is furious about her parents (us baby boomer lot) having all the pensions, property and perks (3 Ps), while her generation is left with nothing but debt, rubbish jobs and pokey flats. (Reminds me a bit of The Whisky Taster by James Graham, which I saw a few years back, though all a bit hazy now.) The sibling rivalry between Kenneth and Henry becomes a metaphor for the clash between traditional and alternative lifestyles. And as for Kenneth and Sandra, well, they're practically competing in infidelity, weaponizing so-called sexual honesty to tear one another down. Hardly a manual for good parenting, if you ask me. All ends in heartbreak, naturally. The cast was marvellous, with Victoria Hamilton and Claire Foy (brilliant in White Heat on the BBC not long ago, another 1960s thing). Honestly, watching the family dysfunction unfold, I can't help but feel ever so lucky to be an only child. Siblings? No, thank you!

Friday, 12 December 2014

On the advice of a friend, ventured out to west London, Bush Theatre, to see Visitors, debut play by one Barney Norris. What a gem of a discovery! Set in a farmhouse on the edge of Salisbury Plain, the story is about Arthur and Edie, a couple in their seventies who've been married for what feels like forever. Edie's memory is failing her more and more, so they bring in a young live-in carer, Kate, to help out. Then, unexpectedly, their son Stephen turns up after years of being distant. Both Kate and Stephen are outsiders in their own way: Kate, the hired helper, and Stephen, who rarely visits but has strong opinions about what's best for his parents, including the prospect of putting Edie into a care home. Norris's writing was beautifully sensitive (quiet, empathetic, full of understanding). He seems to truly grasp what makes older people tick, capturing both the joys and strains of a long marriage. It was so moving to see the older generation (my generation) portrayed with such tenderness. At the same time, Norris also delves into that sense of loss people feel when their independence begins to slip away, not just through memory loss, but also the fading of a rural, idyllic Deep England. Beautifully crafted piece of theatre, and the cast was exceptional: Linda Bassett as Edie and Robin Soans as Arthur were just superb. Country life, eh? Makes me wonder whether I ever will get that country cottage!

Friday, 2 October 2015

Off to the Bush Theatre again, another long slog on the Central Line, which, honestly, isn't my favourite. This time to see Fuck the Polar Bears by Tanya Ronder. Can't say I'm a fan of the title, bit brash for my taste, especially as I adore animals (and cuddly ones most of all!). Thankfully, it turned out to be an absurdist comedy, billed as 'a raucous family drama about the cost of living the life of our dreams'. The play is about on a picture-perfect family: Gordon, the dad, works for an energy company; Serena, his wife, is training to be some sort of alternative health guru; and then there's their little daughter, Rachel. They're what you might call the classic 'golden couple', so rich in cash but woefully short on time. Usual problems: money worries, vanishing intimacy, the creeping sense that life's a bit hollow. Gordon is cursed, everything he touches falls apart: bulbs blow, glass shatters, his phone refuses to charge. He's convinced the drains are clogged, and the stench of sewage becomes almost unbearable. Meanwhile, Rachel's toy polar bear mysteriously vanishes. The symbolism couldn't be clearer: Gordon, the big-shot energy executive, obsessed with his child's lost polar bear, a clear nod to the climate crisis his work exacerbates. Add to the mix Gordon's brother Clarence (recovering addict) and Blundhilde (young Icelandic au pair), the most exploited member of the household. So a clash of lifestyles: Gordon and Serena, the energy-guzzling, status-obsessed middle class, versus Clarence and Blundhilde, who are trying to live simpler, more eco-conscious lives, anti-fracking, cutting back on consumption, that sort of thing. Blend of styles: part farcical family comedy, with polar bear suits, escaped hamsters and eggs flying through the air; part thought-provoking 'play of ideas'. It shows how even the most privileged family can crumble under the weight of its own selfishness, mirroring humanity's careless destruction of the planet. Poor polar bears. Poor us.

Friday, 11 May 2018

After work, took a stroll across Waterloo Bridge to the National Theatre to see Nine Night by Natasha Gordon. A colleague at work raved about it, so I thought I'd give it a go, though I must admit I was slightly distracted by my new shoes, pinching dreadfully, so I had to slip them off discreetly during the show. Needs must. Unwelcome distraction. The play is inspired by the Jamaican tradition of nine nights of wake. It is about Gloria, who has died of cancer, and how her family, particularly her grown-up children, Trudy, Lorraine and Robert, grapple with their loss. The family dynamics are complex: Gloria came to London in the 1950s, leaving Trudy to be raised in Jamaica, while Lorraine and Robert were born in Britain. Dutiful Lorraine, who's organized the wake, has been looking after their mother for the last three months, with some help from her own daughter, Anita. Robert, meanwhile, is married to Sophie, who's white and a teacher, and Gloria's 70-something cousins, Maggie and Vince, are also present. Naturally, as with any family gathering, tensions bubble to the surface. Robert, whose business is struggling, wants Lorraine to sell their mother's house, but Lorraine insists it's more than just bricks and mortar: it's a home, a place filled with their mother's spirit. And then there's the question of race. Sophie might have been welcomed by the Jamaican side of the family, but Robert resents the fact that her white mother refuses to accept him. The standout performance for me was Aunt Maggie (brilliant Cecilia Noble) who brings larger-than-life energy to the stage. The dialogue, rich with the vibrant mix of English and West Indian rhythms, gives the play such vitality. The audience was utterly engaged (spontaneous applause at some points) and I was pleased to see it got a much-deserved West End transfer. Note to self: wear sensible shoes next time. Given the current focus on the Windrush generation, particularly in light of the Windrush scandal, this play feels incredibly timely. It also made me reflect on other instances of racism in Britain, like the tragic murder of Stephen Lawrence. I ended up watching the BBC iPlayer documentary Stephen: The Murder that Changed a Nation. Chilling and heartbreaking.

Wednesday, 15 January 2020

This must have been the last play I saw before theatres went dark because of COVID. It was Alexandra Wood's The Tyler Sisters at the Hampstead Theatre, and I went on the recommendation of a listings website. Quite intriguing concept: it's the story of three sisters from the north of England, spanning an epic 40 years. The format was fascinating: each scene represented one moment from one year, starting in 1990 and going all the way into the future, to 2030. The sisters are Maddy, Gail and Katrina, and they're wonderfully distinct.

Maddy, the eldest at 20, is shy and conflict-averse; Gail, 18, is determined but controlling (straight at first, later a lesbian); and Katrina, just 16, is the confident, passionate one. What's clever is how these core traits remain yet also evolve as the decades roll on. It's really a triple character study, which, I later discovered, was inspired by the Brown sisters, real-life siblings photographed by Nicholas Nixon over 40 years (another gem of a discovery, that). The play about all the highs and lows of family life: love, marriage, pregnancy, childcare, caring for ageing parents, bereavement and eventually grandchildren. It's compelling to watch the alliances between the sisters shift, and there's something so true about how we remember family events differently. One sister recalls an emotional moment vividly, another has completely forgotten it. As the audience, we see the actual events unfold, so we're in on what's remembered or misremembered. A nice touch was that the men (all those husbands, lovers and wayward fathers) are kept entirely offstage. It's refreshing, actually, though their presence is still felt in how they shape the women's lives. My favourite moment? Katrina reeling off an absolutely hilarious list of ways to get revenge on an unfaithful man. Brilliant! But it's the bigger themes that linger, like motherhood, particularly Gail's journey as a lesbian mother, which was beautifully portrayed. It reminded me of that line, 'All happy families are alike, but every unhappy family is unhappy in its own way.' Unhappy families do make the best drama, don't they?

SCENE NINE

Plays about gender

The popularity of personal monologues and plays about family relationships leads inevitably to the question of gender. In the 2010s this became part of the culture wars in which traditionalists insisted that there are only two genders, male and female, while progressives argued that reality is much more fluid: not only are there more than two genders, but some people identify with different genders at different times during their lives, and human sexuality is also fluid, and changeable. Such disputes have existed for years, but in this decade were often weaponized by populist politicians for their own ends. As writer Helen Lewis wrote in her *New Statesman* article, 'What makes you a man or a woman anyway?', published in September 2013: 'The idea of gender has become a battleground, with scientists, philosophers, writers and activists clashing over its definition, and even its usefulness as a category at all.' Gender became central to the culture wars – woke versus anti-woke – which fuelled the intense emotionality of issues that are often difficult to simplify or to view dispassionately.

Simultaneously, British theatre in this decade saw an increase in the numbers of women playwrights, and a boom in plays staged by them. But such progress took place against a background of inequality and negative experiences. The context, of course, was the revitalization of the #MeToo movement following the Harvey Weinstein scandal in 2017, which gave renewed impetus to women to assert themselves in the world of theatre, either by applying in increased numbers for jobs which had real power (such as artistic directorships) or by denouncing their mistreatment by powerful men. The stark facts about harassment and abuse inspired several new plays ranging from sharp satire to crass comedy. *Guardian* theatre critic Arifa Akbar gave an account of these in an article titled 'Theatre and #MeToo: "There's a new anger in women's stories"', published in 2019, which also quoted Lynette Linton, the new artistic director of the Bush Theatre, who pointed out that 'the #MeToo movement was slow to embrace the stories of women of colour'.

Questions of gender, sexuality and the belated emergence of trans artists in British theatre, were articulated in a number of plays. To take two examples from 2019: Martin Crimp's remarkable play *When We Have Sufficiently*

Tortured Each Other (National Theatre) is described by the playwright as 'Twelve variations on Samuel Richardson's *Pamela*'. In it, he transforms the 1740 novel into a powerplay between a Man and a Woman, who repeatedly switch gender roles. In the programme note, Crimp comments on Richardson's original, highlighting two incidents which are, to my mind, unconscious examples of queerness. In one, a cross-dressed abuser fails to rape his vulnerable victim, so both man and woman are unable to perform the roles traditional society has imposed on them; in the other, the abducted Pamela imagines that her escape attempt has been thwarted by two bulls in field, one of which she identifies with a woman, and which both turn out to be cows. These examples of gender fluidity – some 150 years before Freud – animate Crimp's play.

On the subject of masculinity, a gendered subject beloved of many playwrights, Bijan Sheibani's debut play *The Arrival* (Bush Theatre) sets up a neat contrast. Tom, a thirty-five-year-old computer businessman who was adopted at birth, spontaneously seeks out his biological brother, thirty-year-old Samad. For Samad, things definitely shift: once he was the older brother of his sister; now he is Tom's younger brother. So Tom is not only an arrival – he is also a rival. He has some features in common with his new-found brother, but the two men are also different. Still, the drama is about feelings of masculinity. How do two men – linked by shared genes, but separated by different life experiences – manage to connect? When they do physical stuff, like jogging or cycling, they are fine; but how do they talk about emotions? As moments of tenderness follow incidents of aggression, a complex picture emerges of how boys will always be boys.

Plays such as these have provoked debate and discussion, so how better to examine the theme of gender in theatre than by holding a study day on the subject?

Reflections on a gender and performance study day

- As part of my role as a junior arts management consultant, I attended a study day on gender and performance for a BA degree module on Contemporary British Theatre. Basically, my role was primarily that of an external observer and note-taker. While some of the more theoretical concepts were challenging, I've tried to summarize key points in an accessible manner.

Scene 9: Plays about gender

MEET AND GREET

Session One: Introduction

Discussion highlights: The study day began with an introduction to gender theory. A fundamental definition of gender is understanding that while sex is biological, gender refers to the characteristics of women, men, girls and boys that are socially constructed. Basically, this includes norms, behaviours and roles associated with being a woman, man, girl or boy, as well as relationships between them.

In our society, children are assigned a gender at birth, either male or female, a binary classification reinforced by family structures and media in a predominantly heteronormative structure. The discussion introduced key philosopher Judith Butler (preferred pronouns they/them). Their works *Gender Trouble* (1990) and *Bodies That Matter* (1993) argue that gender is not a fixed characteristic, but a fluid and performative identity shaped by choices and actions over time. Essentially, we perform our gender, through a stylized repetition of behaviour, learning to act in ways that align with societal expectations.

A critical point raised by contributors to the discussion was the distinction between gender performativity and theatrical performance. While both involve elements of 'acting', gender performativity refers to how individuals construct their identity in everyday life, whereas theatrical performance is a deliberate act of staged fiction. Moreover, performativity in society precedes and informs theatrical representations. Apparently, British theatre has witnessed an increase in recent plays which have significant things to say about gender.

Open discussion: One person reckons, bluntly, that 'sex is between the legs while gender is between the ears'. Takeaway is that we have some choice about our performance, but very little say as regards its social context, which is one of stereotypes and gender expectations. Basically, according to stereotype, for example, women are to be looked at; men to be listened to. Women have emotional intelligence; men tunnel vision. Women nurture; men fight. My question is: what happens if you don't feel like this? As someone said, 'It's complicated!'

TEA/COFFEE BREAK

Session Two: Masculinities

Following the introductory discussion, we moved into the next session, which focused on masculinity. This began with a reminder that toxic masculinity – a pattern of harmful male behaviours and attitudes – is a significant societal issue. The presentation then explored this theme by means of examples:

Case Study 1: Violence and Son *by Gary Owen (Royal Court, 2015)*

Violence and Son shows how violent behaviour, normalized in certain societal contexts, is passed from one generation to the next. The protagonist, Liam, is a seventeen-year-old boy forced, after his mother's death, to live with his estranged father, Rick (nicknamed 'Vile' because of his propensity for violence). Rick embodies a stereotypical, toxic form of working-class masculinity: tattooed, beer-drinking, manipulative and misogynistic. He encourages Liam to assert dominance over Jen, a teenage classmate. According to him, Jen is acting as if she wants sex (in fact, she is uncertain and confused). He tells Liam: 'She's up for it. Only thing is, have you got the balls.' This culminates in a sexual assault. Basically, the discussion highlighted Owen's convincing critique of how men like Rick perpetuate toxic masculinity by actively encouraging harmful gender stereotypes and aggressive behaviour in their sons. The play exemplifies a broader trend in recent theatre to examine the issue of male violence.

Case Study 2: Lela & Co *by Cordelia Lynn (Royal Court, 2015)*

The second example shifted focus to the exploitation of women within patriarchal society. *Lela & Co* tells the fictional story of Lela, a once-happy teenager living in a distant country whose life spirals into abuse after she is married off to an older man. After a civil war breaks out, he coerces her into sex work thereby turning her body into a commodity. The play's title is a 'grim joke' about this exploitation. Apparently, the original production used theatrical techniques such as total blackouts during intense moments of violence to emphasize the horror of Lela's experience. Written by a woman, this difficult yet powerful play critiques the commodification of women and the normalization of sexual violence.

Case Study 3: Birthday *by Joe Penhall (Royal Court, 2012)*

On a lighter, but thought-provoking note, *Birthday* uses humour to challenge gender stereotypes. In this sci-fi comedy, Ed and Lisa, a couple expecting their second child, reverse traditional roles: Ed carries the pregnancy. In the original production, actor Stephen Mangan's prosthetic bump was a visual gag and, in a reversal of the usual gender roles, it is the man who talks about the physicality of being pregnant: 'Don't talk to me about hormones, I'm like a Bernard Matthews turkey.' By reversing roles, Penhall shows how men make a big fuss about reproduction, being more competitive than women, while also illustrating how the roles of mother and of bread-winner are socially constructed. Apparently the play shows how old stereotypes linger on: at one point Ed says, 'I'm hard wired to go on the attack when I'm cornered', but that Lisa is 'hard wired to tolerate everything'. Basically, Penhall illustrates how societal norms shape perceptions of motherhood and masculinity, his comedy of gender manners exposing the arbitrary construction of gender roles. It also feels like a prediction of a future in which men as well as women might be able to give birth (through womb transplants).

Case Study 4: **Snookered** *by Ishy Din (Oldham Coliseum, 2012)*

The final example focused on masculinity through the lens of young Muslim men navigating cultural and gender expectations. *Snookered* centres on four friends meeting to mark the anniversary of a mutual friend's death. Each character represents a different response to these pressures: Shaf is volatile, Mo is stable, Billy is polished, but distant, and Kamy is naïve and teased by the others. The title reflects both the characters' shared love of pool and their metaphorical sense of being 'snookered', trapped by societal and personal expectations. Each tries to navigate expectations. One says: 'I wanted to be your mate, a proper mate.' The discussion highlighted how the play balances the portrayal of cultural identity with individual experiences, showing the diversity of expressions of masculinity within this Muslim community.

Key Takeaway:

This session demonstrated the range of ways contemporary British theatre interrogates masculinity, from its toxic extremes to its humorous and subversive aspects. Across these works, playwrights critically examine how societal norms shape gender roles, providing audiences with opportunities to reflect on the complexities and consequences of masculinity.

LUNCH BREAK

Session Three: Women

After lunch the next session of the study day explored plays about women, highlighting the themes of female friendship, and of contemporary feminism.

Case Study 1: **Di and Viv and Rose** *by Amelia Bullmore (Hampstead, 2011)*

Female friendship is a central theme in Amelia Bullmore's *Di and Viv and Rose*, the first example in this presentation. The play focuses on three women who meet at university in 1983: Di, a working-class lesbian with a passion for sports; Viv, a career-oriented intellectual from the North; and Rose, an upper-class art history student with a carefree approach to boys. Over three decades, their evolving friendship highlights how each woman navigates her gender identity. Their differences are reflected even in their clothing choices: Di prefers tracksuits, Viv adopts a retro Second World War-vintage-inspired style, and Rose leans into fashionable trends. Rose's persona is generous, funny and she cheerfully has sex with whoever she fancies; Viv is more studious and writes essays with a feminist theme, guards her privacy; while Di loves the physical energy of sport and is monogamous. While their bond is strengthened by means of shared stories and mutual support, Bullmore also examines power dynamics within female friendships. She critiques how acts of kindness can mask manipulation ('You use kindness to ensnare') and how emotional independence can damage relationships ('You didn't phone me').

Case Study 2: Scenes with Girls by Miriam Battye (Royal Court, 2020)

Scenes with Girls offers a different perspective on female friendship within a feminist, middle-class context. Basically, Tosh and Lou, two twenty-four-year-old flatmates, reject heteronormative expectations. Instead of valuing men to confirm their identity, Tosh and Lou want to 'de-programme' themselves from the heteronormative 'narrative that women have to –'. So Lou has sex with different partners, but doesn't have a steady boyfriend; Tosh has nothing to do with men – a kind of radical separatism 2.0. Lou laughs at a guy who, while they are having sex, repeatedly asks, 'Whose pussy is this?' Neither is attracted to other women, perhaps for ideological reasons: 'I already feel such a fucking responsibility to my gender the idea of dating one of my own I mean I'd just forgive them for everything.' Both dismiss women who follow 'the narrative' by settling down, and they mock their friend Fran, who has met Mister Right and conforms to a traditional role. Battye's flat-share drama also touches on other subjects like the way that some women have coercive control over other women, and Tosh and Lou's casual cruelty to Fran shows they are more focused on their own relationship than female solidarity.

Case Study 3: Revolt. She Said. Revolt Again. by Alice Birch (RSC, 2014)

The session then shifted to discussions of feminist ideas, starting with *Revolt. She Said. Revolt Again.*. This provocative piece, part of the Royal Shakespeare

Company's Midsummer Mischief season, is a response to a feminist provocation: 'Well behaved women seldom make history', and also inspired by Valerie Solanas's 1967 classic *SCUM Manifesto*. Birch eschews the conventional constraints of setting, character and plot, instead creating a four-part piece which explores feminist criticism of the clichés of romantic love, marriage and family life. In these sections, a woman critiques what her lover thinks is seductive language; in another, a romantic offer of marriage is refused because the woman doesn't want 'to become your possession'. At one point, apparently, another woman takes her clothes off and lies down in a supermarket – extreme direct action to subvert everyday normality! The playwright protests against sexual violence and consumerism, ending with a call to arms, which subverts itself by acknowledging that calls to arms are bound to fail. Birch shows gender roles are socially constructed and attacks the idea that women are valued only because of their appearance; she questions the inherent maleness of language, especially the language of sex (in which male is active; female passive). Birch stresses that 'this play should not be well behaved', and her work emphasizes that if a woman's body is a battleground, language can be a weapon of resistance and change.

Case Study 4: **How to Date a Feminist** *by Samantha Ellis (Arcola, 2016)*

How to Date a Feminist exemplifies a lighter, feel-good perspective on feminist themes. Framed as a rom-com, the play flips genre clichés to critique and celebrate relationships. Steve, a baker, proposes to Kate, a journalist, with an apology for the patriarchy rather than a traditional declaration of love. He gets down on one knee, and says, 'I want to apologise for the patriarchy.' But his seduction technique of repeatedly asking 'May I' is a turn-off. Their dynamic – Steve as the 'New Man' and Kate as a self-reliant woman interested in bad boys – suggests questions about gender performance. Flashback shows their meet cute at a fancy dress party, with Kate dressed as Wonder Woman ('symbol of female power') and Steve as Robin Hood ('ethical hero'). Basically, Ellis debates issues such as: Can men really be feminists? Why are nice girls attracted to bad boys? How do you balance the head and the heart? She also asks: Can people change, and how much control do we have over our performance of gender? The characters' contradictions include rough sex (a 'neurosis' in women, but a 'sexual taste' for men).

Key Takeaway:

This session looked at how contemporary plays engage with themes of gender, friendship and feminism, by means of humour as well as provocation.

TEA/COFFEE BREAK

Session Four: Motherhood

The next session focused on the subject of couples and mothers.

Case Study 1: **The Distance** *by Deborah Bruce*
(Orange Tree Theatre, 2014)

The Distance examines the unconventional journey of Bea, a forty-something British woman who leaves her Australian husband, Simon, and their two children in Melbourne to return to England. Bea stays with long-standing friends Kate and Alex, who struggle to accept her rejection of motherhood. Bea's decision to leave her children seems incomprehensible, unnatural and monstrous. Women are supposed to always be there, always on call, always nurturing. But Bea feels that motherhood is a mistake. 'I can't do it! I'm shit at it!' Deep down, she rejects this role. Worse of all, her friends don't listen to Bea, so she fights to make her voice heard. 'Why isn't anyone listening to me?' The play challenges the deeply ingrained belief that motherhood is an innate role for women, portraying Bea's struggle with societal judgement and her own inner turmoil.

Case Study 2: **The Village Bike** *by Penelope Skinner*
(Royal Court, 2011)

The Village Bike (title from a sexist joke about everyone getting a ride on an available woman) also explores motherhood. Set in a rural village, it concerns Becky, a pregnant woman grappling with unfulfilled sexual desire. 'It's like your body is literally telling you what it needs.' But John, her husband, doesn't feel aroused; he's more interested in reading books about babies. Basically, they have swapped gender roles, with her performing the role of a porn-watching sexual adventurer, and him playing the homebody obsessed with kids. Skinner contrasts porn (enthusiastic but fake couplings) and reality (unfulfilled longings and sexual misery), and suggests a larger concern with the power of images, especially images of women's bodies. The play boldly contests the double standard that men can be sexually adventurous while women cannot.

Case Study 3: Jack Thorne's **The Solid Life of Sugar Water**
(Graeae/Theatre Royal Plymouth, 2015)

The session then transitioned to a focus on couples navigating physical and emotional intimacy. *The Solid Life of Sugar Water* is a rom-com about Alice and Phil, a couple with physical disabilities. But it's less about disability and more about their love affair: sex and marriage and pregnancy. The play shows how our performance of gender involves different attitudes. It describes in explicit detail what Phil does with his fingers and Alice with her hips. Phil's attitude to masculinity is quite traditional: he has laddish assumptions about women's bodies, rates Alice as 'a seven' out of ten and doesn't like her nipples. But he does realize that sex is 'really not like riding a bike. Sex. It's far more complicated.' When he loses his erection he feels his maleness is threatened. At the centre of the story is Alice's experience of stillbirth, after an antepartum haemorrhage, and its trauma. In one passage, Phil's pleasurable orgasm is shown side-by-side with Alice's excruciating pain as she gives birth to a lifeless baby. 'CUT IT OUT. PLEASE. CUT IT OUT. I HURT.' So the play is also about grief and how your body feels it, but its often gross physicality is balanced by acute humour.

Case Study 4: Tender Napalm *by Philip Ridley* (Southwark Playhouse, 2011)

Tender Napalm concerns a poetic and visceral exploration of a love affair between Man and Woman, and contains some beautiful moments of explicitly sexual dialogue. When the man describes his delight in the woman's genitals and the woman describes her delight in the man's genitals it's a reminder of the biology of sexual difference. He describes 'the deepest, pinkest, tenderest part' of her vagina, while she sees his penis as a 'perky thing'. Both describe sex as 'tweaking the beak'. But both also compete in making up stories to explain their place in the world: every fantasy voiced by Man is countered by an even more fantastical fantasy by Woman. And while Man imagines metaphorically inserting a grenade inside Woman, she imagines cutting off his penis when he comes home drunk and abusive. Through these images, the play probes themes of power, violence and desire.

Finally, one of the participants spoke about *The B*easts* by Monica Dolan (Edinburgh Fringe, 2017), an unsettling monologue about an eight-year-old girl who convinces her mother to take her to Brazil for breast enhancement surgery. When the child returns to school, the teachers are appalled; they contact social workers. This example led to discussion about the sexualization of children, increasing use of pornography and the fetishization of women's bodies. It posed challenging questions about parental agency and societal complicity in harmful gender constructs.

Key Takeaway:

This session showed how theatre can interrogate deeply entrenched norms.

TEA/COFFEE BREAK

Session Five: Queerness

Following the coffee break, the afternoon concerned the central theme of gender fluidity, looking at a range of plays that challenge conventional norms and reflect on queer identities in nuanced ways.

Case Study 1: **Rotterdam** *by Jon Brittain (Theatre503, 2015)*

Rotterdam, set in the Dutch city of the title, concerns British twenty-something Alice, who has decided to come out as a lesbian to her UK-based parents by means of email. Before she presses send, her lover Fiona shocks her by saying: 'I'm a straight man in a woman's body.' In fact, they want to start living as a bloke called Adrian. So basically Alice faces several gender-related questions, including about her own identity: if your lesbian lover becomes a man, what does that say about you? Does it mean you're straight? And have you been straight all along? Two other characters: Josh, a thirty-something Briton who is Adrian's older brother and former lover of Alice, and the Dutch youngster Lelani, a gay work colleague. The play has humour: Alice suggests that Adrian try a binder to flatten their breasts 'as long as it doesn't set off your eczema'. But a trans man is not a problem: Adrian's coming out is the opportunity for all the other characters to consider their identities – and privileges. Key quote when Adrian says, 'I don't want to change the world. I just want people to see me the way I want to be seen. The way I am.' Also questions of how personal identity relates to national identity. Famous English politeness appears increasingly like moral cowardice and micro-aggression.

Case Study 2: **Out of Water** *by Zoe Cooper*
(RSC/Orange Tree Theatre, 2019)

Out of Water is an exploration of inclusivity in practice. Set in South Shields, the story concerns Claire, a London teacher, and her wife Kit, a police officer, and their arrival in Kit's hometown. Claire gets a job as inclusion manager at the same secondary school that Kit once attended, and works with some of the school's less well-integrated pupils, like Fish, a fourteen-year-old non-binary student interested in swimming and fascinated by 'the aquatic ape' theory. (This apparently is the idea, promoted by David Attenborough, that our species spent eons not just on the savannah, but in the sea. The theory was originally formulated as a critical response, by anthropologist Elaine Morgan in the 1970s, to the gendered stereotyping of male anthropologists who ignored women's role in human evolution.) For Fish, the metaphor of the aquatic ape, 'our great-great-great times a million nan', offers a sense of personal freedom in an imagined world where they are not bothered by other people's preconceptions and prejudices. The play's title suggests the image of a fish out of water, and this is emphasized by Fish's suspicion of authority. By means of the image of swimming in the cold sea, 'thinking about how long it takes to warm the sea up', Cooper argues that each individual needs courage to take the plunge into affirming their own identity.

Case Study 3: *Burgerz by Travis Alabanza (Hackney Showroom, 2018)*

Next examples were of the intersections of race and queerness. In *Burgerz*, the author – who is a Black trans writer and performer – tells the story of how someone threw a burger at them and yelled 'tranny' in broad daylight on Waterloo Bridge. Dozens of witnesses, but basically no one did anything. After this, Alabanza became 'obsessed' with burgers, using this as a way of coming to terms with this transphobic incident, and during the show they invite a white cis man on stage to help them make and cook a burger, a means of reclaiming agency. Through this performance, the Black trans victim analyses their experience, processes it and then packages it up for an audience. The show features the central metaphor of deciding between burgers and hot dogs, and whether to first make the burger and then make a box for it or the other way around, as a critique of the gender binary (male/female). Alabanza's queer sensibility is expressed by their questions: 'What if your burger changes into something different? What if you find out halfway through cooking that actually you don't like burgers, you're more of a hotdog person? Or why must you choose a burger box before you've even made the burger?' Alabanza asks the cis white man from the audience, 'How do you know you're a man?' Often, conversations about gender don't mention race or how many Black people, who live outside the binary, risk being misgendered. The show's interactive approach underscores the inseparability of race and gender in discussions of identity.

Case Study 4: *The High Table by Temi Wilkey (Bush Theatre, 2020)*

The final example was *The High Table*, a celebration of Black queerness which addresses the intersection of cultural heritage and LGBTQ+ identity. It concerns Tara and Leah, a young London lesbian couple who want to get married, but receive a negative reaction from Tara's Nigerian parents. There is also Tara's uncle Teju, who lives in Lagos and is persecuted because he is gay. Set in London, Lagos and the afterlife, where Tara's long-dead ancestors – Yetunde, Babatunde and Adebisi – debate whether to bless her same-sex union, and the playwright includes a historical perspective. Before the coming of white Europeans, and Christian gods, the relationships of African women with women and men with men were not labelled and condemned by religion. White men 'polluted our ways'. Wilkey argues that lesbians from the African diaspora are not as visible as other social groups, and social stereotyping makes coming out problematic. Also, public displays of same-sex affection are difficult: Leah would like to give Tara a goodbye kiss 'without checking over your shoulder'. Basically, the longing of gay people for family support comes across with great power, and the story concludes with a warm glow. Yetunde says, 'I want us to bless this wedding.'

Conclusion

Good study day, with several key takeaways. At the end, someone said something like: Ask yourself, does gender have to be such a big issue? Could it, occasionally, just occasionally, be more of a comedy than a problem? Not sure about that, but here is a word cloud of the event:

SCENE TEN

Plays about race

Just as the emergence of women playwrights is one of the big success stories of the 2010s, a genuinely new trend, another one is the increased visibility of playwrights from diverse backgrounds. This was a very good decade for British Black and Asian playwrights, whose dramas can be seen as writing the future as well as the present – they have constantly been innovative in both form and content. This has happened in a context of the fight against racism in the theatre as well as in the wider society. In the 2010s, individual actors such as David Harewood, Idris Elba, Marianne Jean-Baptiste and Daniel Kaluuya pointed out that they had had to seek work in the United States because of the lack of opportunities in the United Kingdom. In 2012, Patricia Cumper, artistic director of Talawa Theatre Company, told *Channel 4 News*: 'Every time we cast a Talawa show, I am reminded how many brilliantly trained and multi-talented Black and Asian actors there are in Britain. Yet they do not find the number or range of roles they want, or in my opinion, deserve.' By 2018, however, there was evidence that the situation was changing. In this crucial year a series of appointments of non-white people changed the landscape of artistic directorships: Kwame Kwei-Armah at the Young Vic, Nadia Fall at the Theatre Royal Stratford East and Lynette Linton at the Bush Theatre, all joined Indhu Rubasingham at the Kiln Theatre, along with many more such as Justin Audibert, Suba Das, Tarek Iskander and Matthew Xia. At the same time, a new wave of Black and Asian playwrights arrived on British stages.

The excitement of discovering new voices from diverse backgrounds was one of the positive highpoints of the 2010s. Two debuts were particularly striking: Theresa Ikoko's *Girls* (Talawa and Soho Theatre, 2016) won the Alfred Fagon Award and was joint-winner of the George Devine Award. Based on the kidnap in 2014 of more than 200 schoolgirls in the Nigerian town of Chibok by the Islamist terrorist group Boko Haram, it examines the life in captivity of Haleema, Ruhab and Tisana, three young teens who now pass the time by playing various games, having humorous fantasies, sharing memories of church services and making spirited parodies of American television shows. Similarly symbolic of the new talent emerging in the decade was Ifeyinwa Frederick's irreverently noisy, and often hilarious, play *The Hoes*

(Hampstead Theatre, 2018). Set in an Ibiza hotel room, the story features three twenty-year-old women who have been best friends since secondary school: Alex, Bim and J (Jasmine). Their alcohol-fuelled holiday gives a highly charged account of what it feels like to be part of sisterhood: the explicit sexual banter, the sudden switches of feeling, the deep understanding of each other's characters, all come across with pace and energy. Such plays depended on theatre companies such as Talawa, Soho Theatre and Hampstead Theatre, but it's also worth noting the role of the Royal Court theatre as well as smaller venues such as Ovalhouse, where in 2011 the mixed-race playwright Shireen Mula — whose work was developed through the Royal Court's 'Unheard Voices' programme for young playwrights of Muslim descent — premiered her *Same Same*, a lyrical story of regret, longing and mixed-race identity about an adopted woman on the eve of her twenty-first birthday. In the 2010s, gems like this were everywhere for the finding.

In a decade when new voices proliferated, here is a selection of writers from diverse backgrounds, who each tell their own stories.

Black and Asian playwrights on race and writing

Roy Williams

Roy Williams is the leading Black British playwright of contemporary theatre. Starting out in the 1990s with plays about his mother's Windrush generation, he quickly moved on to exploring the social tensions of the present time, showing both the racism and the violence of the Black British experience. When he talks about the initial idea for *Sucker Punch* (Royal Court, 2010), his play about young boxers in the 1980s, he stresses how social history is something he feels personally. Watching a television programme about the 1980s, he recalls that: 'The programme makers were discussing the 1980s like it was something that happened many years ago, but for me, it was like yesterday.' It seemed funny to him 'that my most recent past is now a part of history.' The 1980s were an important time as he was twelve when it started and twenty-one when it ended. He says, 'For most young Black men at the time, there was much more anger than there is now.' Remembering the riots in Brixton, Toxteth and Broadwater Farm, he says that they 'were the only way my generation could say to the establishment: "NO! You are not fucking us over like you did our Mums and Dads"' (Williams, 2010).

In *Sucker Punch*, Leon and Troy are two young Black teenagers trying to discover their identities. They both feel they have to abandon their West Indian culture and find something else. Troy is attracted to African-American culture, believing that Blacks are treated better in the States than in Britain, while Leon embraces the white working-class culture where he is loved, yet also ridiculed. For both of them boxing is a means of escape. Their white trainer Charlie is also important. A Conservative voter pushed aside by the Thatcher boom, he backs the new generation of Black boxers in his gym.

Williams says, 'More than ever back then, Black sporting figures were the strongest role models you could find.' In boxing, he remembers many of them: Frank Bruno, Lloyd Honeyghan, Maurice Hope, Sugar Ray Leonard, Nigel Benn, Errol Christie, John Conteh. 'It is alarming to know how much racism most of these guys had to endure' (Williams, 2010). Williams hopes that audiences do not come out from *Sucker Punch* thinking, 'Yeah it was so tough back then, but things are better now.' That's too complacent. 'Yes,' he says, 'things are better, but only just! All it takes is a little nudge sometimes for us to fall back. It's not just boxers who need to keep their guard up, it's all of us' (Otas).

As well as exploring the history of Black Britons, Williams has also responded to contemporary events, writing plays which featured white working-class characters. These include *Sing Yer Heart Out for the Lads* (National Theatre, 2002), *Wildefire* (Hampstead Theatre, 2014) and *Days of Significance* (Royal Shakespeare Company, 2007), a play which has been revived several times in the 2010s. *Days of Significance* was commissioned by the RSC at the time when the Iraq War was freshly controversial. Williams says, 'I was keen to write about how the war impacted on poorer working-class people, who are often perceived as the lowest of the low.' He wasn't interested in writing about the people in power, but about the powerless. And he links this with another theme: 'young people and the binge-drinking culture – the way that city centres are occupied at weekends by crazed youngsters.' He thought 'that would make a powerful stage image. To show that world' (Williams, 2023).

So when the RSC asked Williams to respond to a Shakespeare play, he chose *Much Ado About Nothing*, and created his own Beatrice and Benedick (Trish and Ben). Ben is in the army and Shakespeare's Claudio is reimagined as Jamie, another soldier. As well as showing binge-drinking, he added a strand about the abuse of Iraqi prisoners, a response to the scandal at Abu Ghraib prison. In addition to Trish, he also included another young woman, Hannah, and her step-father Lenny. The politics are clear: 'I think the war was about telling another country that we don't like the way you live, which is very hypocritical.' He asks the rhetorical question: 'What about all the young people in England you're neglecting? And they're the ones you send off to fight, to defend your values.' The playwright wanted to show how a distant war was affecting the lives of young people in the UK, who couldn't ignore it even if they knew very little about it. The Hannah character has a key line: 'I don't want that war to matter to me.' Tough luck, eh? 'I also wanted to say to those young people that no matter how shat on they feel, it's they who are important. "You do have a say; you do have an opinion: voice it"' (Williams, 2023).

As a playwright, Williams has an openness to change that helps him refine his work, especially after seeing how it affects an audience. Originally, the play's conclusion hinged on a revelation, the love that Lenny has for Hannah, his step-daughter. But, says Williams, 'When we were on at Stratford, I could sense that people were uncomfortable with this, they were shifting around in their seats.' The most pivotal scene in the play, 'and I knew we were losing the audience'. With director Maria Aberg he discussed how to replace the Lenny and Hannah moment, 'but nothing was landing'. At first he considered having Hannah profess her love for Lenny, but then he thought of something simpler. 'I sometimes make myself think not literally, but in metaphors', he says. 'I saw Hannah on the edge of a cliff – she's desperately looking for any excuse to leap off. I held onto that image and let it run around in my head.' Then he was on holiday in France, and the solution came. 'If Hannah is searching for any excuse to jump, what better way than by making a drunken pass at her step-father?' This meant that Lenny continues to have feelings for her, but they are paternal not sexual. And this solution was neat because, apart from a few lines and change of location, nothing was lost. The scene worked much better both with actors and audiences. For Williams, the biggest lesson is that rewrites are okay 'if you hold onto where the characters are, and what they want at any point in the play' (Williams, 2020).

Days of Significance is about the white working-class, and Williams firmly believes that the implications of the label 'Black playwright' should be questioned. It seems really reductive that plays by Black writers should only have Black characters. 'Why can't we write about whoever we want? I like to think I know the world of the white working class as much as my own background.' After all, when he was growing up, a lot of his friends were white. 'So how they spoke stayed in my head, and I understand where they're coming from, especially the idea that "No one's sticking up for us."' So if he has an idea for a story which needs an all-white cast, 'no problem. But the story has to come first' (Sierz).

Tanika Gupta

Tanika Gupta is the foremost British-Asian playwright of contemporary theatre. Since the 1990s her work has explored her Bengali heritage as well as current social issues, including racism in the young offenders system, knife crime and sex tourism in the Caribbean. *The Empress* (Royal Shakespeare Company, 2013) is her play about Queen Victoria and the South-East Asian ayahs and lascars of the late nineteenth century, an epic set over the last fourteen years of Victoria's reign. It was commissioned by Michael Boyd, artistic director of the RSC, after she had vaguely pitched 'a costume drama set in the nineteenth century with Asians running around in it'. Her initial inspiration came from Rozina's Visram's book *Ayahs, Lascars and Princes: The Story of Indians in Britain 1700–1947* and an old black and white photograph taken in a home for ayahs in Aldgate, which showed a group of Asian women seated around a table sewing and reading, wearing saris and Victorian dress. This intrigued her: 'What were these women all doing in East London at the turn of the last century?' (Gupta).

During research in the British Library she discovered that the population of Indians in Britain at that time was larger than she'd thought. As well as Abdul Karim, gifted to Queen Victoria by John Tyler, superintendent of the central prison in Agra, to celebrate her Golden Jubilee in 1887 – and who became the old monarch's beloved Munshi (teacher) – there was Dadabhai Naoroji, the first Indian MP, elected in 1892 to Gladstone's Liberal government. Then there was the younger generation, such as Gandhi, who came as students, particularly to study British law, 'and of course there were the Indian ayahs who served as nannies and nurse maids to the many colonial families, both in India and Britain'. Meanwhile, the London docks were full of Indian lascars (sailors) who worked on the British steamers which sailed all over the Empire. Although not slaves, they were often made to work in appalling conditions. All these different 'birds of passage' ended up in London and many laid down roots two generations or more before the post-war Asian immigration (Gupta).

The Empress follows characters from all these walks of life, interweaving their stories and looking at the personal and the political relationships of India and Britain in the heyday of colonial rule. 'I had a wonderful time discovering how Queen Victoria learnt to speak and even read Hindi from Karim.' She became increasingly interested in her double standards: 'at once championing the rights of her Indian servants, even calling her court "racialists", while also revelling in her title Empress of India and happy to pursue the ruinous exploitation of countries she never visited' (Gupta). The 1890s saw the scramble for African colonies while in India, the so-called jewel of the colonial crown, there was a growing nationalist consciousness with a rising demand for Indian Home Rule championed in London by Naoroji, who mentored Gandhi and Mohammad Ali Jinnah.

The Empress was directed by Emma Rice, with whom Gupta had formed a creative partnership while working together on her musical *Wah! Wah! Girls* in 2012. 'From the start her vision of the world of the play was very modern, which I appreciated.' Early readings of the play included a session at Osborne House on the Isle of Wight, the royal home created by Victoria and Albert, where the queen spent her holidays with Karim. 'The play leapt off the page. Emma brought a unique flair to visualising these rich stories, seamlessly moving the action from the grimy East End docks to Victoria's glittering palace.' The result was not a stuffy costume drama, but 'a magical world, at once epic in scale and private in intimate moments – where an unknown history is revealed through songs, music, movement, words and action' (Gupta).

Since then, *The Empress* has become part of the GCSE syllabus and Gupta 'started receiving social media messages from young students who were inspired by the play and asked amazingly astute questions'. It was produced again at the RSC in 2023, this time directed by her long-time collaborator Pooja Ghai. 'It gave me a chance to work with Ghai to rewrite and update parts of the play, being bolder with the politics given the growing momentum around decolonising history' (Gupta). The production transferred to the Lyric Hammersmith where a diverse London audience could appreciate the play for the first time.

Gupta has also explored her own family history in *Lions and Tigers* (Sam Wanamaker Playhouse, 2017), which draws on the story of the radical revolutionary Dinesh Gupta, her grandfather's youngest brother, and his contribution to the battle for Indian independence. The story is that in 1930 Dinesh Gupta and two other teenage Bengal volunteers broke into the Writers' Building in Calcutta, and shot and killed the Inspector General of Prisons. 'This man was responsible for the torture of political prisoners, so he was deliberately targeted.' But once they shot him they couldn't get out, so one of the group took cyanide and died immediately. 'The other friend shot himself and died, and Dinesh also shot himself, but the bullet got stuck behind his ear' (Bowie-Sell). The British operated on him, took the bullet out and six months later executed him.

While Dinesh Gupta was in prison he wrote a number of letters. 'My grandfather collected ninety-two letters, and half of them were written in Bengali and the other half were written in English, and so I grew up seeing these letters.' Because communications were censored, he couldn't write about politics, so 'he talks about books and novels, and the mangoes he's eating'. They 'show what an amazingly educated young man he was, that he can compare Tagore with Shakespeare, and quote Turgenev'. The playwright grew up with 'stories about this dashing young revolutionary who was hanged by the British when he was nineteen. My grandfather died when he was ninety-three and he never stopped talking about him' (Bowie-Sell).

Gupta had been trying to write this story for many years. 'The first time I read the letters was when I was about nineteen myself. They are so beautiful and I was so taken by the fact that this guy was the same age as me.' This was what inspired her to start writing. So in 1995 she wrote *Voices on the Wind* and sent it to Talawa, who were inviting Black women writers to send in stage scripts. 'They really helped me to develop my play. I kept trying to re-write it and in the meantime my career took off. I could never quite get it right – until I tried again with *Lions and Tigers*' (Bowie-Sell).

The lions are the British and the tigers are the Bengalis. 'The phrase comes from the British colonial prison on the Andaman Islands, where a Scottish jailer welcomed transportees by saying, "This is the place where the lions tame the tigers"'. The play tells the story from Dinesh's point of view, and presents the argument between violent insurrection and non-violent civil disobedience. In terms of the fight for Indian independence, these Bengali revolutionaries were radicalized by the Amritsar massacre in 1919. It was a generational struggle. Young Bengali revolutionaries always 'talked about this country being led by old people who are just so set in their ways. "The days of the bullock-cart have gone," they kept saying. They were very anti-Gandhi and non-violence' (Gupta and Verma).

The play also explores the issue of gender: 'Well, in terms of Dinesh's views on women, my grandfather also wrote a journal where he noted how Dinesh used to go off to houses where he had heard that there had been domestic violence, and throw shoes at the man.' Many Bengali revolutionaries were young women. So she thinks it was a very exciting time for women, 'in terms of getting involved politically. Some of them even did the same thing – there was a couple of fourteen-year-old girls who went and shot a district magistrate' (Gupta and Verma). Gupta wanted to make sure that their voices were heard, so that this wasn't just a play about male revolutionaries.

The story continues to resonate. 'My grandfather always used to say, "Dinesh should not have killed, and he should not have been killed."' The family also thought of the young radical as a victim as well as perpetrator: 'He had done wrong, but equally, they felt that he had been duped into it. One of the things I remember is that my grandfather and my grandfather's older brother both said Dinesh was groomed.' The play shows how older revolutionaries exert influence on the young and 'persuade them into martyrdom. However, when you read Dinesh's own words you can also see the depth of his conviction and political understanding' (Gupta and Verma). As well as being brainwashed, young revolutionaries had agency.

Inua Ellams

Inua Ellams is a Nigerian-born poet, playwright, performer, graphic artist and designer. His most successful play is *Barber Shop Chronicles* (National

Theatre, 2017), which looks at Black masculinity in an international context, and featured a lively staging full of dance and music. It was inspired by chance: 'I was dating someone who was an epidemiologist and she talked to me about a counselling project for barbers, to teach them ways of spotting mental health issues while they were cutting hair.' He understood that for Black British men, barber shops are a safe place where they can relax, 'escape racism and talk freely with no fear of being stopped, questioned or moved on by the police, which is a common experience in the world outside' (Akbar). His aim was to explore the variety of African masculinities, although admittedly only from the anglophone part of the continent.

He says, 'My research began in 2009 – all my projects take a long time, with a lot of pruning and fine tuning.' He travelled to each of the six cities that the play is set in – Lagos, Accra, Kampala, Johannesburg and Harare as well as Peckham in south London – and stayed for a week in each one. One visit coincided with a historic moment: he arrived in South Africa the week Nelson Mandela died in December 2013. In each country he met men who then became characters in the play. 'Sometimes I cleaned up their words or merged aspects of them with others, but the characters are all versions of the men I met' (Akbar).

The cast of *Barber Shop Chronicles* is twelve male actors who play thirty characters. 'We had conversations about including female characters early on and I felt that any female character in the play would have been tokenistic by being on stage for a small morsel of time.' At the time, he was also working on an African version of Chekhov's *Three Sisters*, which focuses on a powerful trio of female characters, and he is sensitive to gender differences. 'Hair politics is not as problematic for men as it is for women. They are dealt a far harder hand and they also have to contend with problematic beauty standards, which is a far more difficult thing' (Akbar).

During the run of the production, which transferred to the Roundhouse in 2019, audience members were welcomed on stage, breaking the fourth wall which separates spectators from actors, an attempt, says Ellams, 'to democratize the space. These barber shops are sacred spaces and the Black men in the audiences came knowing that.' He wanted to say, 'This is your space, these are your stories', and 'it was important to invite them on to the stage for that reason, especially in a place like the National Theatre.' But he never excluded non-Black, non-male audience members. 'I wanted to say, "You are all welcome."' Part of being a poet 'is trusting my audience's imagination, to have the ability to speak a word and trust that it will take root in the depth of their imagination' (Akbar).

Gurpreet Kaur Bhatti

Gurpreet Kaur Bhatti is a British Sikh writer whose work has featured in theatre, radio and television. In December 2004, her play *Behzti (Dishonour)* was taken off by the management of the Birmingham Rep after violent protests by Sikh militants, who were offended that its story of sexual abuse was set in a Sikh temple. Following this notorious episode, Bhatti told her side of the story in *Behud (Beyond Belief)* (Soho Theatre, 2010). She says, 'I knew that *Behzti* would be a provocative piece, and I stand by everything that I wrote.' One of the themes of the play is the suppression of women's voices, so it was striking that when she saw an interview with Salman Rushdie on television, he commented on the irony that the woman who wrote a play about a woman being silenced was herself now silenced. 'It felt like such a monumental, extraordinary experience, that I had to process it as a writer. It would have been disingenuous to my own soul, not to have' (Jackson).

So Bhatti decided to create something theatrical, not a literal explanation, not a documentary, not verbatim, 'but a fiction because everything that had happened was surreal, and unbelievable and fantastical' (Sierz). This would include the many different players: the liberal media, the young men who demonstrated, who broke windows, who invaded the stage. Plus the local council and politicians, the police officers who looked after her, plus her own story.

So '*Behud* shows a playwright working on a play about a past event (like *Behzti*)'. She is on stage writing and slowly the other characters take over and she has a kind of psychological breakdown. The resulting drama is about truth, with the playwright asking: 'What is the truth, what is fiction, whose truth is it and how do you locate that? Alongside that, it's about freedom of expression.' She remembers one of the banners at the protests against *Behzti* which stated: 'Shame on Sikh playwright for her corrupt imagination'. 'In writing *Behud*, I wanted to claim my imagination back' (Sierz).

Arinzé Kene

Arinzé Kene is a Nigerian-born actor and playwright whose roles have included Simba in *The Lion King* and Connor Stanley in the BBC's *EastEnders*. His one-person show *Misty* (Bush Theatre, 2018), which he performed himself, was a hit and transferred to the West End. He first got the idea for it after moving back to Hackney, where he'd grown up, and seeing how the gentrification of that London borough affected some of his friends. 'We would meet up and talk about it, and I just thought it might make a really good story or discussion for London to have.' For him 'one of the jobs of the artist is to bring something that's in the dark, into the light, and so that's what I've done' (Longman).

Gentrification is an urban phenomenon which often leaves long-time residents of an area feeling displaced, even homeless. Kene says, 'It erases people, and it erases their culture. There's many ways of looking at it, though, and we do that in the play, and we laugh about it too. We're laughing at a serious matter' (Kene). One of the playwright's favourite books is *Not Without Laughter* by Langston Hughes, which similarly deals with serious issues, but does so in a way that inspires readers to see the best of a situation.

Misty takes the form of an exciting hybrid: it's a gig, it's a performance poem, it's a one-man show, it's theatre about theatre. 'The reason why we made a meta-play was because while I was writing it I realised that we needed to have me tell the story on the stage.' He wasn't sure if it would work because he'd never done anything similar before. And rehearsals were a learning curve. 'It definitely evolved into something that's very energetic. When we did half of it for the first time I collapsed, it was like: "Oh my God, that's a lot."' But Kene got used to the energy of the show. So much so that he missed this when it finished: 'What is really hard is that when a show ends its run, you get phantom adrenaline at the same time every night. It gets to 6pm and I start to get ready to go on stage' (Longman). But then there's nothing to do.

Kene had never put himself on stage before, and to do so was both intimidating and rewarding. 'To have this frank discussion about the changing of London and the career of a creative like me – inner city, working class, Black – I feel like if we were going to have an honest discussion, you have to hold up the mirror to the theatre community.' But this is a two-way process: 'If I'm going to be honest about me, then I'm going to come for you too! I'm going to open you up, and I think that's what the play does' (Longman).

When *Misty* transferred to the Trafalgar Studios in September 2018, audiences were different, much more mixed than at the Bush Theatre where the show had opened earlier that year. 'One of the things young people have said to me most often is they'll be sat next to an old lady bobbing her head, or a really old man on the other side in tears.' *Misty* is a show where Kene talks directly to the audience so he can see 'there are people in hijabs next to old men sat next to a little boy. What's not to love about that? To me, that's utopia' (Longman).

While Kene was growing up, he never felt welcome in the theatre. So he sees *Misty* as an opportunity to embrace new audiences. 'We always knew the play had the capacity to do that. All the extra marketing and press that we did was just to make sure that those audiences knew that they were included.' And to give something to the people 'who might have felt the West End wasn't for them.' He also acknowledges the creatives that came before him, such as

Kwame Kwei-Armah, whose *Elmina's Kitchen* (2003) was the first play by a British-born Black writer to be staged in the West End (in 2005). Kene says, 'I hope *Misty* opens more doors for creators and for people looking to make less mainstream work' (Kene).

Testament

Testament (Andy Brooks) is a mixed-heritage rapper, beatboxer and playwright. His *Black Men Walking* (Royal Exchange Theatre, Manchester, 2018) was the first of Eclipse director Dawn Walton's *Revolution Mix* project, which brought hidden stories of the Black British experience to theatre, radio and film. The play's story follows three Black men from Sheffield as they walk in the Peak District. Each of them have issues that they need to work through. 'As they walk the landscape, we hear about whose footsteps they are walking in from the past.' The audience finds out 'about Black British figures, hear their stories and see how they resonate with the play's characters, in the present'. Testament questions the nature of history, and asks who controls the narrative? He was inspired by historian David Olusoga's 2016 BBC series *Black and British: A Forgotten History*, which 'opened up a treasure trove of voices which have been ignored for a long time'. He adds: 'As a person of colour, I've had to buy into white heroes and white narratives, or find my own – when I was young, Daley Thompson was the only famous guy who looked like me' (Marks).

As part of the Eclipse commission, Testament went on walks with the 100 Black Men Walk for Health group, and participated in their conversations, seeing 'how they spoke to me and each other and what their dynamic was like. These are fiercely intelligent men having intense debates, sharing their life experiences and laughter.' From these walks he began to invent his characters. For the historical context, he did research, used his imagination to convey moments in time, and then gave the text to the actors to breathe life into these figures. The lyrical aspect of the play comes out in the spoken word. As well as the men, it also features a female character, nineteen-year-old Ayeesha, the young female MC, and her poetry, 'as she speaks in her natural idiom. She has got that wit and humour, and even in terms of how her rhyme patterns work, she's conveying who she is' (Marks).

Testament quotes the opening line of Peter Fryer's 1984 book *Staying Power*: 'There were Africans in England before the English came here' – 'it knocked me sideways. I went out and I bought five copies straight off and sent them to family and friends immediately'. He emphasizes the historical fact that in Roman times Black people were 'doing amazing things before the Anglo-Saxons came here'. He also wants white people to 'have the opportunity to buy into Black narratives and say, "Yes we are British, we are John Moore, we are Pablo Fanque as well as Shakespeare."' This contributes to a strong feeling of having an identity, feeling confident, feeling ownership. 'African history is as much a part of my dad's history – a white Londoner – because it's a part of London's history.' He argues that he more we find out about each other's stories, histories and lives, the harder it is to 'other' other people. It's harder to demonize people when you know the history. 'The more we share our stories, the more enlightened we all become' (Marks).

Selina Thompson

Selina Thompson is a Black performance artist and playwright. She performed her own one-woman show *salt*. (Southbank Centre, 2017), some of which was adapted for the BBC. It is the narrative of a forty-two-day sea journey in 2016 which she and filmmaker Hayley Reid took on a cargo ship to retrace the transatlantic slave route from Europe to Africa and the Caribbean, with the aim of showing how the experience of enslavement underlines racism today. She calls this 'a pilgrimage, reflection and meditation on the afterlife of slavery and colonialism, and the UK's place in that triangle'. The work tells the story of that journey, 'and how I got to that point, as well as placing my personal and political histories onto its route' (Thompson). Her intention was to share a space of meditation and thoughtfulness, which includes pain, love, anger and grief. 'Being at sea is very boring', she says, 'but that means you have loads of time to reflect and think deeply. The trip was bigger than work, but it was work, epic – in the traditional sense of the word' (Frizzell).

On board were nineteen Filipino men, six Italians and a Romanian. 'Me and Hayley were sort of stranded. I didn't get seasick but every day my body would be like: "This is bullshit."' She remembers the noise of the journey, the sound of the huge propellers making her feel like 'being inside a migraine' (Frizzell). One day, she turned on her phone to see the little blue blinking dot on the map was right over the words Atlantic Ocean, so she was literally sailing over the bones of those who had come before her. 'In the slave trade, people were disposed of when they were no longer profitable. Women who were pregnant because they had been raped got thrown over the side of the ship' (Thompson).

The show highlights the labour of thinking about postcolonialism. At one point, they arrived in Ghana on Independence Day, and 'when our guide asked if we had Independence Day in the UK, I had to laugh – we're the country who everybody got independence from'. The trip also involved her first visit to Jamaica, which nevertheless felt familiar. 'The things I associate with home are Lovers Rock, certain accents, certain foods eaten in certain ways, a certain pace of doing things. In the UK all of that culture is pocketed away. But when you're in Jamaica it's everywhere.' Emotionally, it was a homecoming: 'If you've never experienced that before, that is a crazy ass feeling. But it was sort of haunting too, because so much of that stuff I associate with my nan.' But this visit was also challenging. 'I was the only Black person in the resort, so people kept assuming I worked there.' And they would 'speak to me really horrendously. Being a tourist in Jamaica is about being a white person surrounded by Black people there to serve you' (Frizzell).

The trip gave her a perspective on life. 'I've bounced about like a ping pong ball between three continents being told none was home and all were home.' She tries to balance 'the four countries my family hail from with the fact that my adoption makes me feel like one day I just appeared in a drawer in Birmingham town hall' (Frizzell). The show is part performance art, part theatre, part historical retelling. She sees identity as a broad and sprawling thing. 'I guess the best place to start is with the overused, but essentially true adage: comfort the disturbed, disturb the comfortable' (Thompson). But also suggests that it's about centring the marginalized and disrupting those that are privileged in society.

Nathaniel Martello-White

Nathaniel Martello-White is a mixed-heritage actor and playwright. He wrote *Torn* (Royal Court, 2016) while on attachment at that venue. It is a family drama which has a vividly experimental form. To achieve this he had to cut down a much longer draft to arrive at the final ninety-minute play: 'I ended up doing a scary and brave thing with *Torn*: I dismantled the entire play so I could ask myself what it was and what it wasn't.' After discarding seventy-five pages, he was left with about twenty-five pages of material to build back the play. In hindsight, he's glad he did that. 'The form of the play is quite unusual. The idea is that a family meet for an AA meeting, but they haven't all been together in a long time.' He discarded all expositional material, so there are a lot of flashbacks, with 'a lot of overlapping, so as a writer you feel as if you're spinning plates' (Snow).

With *Torn*, Martello-White's aim was to explore race through family, and to show how complicated family can be when you examine the generations. 'The family in my play is mixed race and that's what makes it unique. The Black protagonists exist in a world which is also white', a situation that he argues is not often seen on stage. 'But', he points out, 'ultimately they're family: that's the background I come from and it's the multicultural London I see' (Martello-White).

As an actor, Martello-White is able to rapidly see what is required or needed in a scene, having learnt from working with playwrights such as debbie tucker green and Duncan Macmillan. 'You have got to be able to absorb a lot as an actor so I've got used to doing that as well.' Looking back, he says it 'was a bit of a shock getting into RADA, being a south London boy – a culture shock. You kind of have to lose yourself before you find yourself at drama school.' This experience provokes the criticism that there was too much emphasis on RP and being a 'neutral' actor, 'so for the Tom Hiddlestons of this world or people from that background, RADA would have been an easy follow-on from Cambridge, Oxford or Eton.' For people like him, 'you want to hang on to who you are, but you have to evolve' (Snow). Before he graduated, he did a lot of evolving.

The biggest influence on Martello-White has been the American playwright Tarell Alvin McCraney. He performed in one of his plays, *The Brothers Size* (Young Vic, 2007), a piece which has three actors. 'We created an entire universe in what was essentially a chalk circle. It showed me that theatre at its purest doesn't need loads of props.' If the dialogue is good enough and the story strong enough, 'all you need is actors, their bodies, their voices and their emotions' (Snow). For him, that's the most compelling kind of theatre.

Oladipo Agboluaje

Oladipo Agboluaje is a Nigerian-born playwright whose work has explored race and society in some of the poorer parts of south London, and beyond. In *New Nigerians* (Arcola Theatre, 2017), a satire about Nigerian elections, he mixes African and European theatre techniques to comment on populism across the world. He is a political playwright, and says that he wanted to write something current that would resonate with both British and Nigerian audiences. *New Nigerians* is a 'satire about contemporary politics in modern day Nigeria and focuses on a man and the question of whether he can compromise his integrity to foment political revolution'. The play resonates with British politics, with international politics and the current state of the world. It occurred to him that, 'across the world now, we all use the same language that is used in American politics' (Agboluaje).

In 2006, Agboluaje worked with Femi Elufowoju Jr on his play *The Estate* (Soho Theatre), and the director 'encouraged me and urged me to continue bringing African theatre to the public and I am so grateful to him for that.' *The Estate* was an early work and helped the playwright 'to see that other audiences, not just African audiences, and my peers, understood my characters and their stories'. He says that he is always writing for a Black audience: 'I want my work to be accepted and believed by the people who come from the background that I do as they will be the first to reject or accept it.' If he writes something that is not authentic, 'trust me that a Nigerian will be the first and loudest to confront it even whilst they are sitting in the audience' (Agboluaje).

Agboluaje's favourite playwrights include Wole Soyinka and August Wilson, whose work touches him deeply. He notes that Wilson spoke about writing for an African-American audience as an African-American man, while white playwrights write plays with a European sensibility, a European voice. 'When he wrote a play, he was coming from an African-American background so he had an African sensibility and an African voice. I feel very much the same when I write' (Agboluaje). He wants his characters and plays to be a true reflection of modern-day Africa.

Rachel De-lahay

Rachel De-lahay is a mixed-heritage playwright and screenwriter, whose subjects include immigration and national identity. She contributed the play *My White Best Friend* to the Bush Theatre's 2017 *Black Lives, Black Words* season, a series of commissioned pieces that asked: do Black lives matter today? *My White Best Friend* originated when she found herself in Soho the night after the Orlando shooting in 2016, in which forty-nine people were killed at Pulse, a gay nightclub. She recalls: 'There was a big LGBT march and I found myself joining in.' But she realized it was only because she happened to be in Soho by chance. 'I asked myself: why didn't I choose to come here? What the hell does that say about me that I let my gay friends do this on their own?' This experience made her question what it means to fight for other people. 'I have a strong circle of smart, well-educated friends who want to make the world a better place.' But she was interested in 'how sometimes these brilliant people who I love and love me do not necessarily fight for my rights' (Kellaway).

So *My White Best Friend* asks the question: how do you ask your white best friend to try and visibly give a damn? The process involved a dialogue with her friends of colour. 'We'd have nights with a bunch of artists, actors, people in TV who are so successful, they make me look like a meandering fool', and feeling that 'it's a tiny bit harder being a person of colour in this world'. She recognizes the difficulties of talking about race, and gives the example of Jane Elliott, the veteran American anti-racism activist, who 'does a brilliant one-liner where she says: "Put your hand up if you'd change colour to become a Black person."' No one does. The conclusion is: 'This says everything. You know what's going on and that it is not right. You should make it stop.' Thinking about the issue makes her 'wish I had a brilliant, savvy sentence to sum it up. I don't – which is why I write' (Kellaway).

At the Bush, De-lahay put brown, disabled and queer people at the front of the audience, with white able-bodied men right at the back. This was one way of confronting what is going on in the world. 'If you are a white able man you might go: "Oh – but my wife gets to move forward . . .?" Yeah! That is how it feels!' Her plays are nuanced because her world is multicultural, and she likes seeing people who look like her on stage. She says, 'We need to change people's mindset', and uses the example of Noma Dumezweni being cast as the grown-up Hermione in *Harry Potter and the Cursed Child* in the West End. 'My sister is a massive Potter fan. When she read the book, she was sure Hermione looked like me and her.' People read whatever is their normal. 'Lots of little white girls will say: "I thought Hermione looked like me." We have to change that idea of normal' (Kellaway).

De-lahay compares theatre to the cinema as the only spaces where audiences enter a dark room, switch off their phone and listen. 'I still watch TV with my iPhone in my hand. I am multitasking constantly but, in the theatre, the phone goes on silent and into my bag and I listen.' Achieving this level of concentration in the digital age is not easy, but 'If you can hold an audience for ninety minutes, you can change people' (Kellaway).

SCENE ELEVEN

Plays about white privilege

There are not enough plays about white privilege.

SCENE TWELVE

History plays

Looking at the most significant trends in 2010s new writing, it is the theme of identity that is central – as exemplified by the increase in plays by women, and Black and Asian playwrights. But while the most important new development of the decade was the boosted visibility of identity politics, other theatre genres were also thriving. An obvious example is the boom in history plays. Such dramas are so traditional and so popular that they are often dismissed as populist, as being easy evocations of a safe and unchallenging past. In fact, across British culture there is a sense that history is usually presented as a nostalgic evocation of an era that is simpler, more humane and more beautiful than the present, which is riven by crisis, difficult to comprehend and overwhelmingly ugly. On the other hand, compared to television, theatre is more critical of these rose-tinted versions of history – it has no real equivalents to *Downton Abbey* or *The Crown*.

Theatre's relationship to history is actually quite complex. When E.V. Crowe's 2016 play *The Sewing Group*, which at first appears to be set in the seventeenth century, opened at the Royal Court she spoke to Alice Saville for *The Stage* newspaper. In an article titled 'EV Crowe: "People think historical plays are going to be boring"', the playwright is quoted as saying that *The Sewing Group* 'plays with audience perception of the past, and whether or not nostalgia is a sort of disease, or a cure', adding that: 'I think how we perceive history is very interesting, particularly women in history. It's interesting to look at history through women's lives, because you often see what's happening at that moment in time very acutely, very precisely.' The play is a game with our expectations of representing the past, so it is a complex show that keeps audiences guessing. Crowe adds: 'Maybe for younger audiences, there's a perception that historical plays are going to be even more boring than normal plays. But what I'm doing here feels very different. I definitely think the best historical plays are absolutely about the present, even if they're set in the past.'

The Sewing Group was unusual in its theatrical intelligence and in its critical examination of how we use the past. But over the decade most history plays were more straightforward costume dramas. Many were delightful. I remember seeing national treasure Simon Russell Beale playing Soviet dictator Joseph Stalin in John Hodge's comedy *Collaborators* (National

Theatre, 2011), watching him switch from joviality to menace in a nanosecond, proving that a light touch reveals the horror of tyranny more effectively than a heavy hand. On British stages, the great popularity of the history play meant that this genre was almost impossible to avoid. Take some examples of the genre's infinite variety from the year 2015: at the Park Theatre, Jonathan Maitland used a mixture of fact and fiction to illuminate post-war British history in his *Dead Sheep*, about Margaret Thatcher's 1980s colleague Geoffrey Howe, and his *An Audience with Jimmy Savile*, about the predatory celebrity paedophile. Then the early 1970s radical scene was explored by the ubiquitous James Graham in his *The Angry Brigade*, which toured its lively staging to explore the relationship between cops and urban terrorists. Similarly energetic, Tom Morton-Smith's *Oppenheimer*, about the father of the atom bomb, made the trek – during the anniversary year of Hiroshima and Nagasaki – from the Royal Shakespeare Company in Stratford-upon-Avon to the West End. Elsewhere, the past continued to be relevant to the present: *Dara*, adapted by Tanya Ronder for the National Theatre from an original by Shahid Nadeem, visited Mughal India in the mid-seventeenth century to confront once again the problem of militant Islam. As these plays cross my memory, I am reminded above all by the visual impact of plays set in the past so it seems right that a fictional visual artist should describe them.

The history play: an artist's impression

'It's just there's so much of it. The future is real, but . . . the past, well. It's all made up.'

Logan Roy

The past, the cliché goes, is a foreign country – they do things differently there. It's also a place that looks different: different clothes, different furnishings, different stuff. A foreign place where people speak a different language, believe different things and behave differently. As a visual artist, I'm especially interested in the pictorial aspects of theatre, so I'm drawn to plays set in the past which, in some ways, is more colourful and more beautiful to look at than our own mundane world. Its colours are more eye-catching and its atmosphere more theatrical. Seeing red. Feeling blue. Green with envy. Theatres, as well as galleries, are places where I can practise 'slow seeing', concentrated viewing, especially during the long scenes. So I've been to a great many history plays over the past decade, and I've collected a fair number of production photographs as *aide-mémoires* for the way these historical stories look on stage. I remember reading somewhere that the visual aspect of theatre – *viz*, the colour and shape of the set, the costumes and the lighting – are the vital elements that transport the spectator to another place, the world of the play.

It's clear to me that history, and historical fictions, are central to our national identity. For don't we live in an old country, with its visible reminders of historical sites, from castles to country houses, and its profusion of historical novels, as well as non-fiction history books? During the decade I know of dozens of history plays, plays set in the distant past and near past, plays with recognizable historical personages, or obscure figures, or adaptations of historical novels, or made-up stories which need that sense of distance which comes from a historical setting. I adore this kind of playwriting, and I'm pretty sure most British people attending a history play will arrive with a good idea of what to expect. Like me, they'll know it's set in the past; they may have some idea of the story or historical period, or at least some sense of the past as our national narrative, or in some instances a good idea of the historical event being dramatized.

When I think of the 'history play', the first thing that comes to mind is Shakespeare. The national playwright set many of his plays in the past, from Roman times to medieval England, and his work immediately conjures up the image of the doublet and hose; indeed, an Elizabethan figure holding a skull is an icon denoting theatre itself. For people like me, having studied Shakespeare at school means that the idea of the history play starts with the Stratford playwright. It also means that the Royal Shakespeare Company (RSC) and Shakespeare's Globe have great brand recognition. In the 2010s, both these theatres produced a multitude of historical plays. The RSC and Shakespeare's Globe have a particular aesthetic: I call it 'eclectic mash-up'. It's a mixture of pseudo-medieval and modern in design. The actors wear rusty armour (men), or long gowns (women), but also have machine guns or mobile phones, modern overcoats or beany hats.

A more coherent style was adopted by Roxana Silbert and designer Robert Innes Hopkins for their production of David Greig's *Dunsinane* (RSC, 2010), in which the playwright imagines what happens after *Macbeth* ends. In the aftermath of the tyrant's overthrow, the English invaders find themselves unable to understand how to rule a turbulent Scotland. I read somewhere that Greig was influenced by British involvement in Afghanistan and Iraq, and how occupying forces are outwitted by the locals, but the aesthetics of the play were very much Scottish medieval: *viz*, the bare stage a gloomy wasteland, overlooked by a grey Celtic cross and some equally grey trees, an inhospitable canvas to English eyes. One character called it 'rock, bog, forest and loch'. The costumes suggested cold: men in armour and chainmail and animal pelts, while the women were wrapped up tightly. Siobhan Redmond, playing the resurrected Lady Macbeth character now renamed Gruach, a scheming widow, stood out because of the contrast between her red hair and her intensely blue gown, strikingly different to the overall colour palate of greys and muted browns. When the light caught her gown it glowed Klein blue. At the end of the play, a snowstorm covered the stage in a white powdery blanket, a visual indicator of nature's inescapable hostility, which dooms the English invaders.

Like *Dunsinane*, Rona Munro's *The James Plays* (National Theatre of Scotland/National Theatre, 2014) is a good instance of history having resonance today. This ambitious trilogy, whose impeccable timing coincided with the Scottish referendum on independence, was a response to the fact that Shakespeare's history plays are an integral part of the English national myth. Munro looks at three generations of fifteenth-century Scottish kings, and defines Scotland's identity against that of England. So Henry V is not a hero but a bully, and Scotland's search for identity resonates not only with its referendum, but also with the Brexit vote (remember, Scotland voted to Remain). Munro's provocation is to demand that Scottish audiences turn their negative feelings about the south into support for independence. At one point, in the third play, the Danish wife of James III got a big laugh when, looking at the audience, she said: 'You know the problem with you lot? You've got fuck-all except attitude.' She was played by Sofie Gråbøl, familiar from her role as detective Sarah Lund in TV's *The Killing*, when she wore her trademark Faroese jumper. *The James Plays* were directed by Laurie Sansom, and Jon Bausor devised a striking design dominated by a firmly embedded giant sword, shaped like a cross, a symbol of both violence and religious belief in medieval Scotland. The colour tapestry was dour and dark, with even the reds a dull crimson and the greens bleached out. It felt cold, hostile. No sunshine brightness here.

* * *

I fancy the Tudor era is one of the most recognizable in British culture: from Henry VIII, and his wives, to Elizabeth I, all those ruffs, doublets, hose, everything glittering with jewels and fabulous rich fabrics in pearlescent light. It's costume that says Shakespeare as well as a magnificent past we can be proud of. The Tudors reigned from 1485 to 1603, and are still icons of Englishness – they personify the splendour of royalty, and Tudor mania has been a 2010s phenomenon, from history books, historical novels to films and stage plays. From Hampton Court to mock-Tudor buildings in the suburbs, the Tudor style is everywhere. I remember watching a couple of episodes of *The Tudors*, an American romp shown also on the BBC, with jackets featuring lace galore, heaving bosoms and bejewelled bodices. I also visited the National

Portrait Gallery collection to view their wonderful Tudor portraits, with a colour palette from faint blushes of rose to ochres and umbers, ceruleans and ultramarines. This dynasty, someone said, is the real-life *Game of Thrones*. Whether you take a *Horrible Histories* approach or a girl power one, Tudor mania is profitable. For instance, *Six* (Arts Theatre, 2019) is a hit British musical comedy by Toby Marlow and Lucy Moss which reinvents the lives of the wives of Henry VIII in the form of a high-energy girl-band pop concert. Each of the wives – Catherine of Aragon, Anne Boleyn, Jane Seymour, Anna of Cleves, Katherine Howard and Catherine Parr – take turns to tell their stories. It's exuberant, exciting and energizing, with catchy tunes and feminist lyrics. Gabriella Slade's punky corsets, platformed boots, fishnets and bejewelled puff sleeves give a flashy technicoloured punkish feel to this girl power extravaganza.

My favourite chronicler of Henry VIII's court is Hilary Mantel. Her first two bestselling and Man Booker Prize winning novels, *Wolf Hall* and *Bring Up the Bodies*, about Thomas Cromwell, the king's first minister, were adapted by Mike Poulton (RSC, 2014). I remember the stage being dark with a sense of wood panelling, the lack of bright light suggesting the claustrophobia of Henry VIII's court, as he and Cromwell struggle to get a divorce from Katherine of Aragon so that Henry can marry Anne Boleyn. The men looked serious in their black robes, with Henry – one of those monarchs with an instant recognition rating because of Holbein's 1537 portrait him in defiant pose – the most resplendent in richly embroidered, laced and fur-lined costume. Anne by contrast was attired in sensuous crimson – exuding regal intensity – her neck decorated in pearls and a gold B denoting her family. In the early scenes, Cardinal Wolsey's scarlet robes caught my eye, distracting me for a while from the complex politics in director Jeremy Herrin and designer Christopher Oram's uncluttered production. A similar contrast between dark and red is also the memorable stage picture from Helen Edmundson's play about another royal, *Queen Anne* (RSC, 2015), where the pious Anne (Emma Cunniffe) wears a sombre greyish blue while Sarah Churchill (Romola Garai), her scheming intimate friend, wears glowing pinkish red. These are sumptuous clothes you want to run your fingers across. Once again, Natalie Abrahami's direction and Hannah Clark's design show power battles being conducted in claustrophobic panelled rooms, cascading wigs galore.

The story of Anne Boleyn, who was executed in 1536, just three years after her marriage to Henry, is also the story of the long Reformation, a process that started with Henry's break with Rome in the early 1530s and culminated in the English Revolution of 1642–51. I was amazed to see how Howard Brenton's hit play *Anne Boleyn* (Shakespeare's Globe, 2010) began: Miranda Raison's Anne walked onto the stage in pure angelic white with her own decapitated head in a bag. A visual masterstroke. Surreal even. Brenton then challenges the stereotype of Anne by representing her more as a religious activist than a sex kitten. Here, she has two secret meetings with militant Protestant William Tyndale, an imaginative device because in reality she never met him, but that's fine – theatre is fiction (after all, Schiller led the way with his 1800 play *Maria Stuart* which dramatizes an imaginary meeting between Elizabeth I and Mary Queen of Scots). In Brenton's account, Tyndale gives Anne a copy of *The Obedience of a Christian Man*, which argues that monarchs are responsible directly to God rather than the Pope, and this helps persuade Henry to break with Rome. John Dove's production, designed by Michael Taylor, once again featured delicious silks, which flashed as they caught the sunlight on the outdoor stage at Shakespeare's Globe. It also made me feel that light, like life, is so transient and fickle.

In 2011, to mark the 400th anniversary of the King James Bible, the RSC staged *Written on the Heart* by David Edgar. It's about the completion of this Bible in the 1610s, as well as about Tyndale's translation in 1536, and Edgar shows how God's word is man's translation. As he says: 'Whatever their intentions, those first translators of the Bible into the vernacular gave us a means of communication and imagination that led – whether they liked it or not – to a world in which their own beliefs could be questioned and rejected. Or, if you like: no Tyndale, no Kindle.'

Along with Brenton's *Anne Boleyn*, Edgar's play demonstrates the importance of the written word to British identity, but I also remember Gregory Doran's brisk and lively production, with Francis O'Connor's design once again evoking the mysterious rooms and be-ruffed Reformation, with white-haired Oliver Ford Davies in black-and-white clerical robes as the scholarly bishop Lancelot Andrewes. It reminded me that combining warm colours with black makes them appear more dramatic. Combining cool colours with black increases mystery, while combining them with white is more calming and relaxed.

As far as images go, the English Civil War is usually pictured as dour dark-coated Puritan Roundheads taking on the flamboyantly colourful Cavaliers. In Brenton's *55 Days* (Hampstead Theatre, 2012), which focuses on the trial of Charles I which led to his execution in 1649, the colours are more muted. As well as showing scenes from the trial, the play's strongest moment is again a fictional one in which Charles (Mark Gatiss) and Oliver Cromwell (Douglas Henshall) meet, both dressed in black as befits the seriousness of the encounter. Here and in the rest of the play Cromwell and the parliamentarians are in simple and sober modern dress while Charles wears period costume, a veritable symphony of lace decorations, silky materials and a golden medallion. Howard Davies's production, designed by Ashley Martin-Davis, underlines the contrast of Charles's seventeenth-century attire and the modern gear of the others, referencing the Second World War, another era of radical politics. This visual difference reflects both the men's characters and the tides of history: *viz*, Charles appeals to a romantic past, while his opponents are struggling towards a new Jerusalem. Cromwell is sincere, Charles is vain; the middle classes are on the rise; the aristocracy is in decline.

* * *

There is a sub-genre of history plays that are about the history of theatre, and these tend to emphasize both the fun of the art form and what it can teach us about the past, an uneasy marriage of entertainment and education. Yet some are a hoot. For instance, Jessica Swale's hit play *Nell Gwynn* (Shakespeare's Globe, 2015) is so enjoyable partly because of its subject matter, the Merry Monarch Charles II and his mistress, actor Nell Gwynn, in the bawdy world of Restoration drama, and partly its comedy, especially the bit with the real-life dog, a lovely spaniel. Funny how a dog on stage always draws my attention. As a counterblast to the muted colours of Reformation plays, this one was a blaze of lively tints, helped by the fact that on the stage of Shakespeare's Globe outdoors the bright sunshine (if you're lucky) lights up the whole show. As well as the bawdiness and levity, the play also has a message about visibility, highlighted by casting a non-white actor, Gugu Mbatha-Raw, radiant in the title role. Christopher Luscombe's production was designed by Hugh Durrant as a visual extravaganza, all baroque drapes and tassels, rich textures and bright hues. Visually a feast for the eyes, so beautiful I felt like the past was beckoning: things were so much prettier in the olden days.

Equally successful was Lolita Chakrabarti's *Red Velvet* (Tricycle Theatre, 2012), which starred Adrian Lester as the expat Black American actor Ira Aldridge, who took to the stage at the Theatre Royal Covent Garden after Edmund Kean collapsed one night in 1833. The play? You guessed: it was *Othello*. Chakrabarti tells the story of what happened with remarkable economy in a handful of scenes. And she bookends this London episode with glimpses of Aldridge at the end of his career in 1867, as he tours Europe, this time playing King Lear. Seeing him as a sixty-year-old man transformed into the bearded king of Shakespeare's play is Chakrabarti's haunting final image. Directed by Indhu Rubasingham and designed by Tom Piper, the staging had practically no props, but it did feature a beautifully full-red velvet back cloth, looking like a theatre curtain. Curtains also featured in Ian Kelly's *Mr Foote's Other Leg* (Hampstead Theatre, 2015), which starred Simon Russell Beale as the eighteenth-century actor Samuel Foote, and included, as a contrast to *Red Velvet*, a comic version of *Othello*, which involves him dressing and blacking up just like the era's superstar thespian David Garrick. Richard Eyre's masterly production on Tim Hatley's richly embroidered set created an atmosphere of post-Hogarthian and pre-Dickensian London, with neatly tailored theatre folk and resplendent royals. SRB's Foote was a masterclass in comic timing, a delicious portrait of a freewheeling chancer, for ever ducking and diving, the keynote being the subversive joy of laughter, comedy always giving a play an extra brightness of colouring.

* * *

The Empire is so central to Britain's national identity that images of colonialism in India and the West Indies haunt our culture. Some accounts of Indian history such as Brenton's *Drawing the Line* (Hampstead Theatre, 2013) take a straightforward approach. The play told the story of Cyril Radcliffe, a British judge to whom British prime minister Clement Attlee delegated the task of drawing the boundary line between the newly independent countries of India and Pakistan in 1947. Director Howard Davies and designer Tom Hatley's compelling production emphasized the similarities between the Brits, white shirts and muted waistcoats, and Indian politicians such as Gandhi and Jinnah in equally muted bone beige and light-brown clothing. Even Edwina Mountbatten, who is having an affair with Nehru, has a perfectly restrained wardrobe. As a background, giant light-brown filigree screens suggested the constraints the politicians labour under, and the one big splash of colour was an Indian deity, whose shining bright blue body paint and costume radiantly suggest the riches of the East, which are being pilfered by the Europeans. Other stagings played with the idea of Empire and race in an even more imaginative way.

One instance is Janice Okoh's *The Gift* (Belgrade Theatre, 2020), symbolic of how the 2010s were distinguished by the way global majority playwrights made a strong contribution to the genre of the history play. She tells the story of the Egbado princess Sarah Bonetta, who was given to Queen Victoria in 1850 as a gift, and raised as her goddaughter. In the first act, Okoh features the historical story of Bonetta being cross-culturally adopted, and then, in the second act, she creates a similar situation in a contemporary setting, a fictional story about two Black people adopting a white child. The staging, directed by Dawn Walton and designed by Simon Kenny, opens with two Victorian women, dressed in black crinolines and tightly corseted, sitting on a bright white sofa, taking tea. Both are played by Black actors: one is Bonetta, mistress of the house, and the other is Aggie, a servant. This scene offers a vivid contrast between the dazzling white background furnishings, the silver tea pots and the black skin and clothes of the characters. This vivid contrast underlines the comedy of Okoh's play at the same time as subverting audience expectations about what a Victorian picture can look like.

Scene 12: History plays

A similarly subversive take on the British Empire and its legacy can be seen in two plays from 2019, each an adaptation of a classic European play into settings more reflective of the global majority. The first was Tanika Gupta's *A Doll's House* (Lyric Hammersmith), her radical version of Henrik Ibsen's 1879 play, transposed to Calcutta in Victorian India, under the Raj, with husband Helmer becoming Tom the colonial administrator and his wife Nora the Bengali Niru. The story gets additional resonance from the racial politics of India during the British Empire. Rachel O'Riordan and designer Lily Arnold's production had a hot, sun-speckled courtyard set which effortlessly passed for any of the rooms in the Helmer household. At the back were two huge doors, an allusion to the fact that in the original play Nora slams the door when she leaves her husband. The casting also emphasized power dynamics: Anjana Vasan played Niru, looking small and fragile when Tom (Elliot Cowan) towered over her, this image illustrating the mixture of masculine and colonial power at the core of this adaptation. Cowan's Tom could take Niru into his arms as if she really was just a doll, holding her up playfully in the air.

The other great play that transposed a European classic to a different context is Inua Ellams's *Three Sisters* (National Theatre), his version of Anton Chekhov's 1901 original. Ellams sets his adaptation in a village in Owerri, Nigeria, where three sisters think back longingly to their previous life in Lagos. The time period is 1967–70, during Biafra's attempted but doomed secession from Nigeria, making this a fascinating account of the clash of cultural identity between Igbo, Yoruba and Hausa peoples. The hostility of the sisters to their brother's wife is here explained by their belonging to the dominant Igbo ethnic group, while she is Yoruba. Director Nadia Fall and designer Katrina Lindsay's visually impressive production used the dresses of the sisters to express their characters, whether well-defined and ankle-length, elegant but restrictive, or flowingly silky green. The set is at first luxurious and sun-lit, a Biafran flag brightly standing out against the pale walls of the family house. As war approaches, the weather turns grey and foggy, before the house finally disappears and the sisters, now dressed in sacrificial white, move among a tapestry of long grasses and reeds. This atmosphere of quiet desolation underlines the way that Ellams condemns the British for creating the state of Nigeria out of a variety of ethnic groups, thus being ultimately responsible for the civil war.

Now I'm completely aware that I'm a case of the 'white gaze' on global majority culture, but I don't think that stops me from applauding the way that 'colour conscious' casting and plays by non-white playwrights have radically changed the way the stage pictures of history plays represent the British population. Like *Bridgerton*, these British history plays of the 2010s were a radical intervention which visually contests the hegemony of the majority culture. Such casting also foregrounds urgent questions of gender as well as race, *viz*, Phyllida Lloyd's all-female Shakespeare productions. What's striking about these casting choices is that they completely alter the image of British history, in a good way.

* * *

This decade also witnessed female playwrights using the genre of the history play for female empowerment, especially when they seized the chance to work in previously male-dominated bastions. Following in the 2008 footsteps of Rebecca Lenkiewicz's *Her Naked Skin* – a history play about the suffragettes and the first play by a living woman writer to be staged on the Olivier stage, the largest at the National Theatre – in 2010 Nell Leyshon's *Bedlam* was the first play by a woman at Shakespeare's Globe. It's a fictional account of the Bethlem – London hospital for the mentally ill – set during the mid-eighteenth-century gin craze. Its aesthetic was a kind of historical dirty realism, with artfully tousled big hair, artistically stained aprons and grimy faces for the inmates, and tightly laced bodices and pastel-coloured frock coats for the rest. In the same year, Katori Hall won an Olivier Award for *The Mountaintop*, a history play about Martin Luther King, making her the first Black woman to receive this accolade. But it's another play by Lenkiewicz that I remember most. The eighteenth century, the so-called Age of Enlightenment, was anything but for many women. Set in Hertfordshire in 1712, Lenkiewicz's *Jane Wenham: The Witch of Walkern* (Out of Joint, 2015) features an independent herbalist and wise woman who faced persecution as a witch, a symbol for all women who challenge social norms. Ria Parry's production, with a design by James Button, had the villagers, dressed in a patchwork of autumnal golds and russets, sit round the circular space, as if watching each other. The focus of the design was a gruesome gibbet, which also suggested a crucifix, a combination that symbolized the role of clergy in the persecution of women. The tour of the play also proved controversial: *viz*, its 13 October 2015 performance at Ipswich High School for Girls was cancelled by the venue because of concerns over the play's language and themes of abuse.

Another outstanding instance of an eighteenth-century story was Lucy Kirkwood's *The Welkin* (National, 2020), a similarly acute critique of the patriarchy. The plot features Sally, who is sentenced to hang for murder; when she claims to be pregnant, a jury of twelve matrons have to decide if she's telling the truth, and can escape death. Kirkwood's linking of past and present is clear from the author's 'Note on the Play' about casting: 'It is crucial the group [of women] reflects the present-day population of the place the play is being performed in, not East Anglia in the 1750s.' So James Macdonald's production, designed by Bunny Christie, had a diverse cast, a visual reminder that the play is about us as well as the past. The central issue of the play is the question of who controls women's bodies, and the matrons – modestly dressed in domestic aprons, rough beiges and light browns – of course have a much better understanding of this than the male doctor. The play began with a breathtakingly tall multi-level tableau showing black silhouettes of women at work, then it plunged into a crepuscular candle-lit scene for the murder, before finally opening out into a wide room, decorated in mild greys. The dramatic highpoints – Sally's attempt to produce milk and an exploding chimney – used the colour black as an extreme contrast to the muted canvas of the room and costumes. Actors were led by Maxine Peake, as the matrons' spokeswoman, and Ria Zmitrowicz as Sally, achieving an alchemy of intensity.

Finally, another instance of Shakespeare being our contemporary was Morgan Lloyd Malcolm's feminist hit *Emilia* (Shakespeare's Globe, 2018). This is about Emilia Bassano Lanier, born in 1569, and one of the first English women to publish her own poetry, and the play speculates that she was also the 'dark lady' of Shakespeare's sonnets and his chief inspiration (in fact, the claim is that he stole her ideas). In Nicole Charles's production Emilia – played by three actors at different stages of her life – is a metaphor for women today: find your voice and own your anger. The play had a diverse all-woman cast, who – in a neat reversal of Elizabethan theatre conventions – played all the male as well as the female parts, and featured some vigorous disco dancing and boisterous humour. Designed by Joanna Scotcher, the staging highlighted gorgeously blue gowns, a tapestry of shimmering ultramarine and summer sky blue, partly Renaissance and partly modern in cut, for the actors playing Emilia, which tended to grab attention, as they should. The play's ending delivers a rousing cheer for women's emancipation.

* * *

Design creates vivid worlds on stage. For instance, Mark Ravenhill's imaginative adaptation of Voltaire's 1759 novella *Candide* (RSC, 2013) attacks our current obsession with positive thinking while acknowledging the difficulty of finding either a new form for adapting novels or a new language to express historical awareness on stage. The playwright adopts a radical form of five episodes, which not only dramatize Voltaire's original novel, but also invent scenes set in different eras and in different genres. Ravenhill says, 'Although the play is not written in strict verse form, there is an underlying beat of rhyming couplets, with echoes of Pope and the tradition of eighteenth-century philosophical verse.' Whatever the success of such experiments, they demonstrate that the search for new forms of language, as well as stage pictures, is one of the missions of a history play. Because Ravenhill's drama takes place in different locations and in different eras, Lyndsey Turner and designer Soutra Gilmour's production had an eclectic design, *viz*, one scene glowing in the reds and orange of eighteenth-century dress, another more white and blue, yet another beige and washed out; one with muskets, another with a hand gun; one scene looking like a cartoon, another like a historical re-enactment. Together they make the point that visualizing the past is search and research, an experiment.

Fringe theatre has less resources than the big national companies, but that doesn't mean it can't successfully evoke the past. For instance, Neil McPherson's *I Wish to Die Singing* (Finborough Theatre, 2015) is a docu-drama about the Armenian genocide of 1915, which opened on the exact centenary of the crime's mass deportations, which resulted in the Ottoman Turks killing 1.5 million people. The play both recounts the story of the events, and indicts the Turkish state for its consistent denial of them. McPherson points out that the word genocide was coined to describe these state-sponsored atrocities, while the show's video projections offer snapshots of the grizzly events as well as quotes from those, including Adolf Hitler, who were encouraged by this horrific ethnic cleansing. Tommo Fowler's strong and often uncomfortable production featured a multiracial cast, who all play several roles each, dressed simply – without elaborate costumes – and often on an aptly dark stage. Likewise, lack of a big budget did not prevent Joy Wilkinson's *The Sweet Science of Bruising* (Southwark Playhouse, 2018), whose subject is Victorian female boxing, from having a strong stage presence. Kirsty Patrick Ward's production used some memorably balletic fight sequences, with Alison de Burgh's movement skills and Anna Reid's design. One of several symbolic images was the corset, representing the physical restraint of women, an item of clothing which is shed in the climactic scene.

Of course, plays set in more recent decades need to acknowledge popular ideas about retro fashions. For instance, anything set in the hippie circles of the 1970s requires Afghan coats, flares and frilly shirts – at least until punk comes along. But some other design references are more specific: Steve Thompson's *No Naughty Bits* (Hampstead Theatre, 2011) is set in 1975 and tells the story of the censorship of the surreal BBC comedy series *Monty Python's Flying Circus* in the United States. Edward Hall's production, designed by Francis O'Connor, framed the stage in a huge television, and gave the story an aptly Python-esque feel, with a blue cloud-flecked summer sky which occasionally displayed the iconic Python foot and other visual gags referring to the original series.

Plays set in the twentieth century often seem drab, but some succeed in creating memorable stage images. I'm thinking of plays such as Nicholas Wright's *Travelling Light* (National Theatre, 2012), which is set in a pre-First

Scene 12: History plays 143

World War Russian-Jewish shtetl, and evokes the early years of film-making using not only a *Fiddler on the Roof* aesthetic, but also a re-created Lumière brothers' Cinématographe. The same playwright's *The Last of the Duchess* (Hampstead Theatre, 2011) is about the aged Wallis Simpson – widow of the abdicated King Edward VIII – living as a recluse in her Bois de Boulogne mansion in 1980. As an image of old age, decay and vanity, its emotions were enhanced by Anthony Ward's mouldering set. And the themes of snobbery, secrecy and sex are refracted through the cracked champagne glass whose crystal threw eerie lights over the gloomy mansion. By contrast, Amanda Whittington's *The Thrill of Love* (St James Theatre, 2013), about the life of Ruth Ellis, is a sad story which nevertheless offers the chance of seeing women dressed in nicer frocks. Finally, early twentieth-century Englishness can be evoked by the retro baggy suits of, for instance, David Hare's *The Moderate Soprano* (Hampstead Theatre, 2015), about John Christie, an eccentric English businessman who in the 1930s built an opera house next to his house, thus creating Glyndebourne, or Nick Dear's *The Dark Earth and the Light Sky* (Almeida Theatre, 2012), about the poet Edward Thomas, who dies in the First World War, a conflict whose military aesthetic – our boys in khaki – is as recognizable as that of the Tudors. So Owen Sheers's *Mametz* (National Theatre of Wales, 2014) put us in the trenches, while history man Howard Brenton's *Doctor Scroggy's War* (Shakespeare's Globe, 2014), about Harold Gillies, a First World War facial reconstruction surgeon, features soldiers in khaki, doctors in white coats, nurses in capes and the figure of the Gillies himself, resplendent in vibrant kilt and military reds as he creates his surreally entertaining Doctor Scroggy persona – an antidote to fear and despair. Combining neutral tones like brown, tan, grey, white and black with other colours often enhances their effects.

* * *

My conclusion is that the art of theatre is not just a literary one, not merely verbal; it's a visual live performance. The *mise-en-scène*, light and shadow, texture and form, and the physical appearance of the actors not only represent images of our national past, but actively create new pictures in our minds. To design is to bear witness. To watch is to identify. This is especially true when it comes to casting non-white and female actors, a radical gesture which reclaims the past for the present – surely the essence of theatre.

SCENE THIRTEEN

Adaptations

The popularity of history plays was, and is, rivalled only by the popularity of stage adaptations, all those theatre versions of well-known novels, films and television series. Across the decade, West End audiences could enjoy transfers from the National Theatre such as *The Curious Incident of the Dog in the Night-Time* (by Simon Stephens from Mark Haddon's novel) and *The Ocean at the End of the Lane* (by Joel Horwood from Neil Gaiman's novel). Like many history plays, these adaptations offer reasonably comfortable viewing experiences and their popularity with audiences has been criticized as evidence of a populist turn in West End theatre. On the other hand, adaptations offer a fabulous range of pleasurable experiences, being essentially remakes in a different medium of favourite books and films, for fans and casual theatregoers alike. And the range is amazing: there are plays that have been adapted from novels, short stories, films, television shows, biographies, autobiographies, news reports, interviews, court transcripts, treatises, histories and comic books. A limitless range. Some source books were positively inspirational: in 2012, F. Scott Fitzgerald's 1925 novel *The Great Gatsby* got three stage adaptations. It began its long run as an immersive production at Wilton's Music Hall. This was followed by *Gatz*, an eight-hour-long version by the Elevator Repair Service company, in which a cast of thirteen read every single word of the book on stage, and then a musical version by Joe Evans opened on the fringe.

Noting this phenomenon, *Guardian* theatre critic Arifa Akbar wrote an article titled '"Any attempt is perilous!" How do you adapt a novel for the stage?', published in early 2020. Here she asked: 'How does a well-loved novel become a stage production without incurring the wrath of book lovers and theatre audiences alike?' And she quoted Bryony Shanahan, who with Andrew Sheridan adapted Emily Brontë's *Wuthering Heights*, saying that 'while purity of vision is vital, an adaptation should ultimately be free to be as faithful or irreverent as it chooses'. As Mark Gatiss has said of his book-to-television adaptations of Arthur Conan Doyle's Sherlock Holmes series, this genre is not just about 'drearily reproducing' a classic. It is also about bold reinvention.

During the 2010s, not only did adaptations become big box-office hits at the National Theatre, the Royal Shakespeare Company and in the West End, they were also welcomed at theatres such as the Royal Court, which previously staged only original plays. Examples include the West Coast American couple She and He's story about a love affair, called *The Mistress Contract* (adapted by Abi Morgan) and Roald Dahl's *The Twits* (by Enda Walsh). At the National Theatre, I also remember powerful stage versions of many classics, such as Sally Cookson's spirited adaptation of *Jane Eyre* (2015) and Anthony Neilson's quirky postmodern take on Edgar Allan Poe's *The Tell-Tale Heart* (2018). Other highpoints for me include Duncan Macmillan's spectacular version of Paul Auster's *City of Glass* at the Lyric Hammersmith in 2017. Such adaptations have been so successful that a documentary about this phenomenon could easily be suitable for broadcast on, for example, BBC Four. Below is an extract of a treatment, meaning a summary of essential scenes intended to be a pitch to producers, of just such a documentary. It's called *Stages of Adaptation*.

Stages of Adaptation

Treatment

Scene One – Introduction

A slow street-level panning shot of Shaftesbury Avenue in the daytime with a voiceover describing the boom in the West End's commercial sector in the 2010s. Using some brief clips from the shows, we are introduced to the economic advantages of theatre adaptations: because they are based on already well-loved books or films they have titles and stories that are instantly recognizable to audiences; they enable people to relive their experiences of reading or watching via the new medium of the stage. With the glitter and glamour of theatres, both buildings and stars, they offer a thrilling audience experience. Some statistics about West End mega-hits of this decade (source: Society of London Theatre), and then focus on two musical versions of books by Roald Dahl, which top the list of recent record-breaking shows: the two musicals are *Matilda the Musical* by Tim Minchin and Dennis Kelly, which opened in 2011 (still running today) and *Charlie and the Chocolate Factory* by Marc Shaiman and David Greig, which when it opened in 2013 broke the then-record for weekly ticket sales.

Scene Two – National Theatre

Even if such adaptations as *Matilda* are big commercial successes, it is often state-funded theatres, such as the National Theatre and the Royal Shakespeare Company that have developed them – before they transfer to the West End. Interview with Nicholas Hytner, artistic director of the National Theatre until 2015, about his theatre's development of playwright Simon Stephens's adaptation of Mark Haddon's *The Curious Incident of the Dog in the Night-Time* (2013).

Then a brief interview with Rufus Norris, Hytner's successor, and his theatre's version of *Small Island*, a 2019 adaptation by playwright Helen Edmundson of Andrea Levy's 2004 award-winning novel about the Windrush generation.

Scene Three – Royal Court

The National Theatre is not the only theatre that uses adaptations to boost audiences. One other factory of new ideas is the Royal Court Theatre in London's Sloane Square. In 2013 this venue joined forces with the National Theatre of Scotland to stage *Let the Right One In*. This example of the vampire romance genre began life as a 2004 novel by Swedish writer John Ajvide Lindqvist, and had already been adapted into a Swedish film version (2008) and then as an American film adaptation with the title *Let Me In* (2010). The stage version is adapted by playwright Jack Thorne, who is one of the handful of go-to theatre adapters (he also adapted *A Christmas Carol* for the Old Vic Theatre, and collaborated on *Harry Potter and the Cursed Child*, both big hits). Short interview with Thorne. *Let the Right One In* has creepy stage music by multi-talented Icelandic musician Ólafur Arnalds, who wrote the soundtrack to the ITV's *Broadchurch*.

Scene Four – American imports

Some of the most successful adaptations have either come from the USA, or been inspired by American classics. Critic Matt Wolf of the *New York Times* talks us through some examples, such as *Kinky Boots* by Harvey Fierstein, who also wrote the book for *La Cage aux Folles*, and had another big hit with this feelgood story of a drag queen who saves a failing English shoe factory. Based on a 2005 British film, pop idol Cyndi Lauper wrote the music, and became the first solo woman to win a Tony Award for Best Score. Then there's *An American in Paris*, based on Vincente Minnelli's 1951 movie musical, with director Christopher Wheeldon's choreography to George Gershwin's music. Or *All About Eve*, the 1950 Joseph L Mankiewicz Hollywood classic which starred Bette Davis and Anne Baxter: in 2019, Amsterdam-based superstar *auteur* Ivo van Hove brought Mankiewicz's script to the West End, starring Gillian Anderson and Lily James. Less successful was *The Exorcist*, William Peter Blatty's 1971 horror classic, made into a theatre show by John Pielmeier, which premiered in the West End in 2017.

Scene Five – A bumper year

2018 was a bumper year for stage adaptations. A couple of artistic directors sum up the successes of, for example, *A Monster Calls*: Patrick Ness's award-winning bestseller tells the story of lonely thirteen-year-old Conor O'Malley, whose mum is sick with cancer, and shows how he experiences the feelings that arise from the illness. Sally Cookson's adaptation was a co-production between the Old Vic in London and the Bristol Old Vic, where it opened at the end of May. Devised by the thirteen-strong company of actors, it is a feast of visual and aural stimulation. Another example is *Imperium*, adapted by Mike Poulton for the RSC from Robert Harris's Ancient Rome trilogy of novels about Cicero. This two-part drama transfers to the West End after opening in Stratford. Called *Conspirator* and *Dictator*, they tell the thirty-year story of the last days of the Roman republic as it first resists the conspiracies of Catiline and Clodius, before succumbing to the power grabs of Julius Caesar and Augustus. Last example is *White Teeth*, Stephen Sharkey's version of Zadie Smith's classic and part of the north London Kiln Theatre's opening season. Her bestselling 2000 debut novel is set in Willesden, Kilburn, and thereabouts so it's a good fit for what is essentially a tribute to the area's multicultural character.

¶ Unlike a treatment, which is an introductory set of ideas, a documentary film script contains much more detail about the material which constitutes the actual film. Below is an extract from an early episode, the sixth one, in the initial script for *Stages of Adaptation*:

VIDEO	AUDIO
1. Ext of Shaftesbury Avenue, West End of London, in the evening. Visuals of theatre exteriors and billboards.	Showtime music
	Presenter V/O: 'The bumper year for adaptations of novels was 2018, but British theatre's creativity did not stop there. In fact, the following year was equally outstanding.'
Close-up of the poster for Enda Walsh's adaptation of *Grief Is the Thing with Feathers*; fade to poster for David Greig's *Touching the Void*.	
	'This time, two other bestsellers lit up the West End stage. And both were books whose themes of death and disaster were quite challenging.'
2. Close-up of book cover: Max Porter, *Grief Is the Thing with Feathers*.	Presenter V/O: '*Grief Is the Thing with Feathers* is a debut novel by Max Porter, first published in 2015. It rapidly found a committed following despite the fact that it's so hard to classify: is it a novel, a poem or a personal memoir, fact or fiction? However you label it the book soon won great reviews, devoted readers, and many awards.'
Book reviews from newspapers.	
Production photograph of Crow from Enda Walsh's adaptation, starring Cillian Murphy, originally staged at Galway Theatre in 2018.	
	'The story is about a father and his two boys trying to make sense of the sudden death of his wife and their mother. As they attempt to cope with this devastating bereavement, their London flat is invaded by a huge talking Crow. The stage version is basically a one-man show starring Cillian Murphy, familiar to viewers from BBC Television's *Peaky Blinders*.'

Scene 13: Adaptations

3. Interview with Enda Walsh, ID'd in lower third left as Playwright Enda Walsh.	Interviewer: 'When did you first come across Max Porter's book?'
	Walsh: 'The London theatre company Complicite approached me and asked if I'd read the book. It was in the book pile on my wife's side of the bed, and she hadn't read it, so I read it in a sitting and thought, Maybe I'll do every word of it. It certainly doesn't need much adapting. I'm certainly not going to use my words, because his words are fucking brilliant.'
	Interviewer: 'Your adaptation focuses on the father and the boys don't appear on stage at first.'
	Walsh: 'I didn't want the boys talking on stage until much later on. I thought, Well, how do I keep them present? I came up with this idea by going back to my own childhood, when my brother and I would tape conversations and listen to them. We used to tape our thoughts or our parents arguing with one another and then listen to them later on when we were playing darts in our bedroom. So the boys, who are taped, have all these cassette tapes. The dad finds the tapes, and we get to know them through these. That was a device to introduce the boys into the soundtrack. By the third act, they begin to talk out to us, and that's a real shock to the audience. Also, I knew I wanted the wife in it in some way. We shot some Super 8 footage of her out on the beach with the kids and took some really badly out-of-focus Polaroids.'
4. Interview with Max Porter, ID'd in lower third left as Writer Max Porter.	Interviewer: 'What do you think of this version of your novel?'
	Porter: 'It isn't being twisted in any direction it's not comfortable with – it's just being given wings. The minute I met Enda, I knew this was going to be no problem at all because he just gets it. He's got this weird combination of playful energy and intellectual seriousness.'
6. Book cover of Joe Simpson's *Touching the Void*, fade to extract of film version by Kevin Macdonald: West Face of Siula Grande mountain in Peru.	Presenter V/O: 'Joe Simpson's book *Touching the Void* is the compelling story of how he, together with Simon Yates, were the first mountain climbers to reach the summit of Siula Grande, a 20,000 foot peak in the Peruvian Andes, using the previously unclimbed West Face.'
	'The book, published in 1988, has sold over a million copies, and has been translated into twenty languages.'

VIDEO	AUDIO
	'After the pair reached the top of the mountain, their problems began when, during their descent, Simpson slipped, plummeted down and broke his leg. Yates managed to reach him and then lowered him further down, but – in order to save himself – was forced to drop him into a crevasse. Since they couldn't communicate, Yates assumed that his climbing partner was dead and gradually made his way back to base camp. Many feet below, Simpson realized he had been abandoned and decided to crawl to safety – it took him three days.'
	'And he made it: It's a quintessential tale of survival against the odds.'
	'David Greig's adaptation of the book reached the West End in 2019 after being first staged at the Bristol Old Vic.'
7. Interview with David Greig, ID'd in lower third left as Playwright David Greig.	Interviewer: 'What grabbed you about Joe Simpson's story?'
	Greig: 'I'm fascinated by the thought of, How do you come back from a point where death is so close to you that it's easier to let go, than to fight on? And what attracts me to this story is Joe Simpson's incredible determination and courage, and where he finds the resources to continue and struggle through an unimaginable situation.'
	'One of the things I love about theatre is that it's a type of poetry, a type of metaphor: You obviously can't realistically stage a mountain on stage, so that means inventing some really imaginative, clever, thoughtful ways to bring this story out.'
	'Some people will know the story already, it was an incredibly successful book and film, and I think that those people are going to get a pleasant surprise at how we've chosen to tell it.'
7. Interview with Tom Morris, ID'd in lower third left as Director Tom Morris.	Presenter V/O: 'David Greig's adaptation of *Touching the Void* was realized on stage by director Tom Morris, who is artistic director of the Bristol Old Vic.'
	Interviewer: 'Could you tell us how you approached this adaptation?'

Morris: 'Ever since I read the book, this story has been lodged in my mind like a splinter. I can't get rid of it. And I'm not alone either. There's a whole generation of people whose minds were dented by it and for whom it has become a permanent reference point for life.'

'All I knew was that we couldn't try to recreate the film. We had to do something that could only work in a theatre and that was to appeal to the audience's imagination.'

'Set designer Ti Green and I tried to produce a staging which gives the audience the sensation not of what it feels like to look at the mountain but of what it feels like to be on the mountain, in that situation of jeopardy facing your own death.'

'The most powerful storytelling tool in theatre is the audience's imagination. The writing, the acting and the scenery are there in order to stimulate the audience's imagination.'

'This is a story about humanity at the very limits of its endurance – and the things we might be capable of – and our staging is a fantastic way to introduce people to it in a theatre.'

[And here is the final extract from a treatment for *Stages in Adaptation*:]

Conclusion

Our documentary not only celebrates the creativity of theatre adaptations, which bring joy to millions of theatregoers, but also illustrates the partnerships – between commercial sector and state-subsidized theatres, and between the metropolis and venues outside London – that make all of these big hits happen. The film also examines how theatre adaptations, both musicals and straight plays, differ from their original sources – whether these are books or films – and shows what wonderful things theatre can add to the original tellings of these familiar stories.

SCENE FOURTEEN

Valediction

Daisy and Jack's decade

So far, the central theme of 2010s new writing has been identified as identity politics, personal accounts of being female, non-white or queer. At the same time, traditional genres such as the political play, the monologue, the family play, the history play or the adaptation also received a renewed creative boost. The result was an unparalleled sense of variety. So when Susannah Clapp, theatre critic of the *Observer*, looked back on the decade in an article aptly titled 'All change!', published in June 2019, she wrote: 'British theatre is in the process of a massive change. More far-reaching than any I have seen in more than 20 years as the *Observer*'s drama critic. Accelerating. Overdue. Irrevocable. Welcome.'

This neatly sums up the dynamic variety of this crisis-prone decade. Now, coming to the end of my own journey through the different genres and styles of contemporary drama it is clear that although the greater visibility of female, Black and Asian playwrights, as well as the key themes of gender and identity, are central to the story of the decade, there was so much more happening in British theatre at the time. So, of course, most individual theatregoing experiences could be much more personal – not everyone saw the same shows at the same time. To give this variety its due, this penultimate chapter is a fictional memoir that tells another side to the story of 2010s drama – this time from the perspective of three millennials.

Lewis's notebook

Say bye-bye to the twenty-tens (just don't call them the tweenies),,,

I never go to the theatre; BORING. Gigs yes, clubs yes, films yes, West End no-ho. But I know a couple who do, who love glitzy shows and all that. I was interested in why so one of my lockdown projects was to ask them what they remembered of the decade, like theatrewise.

But, first, a bit about us: I'm Lewis, and they're Daisy and Jack, and we were all born in 1989.

We're mates, yeah, even if we don't always see eye to eye. But one thing we all agree on? The label 'millennial' is the WORST. Like, no thanks. We are

NOT Generation Rent, we're not Lost, and we're definitely not Confused. FOMO? Not really. Hard pass on all that. Yeah, we're young, but we're also individuals. I vaguely remember stumbling across an old issue of *Dazed* ages ago with the headline: 'The Millennial Does Not Exist' #dazedgeneration. Honestly? Alright, if you can't sum up millions of young people in the UK without leaning on the most tired, cringe-worthy stereotypes, why even try? And Seriously, who's actually calling themselves Gen Y? Like, do you even know anyone named India? Exactly. What I can say about our age group, though, is that our attitudes are all over the map – and what's wrong with that? We've got everything from 'burn it all down' energy to 'raise the minimum wage'. From 'make travel ridiculously cheap' to 'cut tuition fees in half'. From adulting vibes to 'stop taxing periods already'. See? Variety.

Anyway, let's talk about Daisy and Jack.

Here are their profiles:

- Daisy's assets: degree in Eng Lit (job in marketing); shared ownership of London flat; discreet tattoos; all the birthday cards she's ever got, but not thrown away; Granny's lemon pie recipe; Victorian copy of *A Christmas Carol* (18th birthday present); vintage Swatch watch; picture album of Vinny, the family dog; 2,000 Instagram followers.
- Jack's assets: degree in media studies (job in PR); hipster beard; overdraft facility of £2,000; 35,000 photos on his iPhone (not downloaded yet); Glastonbury festival wristbands; 320-song playlist from Ibiza 2011; homebrew beer-making kit (unopened); Armani sunglasses; leather brief case in retro 1950s style. Twisted TikTok algorithms.

Daisy and Jack have been a thing since 2010. 🤷 No kids yet, so they've got time to spare – and they're making the most of it. They're all about films, gigs and, being Londoners, hitting up theatre a few times a year. They know their vibe: plays and musicals that everyone's hyped about. If it's buzzing on Twitter, they're probably buying tickets. Shakespeare? Hard pass. They've had enough of that from school, thanks. Haven't we all? And if a show doesn't hit the mark, you will see their tweet: 'Boring' 😒 🤮

We still crack up about that time the legendary West End Whingers blog renamed *Love Never Dies* (yeah, Andrew Lloyd Webber's sequel to *Phantom of the Opera*) as *Paint Never Dries*. Absolute gold. Daisy and Jack retweeted it so many times we lost count.

Anyway, I've sorted our decade into three bits:

The first bit is the early twenty-tens, about 2010–13:

Shows? Honestly, Daisy and Jack don't remember much from the start of the decade (relatable), but scrolling through their old Facebook posts gave them a

Scene 14: Valediction

little brain refresh. Daisy's timelines are kind of blurry, but one thing's crystal clear: they're all about fun nights out. Case in point? My squad loved *Legally Blonde: The Musical* – the stage version of that iconic American rom-com film.

Daisy's still HYPED about it. She's practically glowing as she gushes over Sheridan Smith as Elle, the sorority queen-turned-Harvard-law-student who crushes a murder trial like it's NBD. Even Jack admits she was a total powerhouse: singing, dancing and just radiating main-character energy. Words like 'radiant' and 'totally smiling' were thrown around, and you know what? Fair™.

Elle's big entrance – decked out in pink, holding a tiny Chihuahua and defying everyone's expectations – was just incredible. Fleek. And, of course, who can forget the moment the lawyer chorus belts out 'Is he gay – or European?' 😉 An absolute classic.

Apparently, some newspaper called *Legally Blonde* 'a musical for the Twitter generation'. Yeah, why not? Daisy and Jack are living proof.

And more. Honestly, Daisy and Jack are totally obsessed with *Matilda the Musical* – like, who wouldn't be? Based on Roald Dahl's book, it's been running in the West End for over a decade. Neither of them ever read the book (oops), but they're all into its icon value: a whip-smart, book-loving little girl who basically flips the script of her awful family and a nightmare of a headmistress to carve out her own happiness. Uplifting? ABSOLUTELY.

Now, of all the small things, taking care 'bout what truth brings, they can't remember which of the pint-sized stars played Matilda (classic), but they're still raving about Bertie Carvel as Miss Trunchbull. Apparently, his performance was next-level. Oh, and by the end of the show, half the audience was in tears – pass the cry tissues. Daisy swears she wasn't, though Jack's not so sure. 😉

The BIG takeaway? The idea that you can totally rewrite your life's story if you're bold enough. Jack calls it a 'valuable life lesson' (a bit preachy, but we'll let that slide). Bottom line: they're into it, and they think everyone else should be too.

Around the same time, Daisy and Jack were all about *One Man, Two Guvnors*, Richard Bean's chaotic, laugh-until-you-cry farce that had audiences rocking in the aisles. Sort of. Did they care that it was based on some fancy 1743 Italian commedia dell'arte play (*The Servant of Two Masters*, for those keeping score)? Absolutely not. They showed up for the fun – and yeah, boy, did it deliver.

The star of the show? None other than James Corden (yes, his middle name is Kimberley, and no, they didn't know that either). Everyone knows him from *Gavin & Stacey*, and he proved to be the ultimate comedy pro. His stage character? A clueless, love-starved, small-time musician bumbling through 1960s Brighton, tangled up with gangsters and a whole bunch of oddballs. Daisy and Jack still swear they were practically sick from laughing 😂

The HIGHLIGHT? The now-iconic 20-minute scene where Corden's character tries to serve two meals to two bosses at the same time. Pure madness. They were dining out on that story for months. Daisy even compares it (with a big grin) to the random Labrador puppy that stole the show at the end of *The Curious Incident of the Dog in the Night-Time*. High praise. HIGH FIVE.

When the filmed version of *One Man, Two Guvnors* got streamed later, Daisy and Jack became obsessed with Corden's catchphrases, mimicking his nasal Cockney whine at every op: 'I got two jobs – how did that 'appen?', 'You gotta concentrate, 'ain'cha?', 'I gotta be verrry careful what I say here'. And the ultimate fave? When he's asked whether he prefers eating or making love: 'It's a tough one, that, innit?' Absolute legend.

Way back at the start of the decade, Jack was all about Kate Tempest (now Kae). Tempest was everywhere for a hot minute: telly, radio, live gigs. Yeah, they even trekked to Battersea Arts Centre to catch their show *Brand New Ancients*. A mix of performance poetry, music and lighting effects. What kind of effects? NO CLUE. 🤷 That part's fuzzy. But hey, vibes were immaculate.

When it comes to the West End, though, their memories get sharper. *The Book of Mormon*? Absolutely unforgettable. This American musical comedy – one of their go-to genres – comes from the creative geniuses behind *South Park*, with music by Robert Lopez (*Avenue Q* fans, you know). The story? Two clueless Mormon missionaries trying to spread the good word in a Ugandan village, with predictably chaotic and hilarious results. Oh, and fun fact from WIKI: it's raked in over $700 million in the US alone. Wild.

And, living in London, who could miss those iconic Tube ads? 'The best musical of this century.' Turns out, the hype was REAL. Daisy and Jack were all over the satire and the jokes – pure gold they say. Jack even remembers snapping a selfie with Daisy during the interval and proudly making it his very first Instagram post. Talk about a moment!

The second bit is the mid twenty-tens, about 2014–17:

Daisy and Jack aren't big on birthdays (same here), but they do like to mark Valentine's Day. So, they were thrilled when her mom got them tickets to *Shakespeare in Love* for 14 February 2015. It's another rom-com, this time adapted by Lee Hall (the guy behind *Billy Elliot the Musical*) from the film written (or maybe co-written?) by the legendary Tom Stoppard. Sure, some of the best lines came straight from the movie, but the play still delivered a beautifully romantic vibe, full of wit and warmth. Bonus points for the live dog on stage (yes, again!).

Around the same time, they also caught *Kinky Boots*. Written by Cyndi Lauper, the musical follows Charlie, who inherits a struggling shoe factory in Northampton and teams up with drag queen Lola to create a line of high-heeled boots that save the business. It's a high-energy show that hit all the right notes for Daisy and Jack, with its over-the-top camp appeal and Lola's demand for 'two-and-a-half feet of irresistible tubular sex' in the form of red thigh-high boots. Matt Henry (a finalist from *The Voice*) absolutely owned the role of Lola – bold, proud and hilarious, especially when throwing shade at 'weekend transvestites' who look 'like Winston Churchill in their mum's knickers.'

As one of Daisy's friends put it on Twitter: 'There's no business like shoe business.' 👀

I've made Daisy and Jack sound like they're all fun and games, but that's not the full picture. They're into the serious stuff too. Case in point: Simon McBurney (middle name Montagu, apparently). Most people know him as an actor from *The Vicar of Dibley* on the telly, or *The Theory of Everything* film, but they told me about his one-man show *The Encounter* at the Barbican.

It's based on a 1969 adventure when a *National Geographic* photographer, Loren McIntyre, gets lost in the Amazon rainforest while searching for an indigenous tribe called the 'cat people' (Daisy loves that name). When he finds them, he can't speak their language, but believes they communicate telepathically, a process he calls 'beaming'. A voice in your head that bridges the gap. Kind of poetic, right?

Jack explained that McBurney used headphones for the audience to tell this story. Instead of sharing a traditional theatre experience, each person listens in isolation, a mirror of McBurney's ideas about perception and communication. You're not just watching the show; you're in it, trapped within your own head while being taken into the jungle, like physically and mentally. It's a challenging, immersive and completely brilliant piece of theatre.

Time to switch. Let's talk Potterverse. No need for backstory, right? Daisy and Jack dived into *Harry Potter and the Cursed Child*, based on J.K. Rowling's idea. It's set 19 years after *Deathly Hallows* (side note: Simon McBurney pops up in one of the films). 💜 Rowling calls it 'the eighth Harry Potter story', where Harry (now Head of Magical Law Enforcement) navigates life as his son, Albus Severus, starts at Hogwarts.

So cue magic, illusions and stage wizardry. Totally enchanting, yeah. They saw both parts over two nights at the Palace Theatre, which had been decked out in full gothic, Potter-esque glory – right down to the Hogwarts wallpaper. They were into every detail: the ornate lobby, the themed carpets, even the light fixtures.

They'd probably agree with *Forbes* (which I found online) calling the play 'one of the most defining pop culture events of the decade'. In fact, they loved it all on Instagram and YouTube, and, of course, the online gift shop. Perfect spot for souvenirs like wands, scarves and the usual T-shirts (great gifts for younger nephews and nieces). Just don't ask me to watch any TikToks of it.

Okay, so most of this was fine, but I wasn't ready for the full-on enthusiasm Daisy and Jack unleashed when they brought up what they called – exact quote – 'two phenomenal musical experiences'. One I'd never heard of; the other was everywhere at the time.

First, Lee Hall again, adapting Alan Warner's novel *Sopranos* (no, not the mafia telly show). It's called *Our Ladies of Perpetual Succour* and they tell me it follows six Scottish 17-year-old convent schoolgirls from Our Lady of Perpetual Succour on a trip to Edinburgh for a choir competition. A classic coming-of-age story, apparently. On the way, they go full chaos mode, teenagers being teenagers: sex, drugs, rock 'n' roll. The soundtrack? Electric Light Orchestra deep cuts by Jeff Lynne. Basically, a wild, unapologetic celebration of life.

Accolade time: the most memorable musical of the decade – and yes, even I've heard of it – *Hamilton* by Lin-Manuel Miranda. It's a history lesson with a twist: the story of US Founding Father Alexander Hamilton, told with an ethnically diverse cast. Miranda calls it: 'America then, as told by America now.' Most Brits never heard of this Founding Guy, but everyone loves the music and dancing.

Daisy says they were drawn in by the rave reviews, like the *Guardian*'s five-star take: 'A rollercoaster of a show in which a bare-headed, largely non-white cast captures the fervour and excitement of revolution while reminding us how much America's identity was shaped by a buccaneering immigrant, Alexander Hamilton. Miranda's use of rap, hip-hop and R&B becomes the ideal vehicle for exploring the birth of a nation.' Yeah, okay, I get it.

Jack can still name the leads (Jamael Westman as Hamilton and Giles Terera as Aaron Burr) and everyone was blown away by Miranda's hip-hop score, sharp lyrics and game-changing dance numbers. And diverse cast reflected in diverse young audiences. The full soundtrack was on repeat on YouTube (even I gave it a listen now and then). As WestEndProducer tweeted: 'Bravo!' 😁

The last bit is the late twenty-tens, about 2018–20:

By now, I'm feeling a little overloaded with musicals. Seriously, do you guys ever watch straight plays? Daisy and Jack flash matching smiles: okay, fair play, they do. The one they remember most vividly is *Cyprus Avenue*, a play they say sticks with you because of its sheer stage power.

The title comes from a Van Morrison song, but the big draw was Stephen Rea, the Irish actor known for *Greta* (Neil Jordan is his frequent collaborator) and *The Honourable Woman* on TV. In *Cyprus Avenue*, he plays a Belfast loyalist whose paranoid mental state led him to believe his five-week-old granddaughter is Gerry Adams. Yes, it's as strange as it sounds. Daisy calls it the most shocking play she's ever seen, with its raw depictions of racism and extreme violence. Jack, on the other hand, argues that the brutality is justified by the play's exploration of identity crises within Northern Ireland loyalism and the lingering legacy of urban terrorism. He's read about the Troubles and their aftermath and seemed ready to dive into a detailed mansplaination, until we stopped him with a collective, 'We know, we know!'

Things settled down as they moved on to another serious piece: *Beginning* by David Eldridge. It's a two-hander about a man and a woman, both in their late 30s, navigating the awkwardness of meeting after a party and starting the early stages of a relationship. Daisy recalls that it wasn't just about the cringeworthy social awkwardness (something English people are great at) but also class. The woman is middle-class; the man working-class. The tensions that arise from their differences were kind of subtle, but compelling.

Despite my protests, Daisy and Jack insist on a final recap of their recent musical highlights. Fair enough. So, what made the cut?

First up: *Everybody's Talking About Jamie*, inspired by a British TV documentary, *Jamie: Drag Queen at 16*. Based on the real-life story of Jamie Campbell, it's about a schoolboy overcoming prejudice and bullying to become a drag queen. Heartwarming and uplifting, says Daisy, who much preferred it to *Girl from the North Country*. Why? She can't stand Bob Dylan, whose music features heavily in that one.

Next: *Come from Away*, written by a Canadian husband-and-wife team. It's based on the true events in Gander, Newfoundland, where 40 planes carrying approximately 7,000 passengers were diverted after 9/11. The musical celebrates the town's generosity in hosting these unexpected guests for a week. Daisy and Jack describe it as life-affirming, with standout choral singing and foot-stomping Canadian folk tunes. You know, fiddles, penny whistles, the works.

Jack isn't done yet. He brings up *Dear Evan Hansen*, the American musical by Benj Pasek and collaborators (of *La La Land* fame). It follows Evan Hansen, a socially anxious high school senior who fabricates a relationship with a classmate who has died by suicide. Emotional and intense, says Daisy. Sam Tutty, who played Evan, won an Olivier Award at just 22 for his performance.

Finally, *& Juliet*. Having loved *Shakespeare in Love* (despite their usual bard aversion), Daisy and Jack were drawn to this modern take on the Tudors. The jukebox musical, featuring songs by Swedish pop songwriter Max Martin, imagines a world where Juliet survives at the end of Romeo and Juliet. Daisy calls it a fun, feminist, feel-good fantasy, and it's packed with hits from Britney

Spears, Katy Perry and Ariana Grande. Or, as YouTuber Mickey Jo would say, 'Oh my God, hey!'

I think that's everything musical. Big relief, yeah?

This brings us to 2019 – a milestone year when all three of us hit 30. Jack and I took it in our stride, shrugging off the big day. Daisy, on the other hand, was deep into *Everything I Know About Love* by Dolly Alderton. The book lists all the life lessons she'd learned by 30, but we wisely avoided comparing ourselves to her.

Back to the theatre round-up. More straight plays. Jack and Daisy couldn't resist the buzz around *The Lehman Trilogy*, directed by Sam Mendes of Bond films fame. Instead of being split into three separate plays, it's a single three-hour show with three actors (led, oh yeah, by cuddly Simon Russell Beale) playing every role. The play traces the rise and fall of the Lehman Brothers, a financial powerhouse founded by a German-Jewish migrant family. It follows their incredible success in America, culminating in their infamous collapse during the 2008 global financial crash.

Jack and Daisy reminded me of those iconic images of Lehman employees leaving their offices with cardboard boxes, and the staging echoed that imagery with boxes scattered across the set. But it was the acting that truly gripped them, so compelling that the three-hour runtime flew by. Given how many people our age work in offices, they found it refreshing to see some historical context on the shadowy world of finance.

Daisy and Jack aren't the biggest fans of classic European plays, more likely to admire them than fall head over heels. But star power? That's a different story. When they heard James McAvoy was starring in Martin Crimp's version of *Cyrano de Bergerac* at the Playhouse Theatre, they were in. (Earlier that year, they missed out on tickets to see Cate Blanchett in another Crimp play, an adaptation of *Pamela* from the 18th-century novel.)

Crimp's adaptation reimagines Cyrano in a modern context, directed by Jamie Lloyd, who'd already made waves in both the West End and Broadway with his revival of Harold Pinter's *Betrayal* starring Tom Hiddleston. The story itself is a familiar one, thanks to its Hollywood adaptations: Cyrano, a soldier and poet, is in love with his cousin Roxane but can't bring himself to tell her because of his huge nose, which makes him deeply self-conscious. Of course, plot twist and spoiler alert, she ends up falling for Christian, a soldier who can't string a sentence together. The most famous scene is a balcony moment in which Christian is wooing Roxane, while Cyrano stays hidden in the bushes, feeding him eloquent, poetic lines.

This modern-dress production was a hit in Daisy and Jack's eyes. They loved McAvoy for his electrifying energy and performance. And he didn't even need a big fake nose to embody Cyrano's 'ugliness'. His struggle felt more psychological than physical. The highlights? A rap duel and that iconic balcony scene where the actors broke the fourth wall, speaking directly to the audience rather than one another. The language was amazing – performance poetry vibes, drawing more from Kae Tempest and Stormzy than the typical Eng Lit fare.

They couldn't get enough. Both Daisy and Jack spent a week tweeting about it. 'Unmissable' was the word on repeat.

By early 2020, Daisy figured that Tom Stoppard was 82, mainly known to them from *Shakespeare in Love*. So she was curious about *Leopoldstadt*, advertised as his most personal (and even possibly his last) play. The title brought to mind one of their favourite weekend trips to Vienna, which they'd enjoyed immensely. So, they grabbed tickets not long after its West End premiere at the end of January.

Leopoldstadt is a sprawling, heartfelt story tracing the lives of Viennese Jews from 1899 to 1955. The play follows the secular middle-class Merz family (working in business, academia and health) as they increasingly encounter the horrors of anti-Semitism, culminating in its devastating effects in the final scene when a chilling family list reveals how many of them were victims of the Holocaust. The play felt like an elegy, full of historical weight and emotional resonance.

Jack described it as engrossing, satisfying and deeply moving. The play was much more than a historical narrative; it explored themes of identity, heritage and connection that felt deeply personal. This turned out to be the last show they saw before the pandemic brought all theatre to a halt. COVID-19 – what a shit way to close out the decade. 💀

During lockdown, while I bombarded them with questions about all the plays and shows they'd seen, they didn't lose their passion for drama. But they had to pivot to streaming National Theatre productions online instead. Daisy and Jack joked about swapping their plush red West End velvet seats for their black leather living-room sofa. It wasn't quite the same, but it was better than nothing at all.

SCENE FIFTEEN

Conclusion

Ten flash essays about 2010s British theatre (*vita longa, ars brevis*):
1. British theatre in the 2010s is crisis theatre. In other words, it reflects the sense of emergency, social, economic and political, of the decade. For example, the growing climate change catastrophe. The result of this global feeling of calamity is often confusion: I don't know what to think, what can be done or what I should do. But crisis also offers opportunities, and confusion can result in clarity.
2. Crisis theatre exists in a mixed economy. Some of the most successful shows of the decade were staged in the commercial sector, or transferred to Theatreland from the state-subsidized sector. I have watched the same show at the National Theatre or at the Royal Shakespeare Company and in the West End, and the experience has been equally pleasurable. So the commercial sector needs state-funded theatre to thrive, and the state-funded sector needs commercial success to survive. This is the meaning of the mixed economy.
3. Crisis theatre is a theatre of variety. What struck me most strongly about new writing in this decade, whether the plays were staged at the Royal Court, the National Theatre or at a fringe venue, is the sheer multifariousness of the subjects, styles and shapes of new work. Yet despite the uncontrollably multifarious character of 2010s theatre, it has one main theme: identity.
4. Crisis theatre is identity theatre. Looking back over the decade I am conscious that the most innovative and inventive examples of new writing were expressions of personal, ethnic or gender identity. Identity was the central theme of the decade – exemplified in the increase in plays by women and Black and Asian playwrights. But maybe, just maybe, theatre itself was facing an identity crisis: who is it for, and what is its cultural role?
5. Crisis theatre is often political. It is useful in articulating the political concerns of its theatre-makers and appeals to the similar politics of its audiences. All political theatre in Britain is progressive; there are no right-wing plays. Or at least I've never seen one. But if most political

theatre aspires to have some public utility, actually most political theatre is useless. It changes nothing.
6. Crisis theatre stages all subjects under the sun, except for one: that subject is Brexit. In vain have I searched for plays about leaving the European Union, which is one subject I care passionately about. British theatre prides itself on being always relevant and contemporary, but it has consistently ignored this, the most important issue of the 2010s. This means that Brexit is so important that it can't be touched by theatre-makers.
7. Crisis theatre is dystopian theatre. One of the new phenomena in British theatre of this decade is the large number of dystopian dramas. I know that the world is a very bad place, but dystopias are even worse places. Obviously a response to the mental climate of acute crisis, they also showed how the theatrical imagination can be more lucid than journalism. As so often happens, fiction is more truthful than fact.
8. Crisis theatre can be popular theatre. In this populist decade I really enjoyed many examples of such popular forms as the history play and the stage adaptation. This dismissal of work that has been commercially successful is an example of a very British kind of snobbery; in this mindset the only good play is the failed play. But suspicion of success is itself a failure, a failure of imagination.
9. Crisis theatre is experimental theatre. The 2010s were a really good decade for new writing which creatively stretches the boundaries of the possible in both form and content. I was often surprised by the sheer inventiveness of both playwrights and directors. Genuinely experimental theatre, a bit like scientific experiment, can sometimes fail as well as succeed. But often the failed experiment is more creative than the successful one.
10. Crisis theatre is polyphonous, it speaks in many different voices. To do this variety justice I chose to write this book in the creative non-fiction style of the hermit crab essay. Or rather fifteen hermit crab essays. The hermit crab genre is one in which the writer uses an existing form such as a letter, a quiz or a product review, as a structure for their writing. It is named after those crustaceans that have adapted by occupying empty scavenged mollusc shells to protect their fragile innards. It's a way of adding meaning to whatever it is you want to say. This writing style proves that by indirection you can find direction out.

Book list

These are some of the publications about the 2010s which I read while writing my own book.

Kim Adrian, *The Shell Game: Writers Play with Borrowed Forms*, University of Nebraska Press, 2018.
Dolly Alderton, *Everything I Know About Love*, Penguin, 2018.
Katherine Angel, *Tomorrow Sex Will Be Good Again: Women and Desire in the Age of Consent*, Verso, 2021.
Mary Beard, *Women & Power: A Manifesto*, Profile, 2017.
Russell Brand, *Revolution*, Arrow, 2015.
Michaela Coel, *Misfits: A Personal Manifesto*, Penguin, 2021.
Virginie Despentes, *King Kong Theory*, Feminist Press, 2010.
Reni Eddo-Lodge, *Why I'm No Longer Talking to White People About Race*, Bloomsbury, 2018.
Extinction Rebellion, *This Is Not a Drill: An Extinction Rebellion Handbook*, Penguin, 2019.
Mark Fisher, *Capitalist Realism: Is There No Alternative?*, Zero, 2009.
Deborah Frances-White, *The Guilty Feminist: From Our Noble Goals to Our Worst Hypocrisies*, Virago, 2019.
Afua Hirsch, *Brit(ish): On Race, Identity and Belonging*, Vintage, 2018.
John Holloway, *Crack Capitalism*, Pluto, 2010.
Owen Jones, *Chavs: The Demonization of the Working Class*, Verso, 2012.
Naomi Klein, *This Changes Everything: Capitalism vs. the Climate*, Penguin, 2015.
Jack Monroe, *A Girl Called Jack: 100 Delicious Budget Recipes*, Michael Joseph, 2014.
Caitlin Moran, *How to Be a Woman*, Ebury, 2012.
Fintan O'Toole, *Heroic Failure: Brexit and the Politics of Pain*, Head of Zeus, 2018.
Will Storr, *The Science of Storytelling*, William Collins, 2019.
Polly Toynbee and David Walker, *Cameron's Coup: How the Tories Took Britain to the Brink*, Faber, 2015.
Polly Toynbee and David Walker, *The Lost Decade 2010–2020: And What Lies Ahead for Britain*, Faber, 2020.
Alwyn Turner, *All in It Together: England in the Early 21st Century*, Profile, 2021.

Play list

Abdulrazzak, Hassan, *The Prophet*, London: Oberon, 2013.
Abdulrazzack, Hassan, *Love, Bombs and Apples*, London: Oberon, 2016.
Adams, Emma, *Animals*, London: Oberon, 2015.
Agboluaje, Oladipo, *New Nigerians*, London: Oberon, 2017.
Alabanza, Travis, *Burgerz*, London: Methuen Drama, 2018 (revised 2021).
Alipoor, Javaad, *The Believers Are But Brothers*, London: Oberon, 2018.
Barnes, Luke, *All We Ever Wanted Was Everything*, London: Oberon, 2017.
Bartlett, Mike, *13*, London: Nick Hern, 2011.
Bartlett, Mike, *King Charles III*, London: Nick Hern, 2014.
Bartlett, Mike, *Love, Love, Love*, with introduction by James Grieve, London: Methuen Drama, 2015.
Bartlett, Mike, *Wild*, London: Nick Hern, 2016.
Bartlett, Mike, *Albion*, London: Nick Hern, 2017.
Bartlett, Mike, *Earthquakes in London*, with introduction by Bridget Escolme, London: Methuen Drama Student Edition, 2021.
Battye, Miriam, *Scenes with Girls*, London: Faber, 2020.
Bean, Richard, *One Man, Two Guvnors: Based on 'The Servant of Two Masters' by Carlo Goldoni*, London: Oberon, 2011.
Bean, Richard, *The Heretic*, London: Oberon, 2011.
Bean, Richard, *Great Britain*, London: Oberon, 2015.
Bhatti, Gurpreet Kaur, *Behud (Beyond Belief)*, London: Oberon, 2010.
Bhatti, Gurpreet Kaur, *Khandan (Family)*, London: Oberon, 2014.
Birch, Alice, *Revolt. She Said. Revolt Again.*, London: Oberon, 2016.
Birch, Alice, *[BLANK]*, London: Oberon, 2019.
Blythe, Alecky, *Little Revolution*, London: Nick Hern, 2014.
Brenton, Howard, *Anne Boleyn*, London: Nick Hern, 2010.
Brenton, Howard, *55 Days*, London: Nick Hern, 2012.
Brenton, Howard, *Drawing the Line*, London: Nick Hern, 2013.
Brenton, Howard, *Doctor Scroggy's War*, London: Nick Hern, 2014.
Brittain, Jon, *Rotterdam*, with commentary and notes by Stephen Farrier, London: Methuen Drama Student Editions, 2021.
Bruce, Deborah, *The Distance*, London: Nick Hern, 2014.
Buffini, Moira, Matt Charman, Penelope Skinner and Jack Thorne, *Greenland*, London: Faber, 2011.
Buffini, Moira, *Handbagged*, London: Faber, 2013 (revised 2022).
Bullmore, Amelia, *Di and Viv and Rose*, London: Methuen Drama, 2010 (revised 2013).
Butler, Leo, *Boy*, London: Methuen Drama, 2016.
Butterworth, Jez, *Jerusalem*, London: Nick Hern, 2009.
Butterworth, Jez, *The Ferryman*, London: Nick Hern, 2017.

Chakrabarti, Lolita, *Red Velvet*, with an introduction by Kenneth Branagh, London: Methuen Drama, 2020.
Churchill, Caryl, *Love and Information*, London: Nick Hern, 2012.
Churchill, Caryl, *Escaped Alone*, London: Nick Hern, 2016.
Churchill, Caryl, *Glass. Kill. Bluebeard. Imp.*, London: Nick Hern, 2019.
Coel, Michaela, *Chewing Gum Dreams*, London: Methuen Drama, 2013.
Cooper, Zoe, *Out of Water*, London: Methuen Drama, 2019.
Craig, Ryan, *The Holy Rosenbergs*, London: Oberon, 2011.
Crimp, Martin, *In the Republic of Happiness*, London: Faber, 2012.
Crimp, Martin, *When We Have Sufficiently Tortured Each Other: Twelve Variations on Samuel Richardson's* Pamela, London: Faber, 2019.
Crimp, Martin, *Cyrano de Bergerac*, London: Faber, 2019.
Crouch, Tim, *Total Immediate Collective Imminent Terrestrial Salvation*, London: Oberon, 2019.
Crowe, E.V., *The Sewing Group*, London: Faber, 2016.
Crowe, E.V., *Shoe Lady*, London: Faber, 2020.
De Angelis, April, *Jumpy*, London: Faber, 2011.
Dear, Nick, *The Dark Earth and the Light Sky*, London: Faber, 2012.
De-lahay, Rachel, *My White Best Friend (And Other Letters Left Unsaid)*, London: Methuen Drama, 2020.
Din, Ishy, *Snookered*, London: Methuen Drama, 2012.
Dolan, Monica, *The B*easts*, London: Samuel French, 2017.
Donnelly, John, *The Knowledge*, London: Faber, 2011.
Duffy, Carol Ann and Rufus Norris, *My Country; A Work in Progress*, London: Faber, 2017.
Eccleshare, Thomas, *Pastoral*, London: Oberon, 2013.
Eccleshare, Thomas, *Instructions for Correct Assembly*, London: Oberon, 2018.
Edgar, David, *Written on the Heart*, London: Nick Hern, 2011.
Edgar, David, *Trying It On*, London: Nick Hern, 2018.
Edmundson, Helen, *Queen Anne*, London: Nick Hern, 2017.
Eldridge, David, Robert Holman and Simon Stephens, *A Thousand Stars Explode in the Sky*, London: Methuen Drama, 2010.
Eldridge, David, *The Knot of the Heart*, London: Methuen Drama, 2011.
Eldridge, David, *In Basildon*, London: Methuen Drama, 2012.
Eldridge, David, *Beginning*, London: Methuen Drama, 2017.
El-Khairy, Omar, *Homegrown*, London: Fly Prates, 2017.
Ellams, Inua, *Barber Shop Chronicles*, with commentary and notes by Oladipo Agboluaje, Methuen Drama Student Editions, 2021.
Ellams, Inua, *Three Sisters*, London, Methuen Drama, 2021.
Ellis, Samantha, *How to Date a Feminist*, London: Nick Hern, 2016.
Feehily, Stella, *This May Hurt a Bit*, London: Nick Hern, 2014.
Franzmann, Vivienne, *Mogadishu*, London: Nick Hern, 2012.
Frederick, Ifeyinwa, *The Hoes*, London: Nick Hern, 2018.
Fritz, James, *Parliament Square*, London: Nick Hern, 2017.
Gadd, Richard, *Baby Reindeer*, London: Methuen Drama, 2019.

Goode, Chris, *Men in the Cities*, London: Oberon, 2014.
Gordon, Natasha, *Nine Night*, London: Nick Hern, 2018.
Graham, James, *The Whisky Taster*, London: Methuen Drama, 2010).
Graham, James, *This House*, with commentary and notes by Nicholas Holden, London: Methuen Drama Student Editions, 2021.
Graham, James, *The Angry Brigade*, London: Methuen Drama, 2014.
Graham, James, *Ink*, London: Methuen Drama, 2017.
Graham, James, *Labour of Love*, London: Methuen Drama, 2017.
Graham, James, *Quiz*, London: Methuen Drama, 2018.
Grauls, Carla, *Occupied*, London: Methuen Drama, 2014.
Greig, David, *Dunsinane*, London: Faber, 2010.
Greig, David, *The Strange Undoing of Prudencia Hart*, London: Faber, 2013.
Greig, David, *Touching the Void*, London: Faber, 2018.
Grosso, Nick, *Ingredient X*, London: Methuen Drama, 2010.
Gupta, Tanika, *Lions and Tigers*, London: Oberon, 2017.
Gupta, Tanika, *A Doll's House*, London: Oberon, 2019.
Gupta, Tanika, *The Empress*, with commentary and notes by Jane Garnett, London: Methuen Drama Student Editions, 2022.
Hall, Lee, *Shakespeare in Love*, London: Faber, 2014.
Hall, Lee, *Our Ladies of Perpetual Succour*, London: Faber, 2015.
Hampton, Christopher, *A German Life*, London: Faber, 2019.
Hare, David, *I'm Not Running*, London: Faber, 2018.
Hare, David, *The Moderate Soprano*, London: Faber, 2018.
Harris, Zinnie, *How to Hold Your Breath*, London: Faber, 2015.
Hickson, Ella, *Oil*, London: Nick Hern, 2016.
Hickson, Ella, *The Writer*, London: Nick Hern, 2018.
Hodge, John, *Collaborators*, London: Faber, 2011.
Holcroft, Sam, *Rules for Living*, London: Nick Hern, 2015.
Hollingworth, John, *Multitudes*, London: Nick Hern, 2015.
Horwood, Joel, *This Changes Everything*, London: Nick Hern, 2015.
Icke, Robert and Duncan Macmillan, *1984*, London: Methuen Drama, 2021.
Ikoko, Theresa, *Girls*, London: Methuen Drama, 2016.
Ireland, David, *Cyprus Avenue*, London: Methuen Drama, 2016.
James, Charlene, *Cuttin' It*, London: Faber, 2016.
Kaye Campbell, Alexi, *Sunset at the Villa Thalia*, London: Nick Hern, 2016.
Kelly, Dennis, *The Ritual Slaughter of Gorge Mastromas*, London: Oberon, 2013.
Kelly, Dennis, *Girls & Boys*, London: Oberon, 2018.
Kelly, Ian, *Mr Foote's Other Leg*, London: Nick Hern, 2015.
Kendrick, Ellie, *Hole*, London: Oberon, 2018.
Kene, Arinzé, *Misty*, London: Nick Hern, 2018.
Kershaw, Ian, *The Greatest Play in the History of the World*, London: Methuen Drama, 2018.
King, Dawn, *Foxfinder*, London: Nick Hern, 2011.
Kirkwood, Lucy, *NSFW*, London: Nick Hern, 2012.
Kirkwood, Lucy, *Chimerica*, London: Nick Hern, 2013.

Kirkwood, Lucy, *The Children*, London: Nick Hern, 2016.
Kirkwood, Lucy, *The Welkin*, London: Nick Hern, 2020.
Kosar, Sarah, *Mumburger*, London: Methuen Drama, 2016.
Lee-Jones, Jasmine, *Seven Methods of Killing Kylie Jenner*, London: Oberon, 2019.
Lecky, Nicôle, *Superhoe*, London: Nick Hern, 2019.
Leigh, Eve, *Midnight Movie*, London: Oberon, 2019.
Lenkiewicz, Rebecca, *The Invisible*, London: Faber, 2015.
Lenkiewicz, Rebecca, *Jane Wenham: The Witch of Walkern*, London: Faber, 2015.
Leyshon, Nell, *Bedlam*, London: Oberon, 2010.
Lloyd Malcolm, Morgan, *Emilia*, London: Oberon, 2018.
Lopez, Matthew, *The Inheritance*, London: Faber, 2018.
Luscombe, Tim, *Hungry Ghosts*, London: Methuen Drama, 2010.
Lustgarten, Anders, *If You Don't Let Us Dream, We Won't Let You Sleep*, London: Methuen Drama, 2013.
Lustgarten, Anders, *Lampedusa*, London: Methuen Drama, 2015.
Lynn, Cordelia, *Lela & Co.*, London: Nick Hern, 2015.
Macmillan, Duncan, *Lungs*, London: Oberon, 2011 (revised 2021).
Macmillan, Duncan, *People, Places and Things*, London: Methuen Drama, 2015 (revised 2024).
Mahfouz, Sabrina, *A History of Water in the Middle East*, London: Methuen Drama, 2019.
Maitland, Jonathan, *Dead Sheep*, Leith: Salamander Street, 2020.
Marshall, Natasha, *Half Breed*, London: Samuel French, 2017.
Martello-White, Nathaniel, *Torn*, London: Methuen Drama, 2016.
McBurney, Simon, *The Encounter*, London: Nick Hern, 2016.
McDonagh, Martin, *Hangmen*, London: Faber, 2015.
McDowall, Alistair, *Pomona*, with commentary and notes by Dan Rebellato, London: Methuen Drama Student Editions, 2020.
McDowall, Alistair, *X*, with introduction by Cristina Delgado-Garcia, London: Methuen Drama, 2021.
McPherson, Neil, *I Wish to Die Singing: Voices from the Armenian Genocide*, London: Oberon, 2015.
Morgan, Peter, *The Audience*, London: Faber, 2013.
Morton-Smith, Tom, *Oppenheimer*, London: Oberon, 2015.
Mula, Shireen, *Same Same*, London: Playdead.Famous, 2011.
Mullarkey, Rory, *The Wolf from the Door*, London: Methuen Drama, 2014.
Mullarkey, Rory, *Pity*, London: Methuen Drama, 2018.
Munro, Rona, *The James Plays*, London: Nick Hern, 2016.
Murphy, Joe, and Joe Robertson, *The Jungle*, London: Faber, 2018.
Nasr, Carmen, *Dubailand*, London: Samuel French, 2017.
Neilson, Anthony, *Unreachable*, in *Plays 3: Relocated; Get Santa!; Narrative; Unreachable; The Prudes*, London: Methuen Drama, 2018.
Norris, Barney, *Visitors*, London: Oberon, 2014.
Okoh, Janice, *The Gift*, London: Nick Hern, 2020.
Outbox Theatre, *And the Rest of Me Floats*, London: Oberon, 2019.

Owen, Gary, *Iphigenia in Splott*, London, Methuen Drama, 2015 (revised 2022).
Owen, Gary, *Violence and Son*, London: Oberon, 2015.
Patel, Vinay, *True Brits*, London: Methuen Drama, 2014.
Payne, Nick, *Wanderlust*, London: Faber, 2010.
Payne, Nick, *Constellations*, London: Faber, 2012 (revised 2021).
Payne, Nick, *The Same Deep Water as Me*, London: Faber, 2013.
Peck, Adam, and Sally Cookson, *A Monster Calls: The Play*, London: Walker Books, 2018.
Penhall, Joe, *Birthday*, London: Methuen Drama, 2012.
Penhall, Joe, *Mood Music*, London: Methuen Drama, 2018.
Poulton, Mike, *Wolf Hall & Bring Up the Bodies*, London: Nick Hern, 2014.
Poulton, Mike, *Imperium: The Cicero Plays*, London: Nick Hern, 2017.
Power, Ben, *The Lehman Trilogy*, London: Samuel French, 2022.
Prebble, Lucy, *A Very Expensive Poison*, London: Methuen Drama, 2019.
Price, Tim, *Protest Song*, London: Methuen Drama, 2013.
Price, Tim, *Teh Internet Is Serious Business*, London: Methuen Drama, 2014 (revised 2021).
Raine, Nina, *Tribes*, London: Nick Hern, 2010.
Raine, Nina, *Tiger Country*, London: Nick Hern, 2014.
Raine, Nina, *Consent*, London: Nick Hern, 2017 (revised 2018).
Ravenhill, Mark, *Candide*, London: Methuen Drama, 2013.
Ravenhill, Mark, *The Cane*, London: Methuen Drama, 2018.
Ridley, Philip, *Tender Napalm*, London: Methuen Drama, 2011.
Ridley, Philip, *Shivered*, London: Methuen Drama, 2012 (revised 2014).
Ridley, Philip, *Dark Vanilla Jungle and Other Monologues*, London: Methuen Drama, 2014.
Ridley, Philip, *Karagula*, London: Methuen Drama, 2016.
Ridley, Philip, *Radiant Vermin*, with an introduction by Aleks Sierz, London: Methuen Drama, 2021.
Road, Ella, *The Phlebotomist*, London: Methuen Drama, 2021.
Ronder, Tanya, *Fuck the Polar Bears*, London: Nick Hern, 2015.
Ronder, Tanya, *Dara*, London: Nick Hern, 2015.
Sheers, Owen, *Mametz*, with a Welsh-language translation by Ceri Wyn Jones, London: Faber, 2017.
Sheibani, Bijan, *The Arrival*, London: Nick Hern, 2019.
Skinner, Penelope, *The Village Bike*, London: Faber, 2011.
Skinner, Penelope, *Linda*, London: Faber, 2015.
Slovo, Gillian, *The Riots*, London: Oberon, 2011.
Slovo, Gillian, *Another World: Losing Our Children to Islamic State*, London: Oberon, 2016.
Smith, Stef, *Human Animals*, London: Nick Hern, 2016.
Smith, Stef, *Girl in the Machine*, London: Nick Hern, 2017.
Stafford, Nick, *War Horse: Adapted for the Stage from the Novel by Michael Morpurgo*, London: Faber, 2007.
Steel, Beth, *Ditch*, London: Methuen Drama, 2010.

Steel, Beth, *Wonderland*, London: Faber, 2014.
Steel, Beth, *Labyrinth*, London: Faber, 2016.
Steiner, Sam, *Lemons Lemons Lemons Lemons Lemons*, London: Nick Hern, 2016 (revised 2023).
Stenham, Polly, *Hotel*, London: Faber, 2014.
Stephens, Simon, *Three Kingdoms*, London: Methuen Drama, 2012.
Stephens, Simon, *The Curious Incident of the Dog in the Night-Time: Adapted from the Novel by Mark Haddon*, rev edn, London: Methuen Drama, 2013.
Stephens, Simon, *Birdland*, London: Methuen Drama, 2014.
Stephens, Simon, *Nuclear War & The Songs for Wende*, London: Methuen Drama, 2017.
Stevenson, Debris, *Poet in da Corner*, London: Oberon, 2018.
Štivičić, Tena, *3 Winters*, London: Nick Hern, 2014.
Stoppard, Tom, *Leopoldstadt*, London: Faber, 2020.
Swale, Jessica, *Nell Gwynn*, London: Nick Hern, 2015 (revised 2016).
Tempest, Kae, *Brand New Ancients*, London: Picador, 2013.
Testament (Andy Brooks), *Black Men Walking*, London: Oberon 2018.
Thomas, Ed, *On Bear Ridge*, London: Methuen Drama, 2019.
Thomas, Ruby, *Either*, London: Faber, 2019.
Thompson, Selina, *salt.*, London: Faber, 2018.
Thompson, Steve, *No Naughty Bits*, London: Nick Hern, 2011.
Thorne, Jack, *Let the Right One In*, London: Nick Hern, 2013.
Thorne, Jack, *Hope*, London: Nick Hern, 2015.
Thorne, Jack, *The Solid Life of Sugar Water*, London: Nick Hern, 2015.
Thorne, Jack, *Harry Potter and the Cursed Child*, New York: Little, Brown, 2016.
Thorne, Jack, *A Christmas Carol*, London: Nick Hern, 2017 (revised 2021).
Thorne, Jack, *The End of History...*, London: Nick Hern, 2019.
Thorpe, Chris, *The Shape of the Pain*, London: Oberon, 2018.
tucker green, debbie, *Nut*, London: Nick Hern, 2013.
tucker green, debbie, *Ear for Eye*, London: Nick Hern, 2018.
Wade, Laura, *Posh*, London: Oberon, 2010 (revised 2012).
Wade, Laura, *Home, I'm Darling*, London: Oberon, 2018.
Waller-Bridge, Phoebe, *Fleabag*, London: Nick Hern, 2013 (revised 2014).
Warden, Anoushka, *My Mum's a Twat*, London: Oberon, 2018 (revised 2019).
Waters, Steve, *Little Platoons*, London: Nick Hern, 2011.
Waters, Steve, *Limehouse*, London: Nick Hern, 2017.
Whittington, Amanda, *The Thrill of Love*, London: Nick Hern, 2013.
Wilkey, Temi, *The High Table*, London: Methuen Drama, 2020.
Wilkinson, Joy, *The Sweet Science of Bruising*, London: Nick Hern, 2018.
Williams, Roy, *Days of Significance*, London: Methuen Drama, 2013.
Williams, Roy, *Sucker Punch*, with an introduction by Harry Derbyshire, London: Methuen Drama, 2015.
Williams, Roy, and Clint Dyer, *Death of England*, London: Methuen Drama, 2020.

Wood, Alexandra, *The Tyler Sisters*, London: Nick Hern, 2019.
Woods, Simon, *Hansard*, London: Faber, 2019.
Wright, Nicholas, *The Last of the Duchess*, London: Nick Hern, 2011.
Wright, Nicholas, *Travelling Light*, London: Nick Hern, 2012.
Wynne, Michael, *Who Cares*, London: Faber, 2015.
Zeldin, Alexander, *Beyond Caring*, London: Methuen Drama, 2015.
Zeldin, Alexander, *Love*, London: Methuen Drama, 2016.

Notes on Sources

Scene One: Overview

Andy Beckett, 'The Age of Perpetual Crisis: How the 2010s Disrupted Everything but Resolved Nothing', *Guardian*, 17 December 2019, https://www.theguardian.com/society/2019/dec/17/decade-of-perpetual-crisis-2010s-disrupted-everything-but-resolved-nothing.

Sound Diplomacy Ltd, *Economic Impact Assessment of UK Theatre Sector*, 8 June 2023, https://uktheatre.org/wp-content/uploads/sites/2/2024/01/Economic-Impact-Assessment-of-UK-Theatre-Sector.pdf.

Scene Two: Social issue plays

David Hare, 'My Ideal Theatre', *Guardian*, 30 December 2017, https://www.theguardian.com/stage/2017/dec/30/david-hare-my-ideal-theatre.

Scene Three: Political plays

Niall Ferguson, 'The People's Decade: How Will History Come to Define the 2010s?', *Spectator*, 18 January 2010, https://www.spectator.co.uk/article/the-people-s-decade-how-will-history-come-to-define-the-2010s/.

Scene Four: Brexit plays

James Graham, *Brexit: The Uncivil War*, Channel Four, 4 January 2019; 'Interview with Writer James Graham for *Brexit: The Uncivil War*', Channel Four website, 28 December 2018, https://www.channel4.com/press/news/interview-writer-james-graham-brexit-uncivil-war.

Albion reviews:

Arifa Akbar, 'Albion review – Mike Bartlett's Thorny Study of Politics and Patriotism', *Guardian*, 6 February 2020, https://www.theguardian.com/stage/2020/feb/06/albion-review-almeida-mike-bartlett-rupert-goold.

Aleks Sierz, 'Albion, Almeida Theatre', *Sierz.Co.Uk*, 17 October 2017, https://www.sierz.co.uk/reviews/albion-almeida-theatre/.

Scene Five: Dystopian plays

Robert Icke, 'Duncan Macmillan and Robert Icke on *1984*', *Leftlion* website, 27 August 2015, https://leftlion.co.uk/legacy-content/duncan-macmillan-and-robert-icke-on-1984-7643/.

Scene Six: Experiments

Lyn Gardner, 'New Voices Challenge Our Idea of "Good" Theatre', *The Stage*, 3 September 2018, https://www.thestage.co.uk/opinion/lyn-gardner-new-voices-challenge-our-idea-of-good-theatre.

Alice Birch:

Ava Wong Davies, 'Audiences, Parasites, and Personal Revelations: Perspectives on Criticism and Playwriting', *Howlround Theatre Commons* website, 20 October 2019, https://howlround.com/audiences-parasites-and-personal-revelations.

Tim Crouch:

Civilian Theatre website, *An Oak Tree* [July 2015], https://civiliantheatre.com/2015-2/an-oak-tree/.

Ella Hickson:

'Ella Hickson and Blanche McIntyre in Conversation: The Writer', Almeida Theatre YouTube Channel, 8 May 2018, https://www.youtube.com/watch?v=jJZi5xCfspQ.

Anthony Neilson:

Trish Reid, 'Finding the Light: Anthony Neilson in Conversation', *The Theatre of Anthony Neilson*, London: Methuen Drama, 2018, p. 148.

Nick Payne:

Beth Stevens, 'Incognito Scribe Nick Payne on Being "Mr. Science Playwright" & Why It's Healthy Not to Be Interested in Theater', Broadway.com website, 25 May 2016, https://www.broadway.com/buzz/184967/incognito-scribe-nick-payne-on-being-mr-science-playwright-why-its-healthy-not-to-be-interested-in-theater/.

Simon Stephens:

'Adapting *The Curious Incident of the Dog in the Night-Time* for the Stage', National Theatre website [2014], https://www.nationaltheatre.org.uk/learn-explore/schools/teacher-resources/adapting-curious-incident/.

Katherine Press, 'An Interview with Playwright Simon Stephens', *John York Story* website, 27 February 2019, https://www.johnyorkestory.com/2019/02/an-interview-with-playwright-simon-stephens/.

debbie tucker green:

Lyn Gardner, '"I Was Messing About"', *Guardian*, 30 March 2005, https://www.theguardian.com/stage/2005/mar/30/theatre.

Laura Wade:
'Chatterbox with Laura Wade', Playbox Theatre website, 7 July 2020, https://www.youtube.com/watch?v=wKlY7Ba-d9k.

Scene Seven: Monologues

Sarah Grochala, 'Subjectivity on Stage', Sarah Grochala website, 2015, http://www.sarahgrochala.com/subjectivity-on-stage.

Scene Eight: Plays about family

Damien Gayle, 'Survey Finds UK Is Abandoning Traditional Views of Gender Roles', *Guardian*, 10 July 2018, https://www.theguardian.com/lifeandstyle/2018/jul/10/survey-finds-uk-is-abandoning-traditional-views-of-gender-roles.

Scene Nine: Plays about gender

Helen Lewis, 'What Makes You a Man or a Woman Anyway? Adrian Dalton, Julie Bindel, Bethany Black and Gia Milinovich Discuss the Controversial Issue', *New Statesman*, 13 September 2013, https://www.newstatesman.com/politics/2013/09/battle-over-gender-what-makes-you-man-or-woman-anyway.

Amber Massie-Blomfield, 'A Year on from #MeToo, How Much Has Theatre Really Changed?', *The Stage*, 15 October 2018, https://www.thestage.co.uk/features/a-year-on-from-metoo-how-much-has-theatre-really-changed.

Arifa Akbar, 'Theatre and #MeToo: "There's a New Anger in Women's Stories", *Guardian*, 27 August 2019, https://www.theguardian.com/stage/2019/aug/27/women-theatre-metoo-movement-sexy-lamp-bitter-wheat-harvey.

Scene Ten: Plays about race

Felicity Spector, 'Hollywood or Bust for Black British Actors?', Channel Four website, 1 February 2012, https://www.channel4.com/news/hollywood-hails-for-black-british-actors.

Roy Williams:
Otas, Belinda, 'The Root Interview: Playwright Roy Williams on Race in the UK', *The Root* website, 23 October 2010, https://www.theroot.com/the-root-interview-playwright-roy-williams-on-race-in-1790881335 (accessed 19 June 2024).

Sierz, Aleks, 'Theartsdesk Q&A: Playwright Roy Williams: The Prolific Playwright Talks About Football and Racism', *The Arts Desk* website, 24 October 2009, https://theartsdesk.com/theatre/theartsdesk-qa-playwright-roy-williams?page=0%2C1.

Williams, Roy (2010), 'Why I Wrote *Sucker Punch*', *Sucker Punch*, Royal Court website, 30 June 2010, https://royalcourttheatre.com/roy-williams-why-i-wrote-sucker-punch/ (accessed 2 July 2024).

Williams, Roy (2020), 'REPOST: Roy Williams – Reflections on *Days of Significance* and Rewrites', The Bruntwood Prize for Playwriting website, 2 December 2020, https://www.writeaplay.co.uk/roy-willaims-reflections-on-days-of-significance-and-rewrites/ (accessed 24 June 2024).

Williams, Roy (2023), 'Roy Williams on *Days of Significance*', Black Plays Archive, National Theatre website [2023], https://www.blackplaysarchive.org.uk/interviews/roy-williams-on-days-of-significance/ (accessed 1 July 2024).

Tanika Gupta:

Bowie-Sell, Daisy, 'Tanika Gupta: "My Great Uncle's Remarkable Story Made Me Want to Write"', *WhatsOnStage* website, 30 August 2017, https://www.whatsonstage.com/london-theatre/news/tanika-gupta-lions-and-tigers-shakespeares-globe_44493.html (accessed 15 December 2023).

Gupta, Tanika, 'Ayahs, Lascars and Munshis: Staging *The Empress*', *The Arts Desk* website, 17 April 2013, https://theartsdesk.com/node/67639/view (accessed 16 December 2023).

Gupta, Tanika, and Jatinder Verma, 'A Passion from Within: Tanika Gupta on Her New Play about the Fight for Indian Independence', Shakespeare's Globe website, 12 September 2017, https://medium.com/@shakespearesglobe/a-passion-from-within-tanika-gupta-on-her-new-play-about-the-fight-for-indian-independence-3886cd0c595c (accessed 15 December 2023).

Inua Ellams:

Akbar, Arifa, 'Interview: Inua Ellams: Barber Shops Are a Safe, Sacred Place for British Black Men', *Guardian*, 13 May 2020, https://www.theguardian.com/stage/2020/may/13/inua-ellams-barber-shop-chronicles-national-theatre-at-home (accessed 11 August 2024).

Gurpreet Kaur Bhatti:

Jackson, Lorne, '*Behzti* Playwright Gurpreet Kaur Bhatti Returns with *Behud*', *Business Live* website, 30 May 2013, https://www.business-live.co.uk/retail-consumer/behzti-playwright-gurpreet-kaur-bhatti-3933421 (accessed 20 August 2024).

Sierz, Aleks, [In Conversation with Gurpreet Kaur Bhatti], 'Surreal and Unbelievable and Fantastical', *Journal of Contemporary Drama in English*, 2(1) (2014): 185–95.

Arinzé Kene:

Kene, Arinzé, '*Misty* Exclusive: Interview with Arinzé Kene', *Box Office* website, 24 October 2018, https://blog.fromtheboxoffice.com/2018/10/24/misty-exclusive-interview-with-arinze-kene/ (accessed 27 July 2024).

Longman, Will, 'Arinzé Kene Interview: "I'm Trying to Use *Misty* to Push Change in the West End"', *London Theatre*, 27 September 2018, https://www.londontheatre.co.uk/theatre-news/interviews/arinze-kene-interview-im-trying-to-use-misty-to-push-change-in-the-west-end (accessed 27 July 2024)

Testament:

Marks, Heather, 'Interview with Playwright and Beatboxer Testament on *Black Men Walking*, the Craft of Playwriting, and Knowing Your History', Words of Colour Productions, 17 April 2018, https://www.facebook.com/wordsofcolourproductions/posts/1895196810492483 (accessed 1 September 2024).

Selina Thompson:

Frizzell, Nell, 'Interview: Bristol, Ghana, Jamaica and Back: My Trip Around the Atlantic Slave Triangle', *Guardian*, 12 May 2016, https://www.theguardian.com/artanddesign/2016/may/12/selina-thompson-salt-mayfest-atlantic-slave-triangle (accessed 18 May 2024).

Thompson, Selina, 'Interview: Selina Thompson Writer of *Salt* at Royal Court Theatre', *Alt Africa Review*, 2019, https://alt-africa.com/2019/05/25/interview-selina-thompson-writer-of-salt-at-royal-court-theatre/ (accessed 18 May 2024).

Nathaniel Martello-White:

Martello-White, Nathaniel, '*Torn* – Interview with Writer Nathaniel Martello-White', Royal Court Theatre YouTube, 13 September 2016, https://www.youtube.com/watch?v=u_c7DT3WMJM (accessed 3 July 2024).

Snow, Georgia, 'Nathaniel Martello-White: "Theatre at Its Purest Doesn't Need Loads of Sets and Props"', *The Stage*, 13 September 2016, https://www.thestage.co.uk/features/nathaniel-martello-white-theatre-at-its-purest-doesnt-need-loads-of-sets-and-props (accessed 9 July 2024).

Oladipo Agboluaje:

Agboluaje, Oladipo, 'Oladipo Agboluaje – Interview', *Afridiziak Theatre News*, [March 2017], http://www.afridiziak.com/interviews/oladipo-agboluaje/ (accessed 7 May 2024).

Rachel De-lahay:

Kellaway, Kate, 'Interview: Rachel De-lahay: "Being a Brown Woman Is Political in Itself"', *Observer*, 19 March 2017, https://www.theguardian.com/stage/2017/mar/19/rache-de-lahay-interview-my-white-best-friend-being-a-brown-woman-is-political (accessed 22 June 2024).

Scene Twelve: History plays

Alice Saville, 'EV Crowe: "People Think Historical Plays Are Going to Be Boring"', *The Stage*, 14 November 2016, https://www.thestage.co.uk/features/ev-crowe-people-think-historical-plays-aregoing-to-be-boring.

Scene Thirteen: Adaptations

Arifa Akbar, '"Any Attempt Is Perilous!" How Do You Adapt a Novel for the Stage?', *Guardian*, 26 February 2020, https://www.theguardian.com/stage/2020/feb/26/how-do-you-adapt-a-novel-for-the-stage-virginia-woolf-angela-carter-emily-bronte

'This Broken, Jarring Thing: Enda Walsh Interviewed by Tadhg Hoey', *Bomb* magazine, 7 May 2019, https://bombmagazine.org/articles/this-broken-jarring-thing-enda-walsh-interviewed/.

Holly Williams, 'Will *Grief Is the Thing with Feathers* Take Flight on the Stage?', *New York Times*, 16 March 2018, https://www.nytimes.com/2018/03/16/theater/grief-is-the-thing-with-feathers-play-cillian-murphy.html.

'David Greig introduces *Touching the Void* – Season 2018/19', Lyceum Theatre YouTube, *YouTube*, 12 June 2018, https://www.youtube.com/watch?v=-4afve_lTVU.

Adam Bloodworth, '*Touching the Void* Director Tom Morris: "There's Something About Stories of Impossible Resilience, Stories About People Who Have Survived Things We Cannot Imagine"', *Run Riot*, 12 November 2019, http://www.run-riot.com/articles/blogs/touching-void-director-tom-morris-%E2%80%9Cthere%E2%80%99s-something-about-stories-impossible-resilie.

Scene Fourteen: Valediction

Susannah Clapp, 'All Change! Meet the New Artistic Directors Shaking up British Theatre', *Observer*, 23 June 2019, https://www.theguardian.com/stage/2019/jun/23/artistic-directors-shaking-up-british-theatre-lynette-linton-suba-das-tarek-iskander.

Zing Tsjeng, 'We Are the #zedgeneration: First-Time Voters and a New Generation of Campaigners Tell Us How They're Taking Their Future Back', *Dazed Digital*, 14 April 2015, https://www.dazeddigital.com/artsandculture/article/24193/1/millenials-british-youth-dazed-generation.

Susannah Clapp, '*Legally Blonde* Review', *Guardian*, 17 January 2010, https://www.theguardian.com/stage/2010/jan/17/review-legally-blonde.

Michael Billington, '*Hamilton* Review', *Guardian*, 23 December 2017, reviewhttps://www.theguardian.com/stage/2017/dec/21/hamilton-review-musical-london-victoria-palace-lin-manuel-miranda.

Acknowledgements

My deepest thanks to Lia Ghilardi, whose shrewd observations and sharp eye for the nuances of place and character were instrumental in shaping the fictional world of this book. Her generous input, thoughtful reflections and instinct for narrative texture brought clarity and depth to the story's unfolding.

Many heartfelt thanks also for discussion of both the original idea and its long gestation: Martin Crimp, William Dixon and Ari Sotiriou. Likewise warm thanks to colleagues who made many helpful suggestions: Vicky Angelaki, Kasia Lech, Chris Megson and Peter Paul Schnierer. Especial thanks to Graham Saunders, whose support I particularly value.

I must of course acknowledge the immense help given to me by playwrights who talked to me about their work and gave me permission to use their words in Scene Ten: Oladipo Agboluaje, Gurpreet Kaur Bhatti, Rachel Delahay, Inua Ellams, Tanika Gupta, Arinzé Kene, Nathaniel Martello-White, Testament, Selina Thompson, Roy Williams, as well as for help in organizing these contacts from Milli Bhatia, Sian Carter, Judy Daish, Valli Dakshinamurthi, Hilary Foster, Ella Gold, Lisa Goldman, Allie Highmore, Lynette Linton, Nick Marston, Martin Shippen and Phoebe Wyatt.

And likewise thanks to other theatre-makers who shared their perceptions about the new writing scene: the late Mike Bradwell, Ben Buratta, Leo Butler, Anthony Clark, Steve Dykes, Dennis Kelly, David Mercatali, Philip Ridley and Alexandra Wood.

Over the decade I participated in a number of platforms and public events, at mainstream theatres and Rose Bruford College: so thank you Natalie Abrahami, Bola Agbaje, Alia Bano, Mike Bartlett, Dan Barnard, Sarah Beck, Sebastian Born, Ian Brown, Stephen Brown, Deborah Bruce, Daniel Bye, Chris Campbell, Nina Caplan, Satinder Chohan, Dominic Cooke, Ryan Craig, Tim Crouch, April De Angelis, Stella Duffy, Phoebe Eclair-Powell, Lucy Ellison, Kenny Emson, Mellissa Flowerdew-Clarke, Emma Frankland, Anna Galkina, Chris Garrard, Rupert Goold, Carla Grauls, Sarah Grochala, Atiha Sen Gupta, Steve Harper, Ben Holland, Joel Horwood, Shaun Hutchinson, Nicholas Hytner, Julian Jones, Lucy Kirkwood, Ruth Little, Carissa Hope Lynch, Jonathan Man, Louise Mari, Martin Murphy, Mary Mazzilli, Guleraana Mir, Carmen Nasr, Lucy Neal, Anthony Neilson, Ben Ockrent, Nick Payne, Ben Power, Lucy Prebble, Stewart Pringle, Nina Raine, Laurie Sansom, Tom Scutt, Alistair Smith, Simon Stephens, Zoe Svendsen, Meera Syal, Colin

Teevan, Simon Usher, Paul Vale, Laura Wade, Che Walker, Michael Walton, Matt Wilde, Joy Wilkinson and Ross Willis.

I had many fruitful discussions of 2010s plays with students at the Universities of Braunschweig, Hamburg, Konstanz and Paderborn: especially Nhi Do, Antonie Huff, Mattea Jolmes, Charlotte Manzella, Angelina Skuratova, Fabian Tegethoff, Eszter Vass, and Professors Ute Berns, Merle Tönnies, Eckart Voigts and Christina Wald. Especial appreciation to Dennis Henneböhl and Sören Sokolowski for help with documentation of history plays.

I am also conscious of the need to acknowledge the encouragement of a great many people while I was writing: Kim Adrian, Simona Aru, Anna Arthur, Maggie Barker, Franco Bianchini, Yeliz Biber, Michael Billington, Irene Bocchetta, David Byrne, Dominic Cavendish, Louise Chantal, Kieron Corless, Michael Coveney, Susan Elkin, Philip Fisher, Alex Gammie, Mesut Gunenc, Sue Healy, Ian Herbert, Dan Horrigan, Fiona Hughes, Nesta Jones, Kate Maltby, Keith Mckenna, Terri Paddock, Fabrizio Palmas, Mary Parker, Andrea Peghinelli, Talia Rodgers, Christiane Schlote, Simon Sladen, Marc Szydlik, Boyd Tonkin, Matt Trueman, Peter Vetter, Elisabet Massana Vidal, Anoushka Warden, Steve Waters. And cheers to Alan Read, my colleague at Boston University in London.

Finally, my sincerest thanks to publishers and editors who have helped with advice and other support: Matt Applewhite, Anna Brewer, Emily Hockley, Laura Hussey, Jessica Lovett, Eileen Srebernik and Dinah Wood. At Methuen Drama my profoundest thanks go to publisher Mark Dudgeon, editor Ella Wilson, copyeditor Neil Dowden and RefineCatch client manager Merv Honeywood, and to the Society of Theatre Research's Trevor Griffiths and Valerie Kaneko-Lucas.

Index

Additional information may be found under the titles of works

2nd May 1997 42
13 56
55 Days 136

abuse 101
accountability 27
activism 11, 41
adaptations 133, 145–6
    stages of 146–51
addiction 18, 25, 26
adrenaline, phantom 122
Agboluaje, Oladipo 126–7
Age of Enlightenment 140
agency 19, 24
Akbar, Arifa 101, 145
    see also Guardian
Albion 49–50
All About Eve 147
All I Ever Wanted Was Everything 29
ambiguity 75
American in Paris, An 147
& Juliet 159
And the Rest of Me Floats 73
Angry 54
Angry Brigade, The 132
Animals 54
Anne Boleyn 135
Another World: Losing Our Children to Islamic State 24
Anti-Naturalism 64–5
Apollo Theatre 7
Arab Spring 37
Arrival, The 102
artificial intelligence (AI) 54–7, 59–61
Audience, The 40
Audience with Jimmy Savile, An 132

audiences 13–14, 19, 131, 145
    experimental theatre 68, 76–7
    racism (race) 120, 122, 128
audiences, experimental theatre 63–8
austerity 17, 20, 21, 34
awards 140
Ayahs, Lascars and Princes: The Story of Indians in Britain 1700-1947 117

Baby Reindeer 87
banks 38
Barber Shop Chronicles 119–20
Bartlett, Mike 18–19
Beast of Blue Yonder, The 66
Beast Will Rise, The 67
*B*easts* 109
beauty standards 120
Beckett, Andy 5
Bedlam 140
Beginning 43, 159
behaviours 103
Behzti 121
belonging 24
Benn, Melissa 22
Beyond Caring 17, 35
Bhatti, Gurpreet Kaur 121
Birch, Alice 65–6
Birdland 28
Birthday 104–5
Black and British: A Forgotten History 123
Black Lives Matter 77
Book of Mormons, The 156
Boy 36
brands 7
Brexit 7, 45–51, 134, 164
Brexit: The Uncivil War 45

Bring Up the Bodies 135
Brooks, Andy *see* Testament
Brothers Size, The 126
Burgerz 111
Butler, Judith 103
Butterworth, Jez 48–9

campaigns 10
Candide 141
Cane, The 21
capitalism, digital 34–6
casting, colour conscious 139–40
celebrities 8
censorship 10
Chewing Gum Dreams 80–1
children 109
Chimerica 37
China 36
Clapp, Susannah 153
class, social 11
climate change 18, 19, 163
climate crisis 97
Climategate 19
clothes 135
    see also costume
coal industry 40
coercive control 106
collaboration 64
Collaborators 131–2
colour palettes, staging 133, 135, 136, 138
Come From Away 159
commercial sector theatre 163
commodification 28, 104
communication 157
complex regional pain syndrome 85
Consent 23
Conspirator 148
Constellations 73
consumerism 107
Contribution to the Critique of Hegel's Philosophy of Right, A 34
controversy 10
conversations, imaginary, South Bank, London 6–16

costume 133–4
COVID-19 (pandemic) 7, 77, 98, 161
criminal justice system (CJS) 22
criminalization 33
Crimp, Martin 160
crises 18, 19
crisis theatre 163
Crouch, Tim 65–6
cultures 6, 24
    British 13
Cumper, Patricia 113
Curious Incident of the Dog in the Night-Time, The 74, 146
curtains 137
Cuttin' It 17
Cyprus Avenue 158–9
Cyrano de Bergerac 160

Daisy and Jack 153–61
Dara 132
Dark Earth and the Light Sky, The 143
Dark Vanilla Jungle 82
Days of Significance 115–16
De-lahay, Rachel 127–8
Dead Sheep 132
Dear Evan Hansen 159
Death of England 88
democracy 41, 42, 43
desire 109
Di and Viv and Rose 105–6
Dictator 148
digital media 66
digital theatre 66–7
Dirty Butterfly 74–5
disabilities 94
disaffection, civil 33
discrimination 33
dissociation 85
Distance, The 108
Ditch 54
diversity 15, 113, 158
diversity, ethnic *see* ethnicity
Doctor Scroggy's War 143
Doll's House, A 139
Drawing the Line 138

Dunsinane 133–4
dystopias 53–61, 164

Earthquakes in London 18
eccentricity 47
economies, local 5
education 18, 21
Either 67
elections 126
elites 32
Ellams, Inua 119–20
Emilia 141
employment contracts, zero-hours 35
Empress, The 117–18
Encounter, The 157
End of History, The 42
English Revolution 135
enslavement 124
entrepreneurs 35
Escaped Alone 54–5
Estate, The 126
ethnic minority groups
    (communities) 23–4
ethnicity 12, 24
    see also identity
Evening with an Immigrant, An 84
events, international 15
events, international (significant) 37
Everything I Know About Love 160
Exeunt 14
Exorcist, The 147
experimental theatre 63–4, 164
    Alice Birch and Tim Crouch 65–6
    Anthony Neilson 71–2
    Anti-Naturalism 64–5
    On Bear Ridge 72
    debbie tucker green 74–5
    digital theatre 66–7
    Either 67
    Ella Hickson 69
    Gig Theatre 68
    King Charles III 70
    Laura Wade 76
    Love and Information 70–1
    Middle East 71

    Nick Payne 72–3
    Queer Theatre 73
    In the Republic of Happiness
        69–70
    Rules for Living 73–4
    Seven Methods of Killing Kylie
        Jenner 70
    Simon Stephens 74
    theatre form 67–8
    Uncertainty 75
    A Very Expensive Poison 75–6
    X 76–7
    youth 77
    Zoom Theatre 77
exploitation 27, 38, 87, 104, 117
extra value added 5
extremism 14

faith 24
families 91–2, 112, 125
    In Basildon 95–6
    Fuck the Polar Bears 97
    The Holy Rosenbergs 94
    Jumpy 94–5
    Love, Love, Love 96
    Nine Night 98
    theatregoer's diary 92–3
    Tribes 93–4
    The Tyler Sisters 98–9
    Visitors 96–7
    Wanderlust 93
fashions, retro 142
feminism 65, 107, 135
Ferguson, Niall 31, 37
Ferryman, The 48–9
fetishization 109
feuds, family 95–6
film scripts 148–51
films 13, 53
Fleabag 81–2
Forbes 158
Foxfinder 59–60
freedom 32
friendship 95, 106
fringe theatre 142

Fuck the Polar Bears 97
funding, cuts in 9

Gardner, Lyn 63
Gate Theatre 37
Gayle, Damien 91
gender 13, 101–2, 153
    experimental theatre 73
    families 91
    history 140
    masculinities 103–5
    motherhood 108–9
    and performance study day 102–3
    queerness 110–12
    racism (race) 120
    social issues 27–8
    women 105–7
    see also identity
genocide 142
gentrification 121–2
Gift, The 138
Gig Theatre 68
Girls 113
Girls & Boys 86–7
globalization 26, 36–9
Great Britain 27
Great Gatsby, The 145
Greece 37–8
Greenland 19
grief 109
Grochala, Sarah 79
grooming 119
Guardian 5, 17, 63, 101, 158
guidelines 11
Gupta, Tanika 116–19

hacking 35–6
Hamilton 158
Handbagged 39
Hangman 47–8
Hansard 40
harassment 28, 101
Hare, David 17
Harry Potter and the Cursed Child 157
healthcare (health) 18, 20, 21, 85

Hegel, G. W. F. 39
Her Naked Skin 140
Heretic, The 19
Hickson, Ella 69
High Table, The 111–12
history 39–41, 123, 124, 131–2
    art of theatre 132–4
    national identity 138–40
    set design 141–3
    of theatre 137–8
    Tudor era 134–7
    women 140–1
History of Water in the Middle East 71
Hoes, The 113
Hole 68
Holocaust 161
Holy Rosenbergs, The 94
Home, I'm Darling 76
homophobia 40
Hope 42
How to Date a Feminist 107
How to Hold Your Breath 59
Human Animals 57–8
humour (comedy) 47–8, 82, 104, 109, 110, 138
Hunger Games, The 54
Hungry Ghosts 36
Hytner, Nick 10

I Wish to Die Singing 142
Icke, Robert 53
identity 153, 159, 161, 163
    Brexit 41
    experimental theatre 73
    gender 103, 105, 110–11
    history 134
    racism (race) 114
    social issues 18, 23–5
    see also national identity
If You Don't Let Us Dream, We Won't Let You Sleep 34
I'm Not Running 42
images 108
Imaginationship 45

immersive experiences 68
immigration 84, 127
Imperium 148
imports, American 147
In Basildon 95–6
In the Republic of Happiness 69–70
independence 97, 134
inequalities 18, 22, 101
Ingredient X 26
Ink 27
innovation 63
Instructions for Correct Assembly 58–9
interactive spaces 64
Invisible, The 23
Iphigenia in Splott 83–4
IRA 49
Iraq War 115

Jack *see* Daisy and Jack
James Plays, The 134
Jane Wenham: The Witch of Walkern 140
Jerusalem 49
Jumpy 94–5
Jungle, The 39

Kelley, Nancy 91
Kene, Arinzé 121–3
Kiln Theatre 11, 148
King Charles III 70
Kinky Boots 147, 157
Know of the Heart, The 26
Knowledge, The 21

Labour of Love 42
Labour Party 41–3
Labyrinth 38
Lampedusa 38
language, forms of 141
Last Days of the Duchess, The 143
Legally Blond: The Musical 155
Lehman Trilogy, The 160
Lela & Co 104
Lemons Lemons Lemons Lemons Lemons 60–1

Leopoldstadt 161
Let Me In 147
Let the Right One In 147
Lewis, Helen 101
Lewis's notebook 153–61
lifestyles 96, 97
Limehouse 43
Linda 35
Lions and Tigers 118–19
Little Platoons 21
Little Revolution 33
Living with the Lights On 84–5
loss, sense of 97
Love 17
Love and Information 70–1
Love, Bombs and Apples 24–5
Love, Love, Love 96
Lungs 32

magazines, online 14
Mametz 143
manipulation 106
Mantel, Hilary 135
marginalization 24, 49
Martello-White, Nathaniel 125–6
Marxism
　digital turbo-capitalism 34–6
　globalization 36–9
　Labour Party 41–3
　politics and history 39–41
　soft socialism 32–4
masculinity 86, 102, 103–5
　Black 120
Matilda 146
Matilda the Musical 155
McBurney, Simon 157
#MeToo 10–11, 28, 101
media 26–7, 28
　digital 66
mental health 84, 120
Middle East 71
Midnight Movie 66
migration 38–9
millennials 153–4
Mills, C. Wright 18

misjudgements 95
Misty 121–3
Moderate Soprano, The 143
Mogadishu 22
monarchs 136
monologues 79–80
   Baby Reindeer 87
   Chewing Gum Dreams 80–1
   Dark Vanilla Jungle 82
   Death of England 88
   An Evening with an Immigrant 84
   Fleabag 81–2
   Girls & Boys 86–7
   Iphigenia in Splott 83–4
   Living with the Lights On 84–5
   My Mum's a Twat 86
   The Shape of the Pain 85
   Shoe Lady 88–9
   Superhoe 87–8
   True Brits 82–3
Monster Calls, A 147–8
Mood Music 28
motherhood 99, 105, 108–9
Mountaintop, The 140
Mr Foote's Other Leg 137–8
multiculturalism 24
   see also diversity
Multitudes 24
multiverse theory 73
music 68
music industry 26, 28–9
My Country: A Work in Progress 46
My Mum's a Twat 86
My White Best Friend (And Other Letters Left Unsaid) 77, 127

narratives 123, 124
National Health Service (NHS) 20–1
national identity 40, 110, 127, 133, 138–40
National Theatre 46, 145–7, 161
naturalism 15
Neilson, Anthony 71–2
New Nigerians 126
New Statesman 101

newspapers 46
nihilism 35
No Naughty Bits 142
norms, societal 105
Norris, Rufus 46–7
nostalgia 131
notebooks 92
novels 53
NSFW 27
Nuclear War 64
nut 75

Obedience of a Christian Man, The 136
Occupied 50
Oil 38
On Bear Ridge 72
One Man, Two Guvners 155–6
openness 116
Oppenheimer 132
Our Ladies of Perpetual Succour 158
Out of Water 110–11

pandemic 67, 92
Parliament Square 43
partnerships 151
Payne, Nick 72–3
People, Places and Things 25
performance art 68
phone-hacking 27
phones, audience use of 13–14
Poet in da Corner 29
politics 115, 126, 137, 163
Pomona 56–7
populism 8, 10, 164
   Brexit 45
   politics 41
   privilege 145
   racism (race) 126
   social issues 18
Posh 31
postcolonialism 124
poverty 17
power 39, 109, 139
power dynamics 106

press 27
　see also media
prices, ticket *see* ticket (prices)
privatization 34
privilege 32, 129
producers, theatre 7
Prophet, The 37
Protest Song 33
Pulse nightclub 127

Queen Anne 135
Queer Theatre 73
queerness 102, 110–12

racism (race) 11–12, 113–14, 140, 159
　Arinzé Kene 121–3
　families 98
　gender 111
　Gurpreet Kaur Bhatti 121
　Inua Ellams 119–20
　monologues 83
　Nathaniel Martello-White 125–6
　Oladipo Agboluaje 126–7
　politics 33
　Rachel De-lahay 127–8
　Roy Williams 114–16
　Selina Thompson 124–5
　social issues 24
　Tanika Gupta 116–19
　Testament 123–4
Radiant Vermin 55–6
Red Velvet 137
Reformation 135
regulations 27
reinvention 145
religion 24, 34–5
responsibilities, social 27
reviews 14
Revolt. She Said. Revolt Again 106–7
revolutionaries 119
rewrites 116
Rice, Emma 11
riots 33, 114
Riots, The 17, 33

Ritual Slaughter of Gorge Mastromas 35
rivalry, sibling 96
role models 115
roof collapses, Apollo Theatre 7
Rotterdam 110
Royal Academy of Dramatic Art (RADA) 126
Royal Court Theatre 31, 64, 68–70, 76, 147
Royal Shakespeare Company (RSC) 115, 117, 132–3, 145–6
Rubasingham, Indhu 11
Rules for Living 73–4

salt 124
Same Deep Water as Me, The 23
Same Same 114
Saville, Alice 131
Scenes with Girls 106
Schularick, Moritz 37
science fiction 64–5, 76–7
　see also dystopias
Screens 45
scripts, film 148–51
secrets 94
self, sense of 79
selfishness 97
set design 141–3
Seven Methods of Killing Kylie Jenner 70
Sewing Group, The 131
sexism 28, 29
sexual violence 104, 107
sexuality 12, 73
Shakespeare in Love 156
Shakespeare, William 133–4
Shakespeare's Globe 133
Shape of the Pain, The 85
Shivered 68
Shoe Lady 88–9
siblings 96
Six 135
Small Island 147
Snookered 105

social change 32
social class 159
social issues 17–29
    see also crises; identity; populism
social justice 36
social media 13–14
social realism 63
socialism, soft 32–4
Society of London Theatre 5
Solid Life of Sugar Water, The 108–9
Spectator 31
Stage, The 63, 131
Stages of Adaptation 146–8
    film script 148–51
stalking 87
Staying Power 123
Stephens, Simon 74
stereotypes 104, 105, 112
storytelling, fragmented 68
Strange Undoing of Prudencia Hart 68
streaming 161
substance abuse 25, 26
subversion 138–9
Sucker Punch 114–15
Sunset at the Villa Thalia 37
Superhoe 87–8
Sweet Science of Bruising, The 142

technologies, digital 66, 77
Teh Internet Is Serious Business 35
television 53
Tender Napalm 109
Testament 123–4
theatre forms 67–8
theatre, state-subsidized 9, 163
This House 39
This May Hurt a Bit 20
Thompson, Selina 124–5
Three Kingdoms 74
Three Sisters 139
Thrill of Love, The 143
tickets (prices) 5, 8
Tiger Country 20
tolerance 24, 40

Torn 125
transnational corporations (TNCs) 27
Travelling Light 142–3
Tribes 93–4
Tricycle Theatre 11
True Brits 82–3
truth 121
Trying It On 41
tucker green, debbie 74–5
Tudor era 134–7
Tudors, The 134
Tyler Sisters, The 98–9

UK Theatre 5
Uncertainty 75

variety 163
venues 7
Very Expensive Poison, A 75–6
Village Bike, The 108
Violence and Sons 104
visibility 153
Visitors 96–7
Voices on the Wind 119

Wade, Laura 76
Wanderlust 93
wars 115
welfare states 36
Welkin, The 140–1
West End, London 6
What Is to Be Done? 41
When We Have Sufficiently Tortured Each Other 101–2
White Teeth 148
Who Cares 21
Williams, Roy 114–16
witches 140
Wolf from the Door, The 57
Wolf Hall 135
Wolf, Matt 147
women 11–12
    gender 105–7
    history 140–1
    politics 41–2

privilege 131
racism (race) 117, 121
social issues 28
women (female) 153
Wonderful World of Dissocia 71
Wonderland 40
writers 13
　new 16
writing, new 17, 63

writing styles 164
Written on the Heart 136

X 76–7
xenophobia 24

youth 77

Zoom Theatre 77